W9-BBK-445

# Risk and Our Pedagogical Relation to Children

WITHDRAWN

SUNY Series, Early Childhood Education: Inquiries and Insights
Mary A. Jensen, editor

WITHDRAWN

STEPHEN J. SMITH

# Risk and Our Pedagogical Relation to Children

*On the Playground and Beyond*

STATE UNIVERSITY OF NEW YORK PRESS

CARL A. RUDISILL LIBRARY
LENOIR-RHYNE COLLEGE

*L B*
*1117*
*. S 573*
*1998*
*Feb. 1999*

Published by
State University of New York Press, Albany

© 1998 State University of New York

All rights reserved

Printed in the United States of America

No part of this book may be used or reproduced in any manner
whatsoever without written permission. No part of this book may be
stored in a retrieval system or transmitted in any form or by any means
including electronic, electrostatic, magnetic tape, mechanical,
photocopying, recording, or otherwise without the prior permission
of the publisher.

For information, address State University of New York Press,
State University Plaza, Albany, N.Y., 12246

Production design by David Ford
Marketing by Patrick Durocher

**Library of Congress Cataloging-in-Publication Data**

Smith, Stephen J., 1954–
    Risk and our pedagogical relation to children : on the playground
and beyond / Stephen J. Smith.
        p.    cm. — (SUNY series, early childhood education)
    Includes bibliographical references (p.   ) and index.
    ISBN 0–7914–3593–8 (alk. paper). — ISBN 0–7914–3594–6 (pbk. :
alk. paper)
    1. Risk-taking (Psychology) in children.  2. Teaching.  3. Active
learning.  4. Knowledge, Sociology of.  5. Playgrounds.  6. Play.
7. Children—Health and hygiene.  I. Title.  II. Series
LB1117.S573 1998
370.15—dc21
                                  97–17264
                                      CIP

10  9  8  7  6  5  4  3  2  1

*To Tyler, Shayle and Benjamin,*
*who reintroduced me to the playground.*

# Contents

# Acknowledgments

"Can you push me?" It is a question reminiscent of being with a child on a playground. "But don't push me too hard!" The exclamation is a reminder of the child's resources and of the limits of being helpful.

I am grateful to those who came with me to the playground and knew how hard to push.

Max van Manen has been an inspiring and challenging mentor. His fundamental, ontological conception of pedagogical relationality permeates this study. If I have made any small contribution myself to understanding the helpful ways we can be with children it is because I have felt his reassuring theoretical hand behind me. Working with him on the journal *Phenomenology + Pedagogy* was a special gift.

To others who have challenged and supported me I give my thanks. Robert Burch gave voice to my antipathy towards skills, techniques, procedures, and methods that prevent us from swinging with gay abandon. Margaret Haughey was a willing partner in the play of ideas about children and their upbringing. Wilfred Schmidt showed me kindness, quiet grace, and dignity through the example of his own work. And Larry Beauchamp, with humor and unfailing support, kept me in touch with the physicality of educating children.

Bas Levering has been a wonderful friend over the years. He has taught me much about the human science tradition of pedagogy in Holland and about the achievements of the Utrecht school of phenomenologists. Going with him to an old-fashioned playground on the outskirts of Montfoort on a leisurely sunday afternoon remains one of my most treasured memories of observing children playfully taking risks.

Donald Vandenberg deserves special mention for first introducing me to the literature of phenomenological pedagogy. His translations and interpretations of certain *Geisteswissenschaftliche Pädagogik* writers gave a young teacher from The Antipodes much needed insight. I thank him for pushing me higher than I would have dared go myself and for remaining my most challenging critic.

I am appreciative of the interactions I have had over the years with participants at the International Human Science and International Invitational Pedagogy Conferences. I have learned much that has influenced my thinking about pedagogical relationality from Marc Briod, Vangie Bergum, Siebren Miedema, Antionette Oberg, David Smith, David Jardine, Jan Jagodzinski, Terry Carson, Ton Beekman, Madeleine Grumet, Rod Evans, Valerie Polakow, David Kennedy, Loren Barritt and Maxine Greene.

The Faculty of Education at Simon Fraser University has provided a valued and playful home these past eight years. Meguido Zola and Sue Montabello have been kindred spirits and deserve special mention for keeping my feet on the playground. I have also profited greatly from working with such gifted graduate students as Carollyne Sinclaire, Celeste Schroeder, Alannah Ireland, Dana Ulveland, Jan Nicol, Francis Graham, and Joyce Bodell who have helped me extend my sense of playground pedagogy into the classroom. I am also grateful for the plentiful opportunities I have had to take risks with my pedagogical theories in the undergraduate and graduate courses I have taught.

Finally, a special thanks to Priscilla Ross and Mary Jensen for believing in this study and to the reviewers of the manuscript I first submitted to SUNY Press for pushing me beyond the playground.

Some parts of this study have been reworked from my previous publications. I thank the following publishers and editors for permission to include this material. Chapter Two first appeared as "The riskiness of the playground," *The Journal of Educational Thought* 24, no. 2, August 1990, pp. 71–85, ©1985, The University of Calgary. Parts of Chapter 3 appeared in "Remembrances of childhood as a source of pedagogical understanding," *Phenomenology + Pedagogy* 9, 1991, pp. 158–71; "Where is the child in physical eduation research?" *Quest* 43, no. 1, 1991, pp. 37–54; and "Studying the lifeworld of physical education: A phenomenological orientation," in *Research in Physical Education and Sport: Exploring Alternative Visions*, edited by Andrew C. Sparkes, London: The Falmer Press, pp. 61–89. Portions of Chapter 4 are drawn from "'Can you push me?': A pedagogy of risk-taking," in *Through the Looking Glass: Children and Health Promotion*, edited by Jane Ross and Vangie Bergum, Ottawa: Canadian Public Health Association, 1990; and "The security of the child's world," *Canadian Journal of Education (Revue canadienne de l'education)* 16, no. 4, 1991, pp. 442–52. Some ideas for Chapters 5 and 6 were first published as "Seeing a Risk," *Phenomenology + Pedagogy* 5, no. 1, 1987, pp. 63–75 and subsequently developed in "Challenges of the Playground," *Journal of Learning About Learning* 1, no. 2, 1989, pp. 37–55.

Extracts from the following books are used with the permission of the publishers. Judith Conaway, *Sometimes It Scares Me*, Milwaukee: Raintree Editions, ©1977, with the permission of the editors of Steck-Vaughn Company. D. H. Lawrence, *Sons and Lovers*, Middlesex: Penguin Books, ©1913, with permission of Laurence Pollinger Limited and the Estate of Frieda Lawrence Ravagli. William Wordsworth, *The Prelude: Or Growth of a Poet's Mind*, edited by Ernest De Selincourt and revised by Helen Darbishere, Oxford: Clarendon Press, E. Moxton edition text ©1850, by permission of Oxford University Press.

# I

## Locating a Pedagogy of Risk

# 1

# Introduction

ave you been with a child on the playground? I don't just mean, have you taken a child to the playground? But have you really been with a child, taking note of what he or she does on a playground? Have you followed a child as he or she explores the different activities afforded by the playground? And in following this child, have you stopped to consider the nature of this playground activity, and whether the child feels secure, or whether he or she should exercise more care, or perhaps if the child appears overly anxious, whether he or she should not be a bit more adventurous, be a little more of a risk-taker on this apparatus of the playground?

I think of taking my daughter to the playground at a local school-yard. No sooner do we arrive than she leaves me behind in her eagerness to explore the slippery slides, climbing frames, platforms and beams that comprise this playground. I watch as she races off to a slide where only moments earlier some older children could be seen playing. For now my child has the slide all to herself. "Can you manage all by yourself?" I ask as she begins to climb the ladder. My question falls on deaf ears. But halfway up, she glances in my direction. A frown creases her brow. She grasps the rungs more tightly, pulls herself closer to the ladder, and cautiously ventures a little higher up. Now two-thirds of the way up, she does not seem to want to go any higher. She calls for me to come over to her, to come and bring her down from this precarious place. So I do as she requests, wondering at the same time how the slide can lose its appeal so quickly, wondering if lifting her down is the best thing to do, and wondering if perhaps the slide would seem less risky were I to follow her up to the top of the ladder and then to come down with her. Should I not respond in a way that is consistent with the enthusiasm she first showed for this activity? Should I not respond in a way that is respectful of the risks of this activity yet mindful of the child's initial inclination to take the risk of going down the slide? What is the best thing to do for this child when a sense of risk impinges upon her enjoyment of the playground?

The situation involving my child on the playground raises questions that have to do with how we should treat children in general. It raises questions regarding a child's experience of the playground, further questions regarding our understanding of a child's experience, and practical questions pertaining to what we ought to do in order to stay in touch with and yet give direction to a child's activity. In particular, it raises questions regarding the riskiness of children's lives: questions that have to do with a child's sense of risk, our understanding of such risk, and of what we might do so that risks can be taken in a prevailing atmosphere of security.

The study upon which we are now embarking is an attempt to grasp the meaning of these questions that arise primarily out of our interactions with children on playgrounds. It begins with a formulation of "risk" which will guide our reflections on these playground interactions with children and help define those encounters which are of most interest.

First and foremost, risk is a term of our pedagogical relation to children. This study aims to show that risk signifies a relation that holds for children on the playground and for the precarious world which children find beyond the playground. For adults, risk is a term for remembering children's activity on the playground and for seeing themselves capable at some point in their lives of engaging in similar activity. Risk suggests the capacity of adults to identify with the very nature of children's playground activity. More fundamentally, it is a reflective term of maturity whereby adults can follow children's activities as they attempt to influence them in ways the child is only beginning to understand. Risk acknowledges positively the difference that maturity creates between an adult's and a child's understanding of playground activity and of the learning which such activity represents. For, as we shall see, children and adults do experience playground events differently; and though adults may at times be indifferent to the riskiness that children feel, there is always the possibility of their becoming involved in what children are doing and of taking pains to do something about the risks of which children might not otherwise be aware. Adults are in a position to lend a sense of security to children's experiences of playground activity because of their much greater experience of the playground and, indeed, the larger world's riskiness. This possibility of bringing adult maturity to bear upon the playground activity of children is what is implied in the statement that risk is, first and foremost, a term of our pedagogical relation to children.

The "playground" is the immediate and obvious reference point for these reflections on the significance of risk. We want to base our reflections on everyday interactions with children, and so we ought to observe children where they are likely to be found. Of course, children are likely to be found elsewhere and mostly everywhere, especially in schools, homes, nurseries, backyards, parks, kindergartens, daycare settings, and elementary schools, and they probably spend more time in these settings than on playgrounds. Yet these are not places that children typically seek out themselves, nor are they places where they freely spend their time. The playground stands out in this regard as an important focus, being not only a place set aside for children but also a place for viewing activities which have a particularly child-like quality. But the playground holds a greater significance than the mere fact of its accessibility and the opportunities it provides for appreciating the unfettered experiences of children. It is at times a risky place and a place where children are often seen to be taking risks. It is where children are encouraged to take risks by their peers and, at times, by the adults who take them there. The playground is a place where risk tends to thematize our interactions with children as well as their responses to one another. Hence the playground serves not only as a focus for our reflections on risk but also as a commonplace reference in our attempts to describe a responsible pedagogy of risk.

By way of introduction, I will attempt to show how such a formulation of risk begins to make sense of the interactions that invariably occur on the playground.

## Venturing Onto the Playground

The school doors open and children come streaming outside. Some run toward the school gates to where their parents stand beside opened car doors. Others head to bicycle racks to join the growing confusion of children already there, each trying to steer his or her way through cluttered exits. Still others join up with friends or with an older brother or sister, and disappear from view along the sidewalks. A number of children, however, seem much less concerned to get away so quickly. In dribs and drabs they cross the playing field to an adjoining playground. Here they climb ladders, chains, platforms, and beams. They swing on tires and bars. They jump down from various heights or from one piece of equipment to another, and slide down poles and slides or off plastic casings. They sit in the sand, sculpture the sand, throw the sand. They chase each other over the playground, stopping every now and then to discuss what's fair and what's not. All sorts of activities take place on this playground. And after a while this playground is where most of the remaining children are to be found.

Some children are on the playground waiting for their parents to collect them. A car pulls up the asphalt driveway skirting the field that adjoins this playground. A car horn signals the arrival of one of the parents. The passenger-side door is thrust open. "I gotta go, Justine. See you tomorrow," says one young girl as she heads off in the direction of the waiting adult. The scene is repeated many times over. A few adults get out of their cars and walk towards the playground before they are spotted. Some even take a cursory look at what their children are doing on the playground before leading them away. One woman arrives in a flurry. She searches anxiously for her child. "Melissa," she says, "I've been looking everywhere for you. Your music lesson is in five minutes. Oh. Hi, Jillian, how are you? How's your mother? Tell her I'll give her a ring tomorrow. . . . Melissa, I told you to come straight home. Get your things and let's go!" And so it goes on this playground. Parents have important things to do. They must pick up children. And children have important things to do. They have homes to go to and lessons to attend.

But what if we were to ask the children themselves; what order of priorities would they give us? "What did you do at school today?" I ask my child. "Nothing," he replies in a rather disinterested manner. "You mean you just stood around all day doing nothing?" "No, we did things," he says matter-of-factly. This line of questioning is not proving very helpful, so I ask: "And what do you like doing at school?" His expression softens. "I like recess. I like playing with Dorian and Michael. I like climbing things, and I like going down the slide, except when the big kids push us down. We don't like the big kids. They say, 'Don't come on the slide! You can't come on the slide, kid!' Do you know Dorian got pushed off the slide? Like, we were on the slide first, and then a big kid was climbing up the slide. He said, 'Don't touch me or I'll push you off.' And he pushed Dorian off and hurt his mouth. Like, he was laughing and Dorian was crying." He pauses for a moment. "So you like going to the playground," I say, hoping to hear more about what happens there (and becoming a little concerned about the safety of the children there). "Yes," he replies, "but the teacher always makes us sit and eat our lunch first. It takes too long. We just want to play."

The playground is an important place. It is a place for children who are waiting for their parents to collect them. It is a place of recess. And it is a place to take the children when there is nothing more pressing to do. But the playground is even more than this. Although ignored by those for whom children are of little consequence or by those who are too pre-occupied with adult concerns to be much bothered with things that matter to children, although taken for granted by those who take children for granted and prefer to see their effective removal from the adult world, the playground is also a place for understanding what is happening to children. It is a child's place, a place for being able to act like a child, and a place for seeing what matters to children.

Of course, this does not mean that an interest in playgrounds is synonymous with an interest in understanding children. Throughout the summer months pictures of children on swings, slides, teeter-totters, and other playground items appear regularly in local newspapers. A child is caught frozen in the arc of a swing, her body parallel to the ground, a teasing smile on her face. Two children sit giggling together on a tire swing. Another child is photographed reclining on a metal slide, her arms extended, eyebrows raised, mouth agape, making sounds we can only imagine. Do these pictures tell us anything about these children? They certainly tell us something about ourselves. Such activity representations express a more playful mood that exists at this time of year, a holiday spirit, an *esprit de jeu*, an adult longing for the summer idyll. The playground interest evoked in these portrayals of children is at the level of sentimentality and nostalgia. Nevertheless, because the playground is reserved for children, by looking at what children do in this context it is more likely that questions related to understanding them on their own terms will be raised than by looking at them in some other domain where they may be expected to be something other than just children.[1]

Still, it must be acknowledged from the outset that not all children relish the thought of going to the playground. It loses its appeal for the older child, for example, the child who has entered a fraternity of skateboarders and is now allowed to travel farther afield than the local park or school ground. This child's access to the streets takes him or her far beyond the domain of the playground. And though such children may return to the playground once in a while, it is now clear the playground holds a different meaning for them than it does for the younger child. They are like adults who, when at the playground, will try some maneuvre on, say, a set of parallel bars, or perhaps will try to pull themselves up a vertical pole to a platform above, just to see if they can still do it. The actions of these older people show that the playground holds few fears for them. They are now too big for what the playground allows. They have outgrown the playground. There are children, however, who are not quite so old, yet they stay clear of the playground as well. At recess they loiter near the buildings, while after school they skirt around the playground on their way home. These children have not outgrown the playground; on the contrary, they seem to see the playground as an intimidating place to be avoided at all costs. So what can we say about such children? How shall we consider them? Perhaps the answer lies in looking more closely at the nature of playground activity, not only to determine the meaning of what children enjoy and then eventually outgrow, but also to come to an understanding of that which is potentially so intimidating to some children. By looking at the normal course of playground activity something might be said even for the sake of children who choose to stay out of sight.

To take an interest in playground activity means to see children doing things many of us have done ourselves: swinging on tires, climbing metal frames, or playing in a sandpit. We see ourselves in the activities of children on a playground, and we follow what they are doing on the basis of our own recollections of childhood. But this is not all there is to understanding playground activity. Beyond the amusement of watching children at play, we are at times concerned for what particular children can and cannot do, and this concern springs from a maturity which enables us to make sense of their activity. We see children, for instance, as they develop physical skills, acquire problem-solving and other cognitive strategies, gain in self-esteem or lose self-confidence, acquire the ability to interact with others, and so on. We see children from the vantage point of our own sense of maturity, and this provides the basis for our coming to terms with their playground activity. And yet, the really practical and responsible task of maturity remains: to try to understand playground activity through our reflective participation as adults who see and formulate the meaning of this activity for the sake of children's own reflective growth towards maturity, or in other words, by engaging and interacting with children in ways that help them become increasingly confident and competent in their actions.

What pedagogical sense do we make of the riskiness of the playground? And how do we act on our pedagogical understanding of risk? A sense of risk arises when, on the basis of our own experiences, we become concerned about children's fears and difficulties and the danger and challenge of their playground activity. We ask: To what extent is the playground a place of risk? Such a question is important historically and sociologically for the way in which playgrounds have developed as "safe" places set aside for children (and places which serve to keep adult places "safe" from children), but it is also important pedagogically for the way it draws us onto the playground and leads us to consider the significance of our adult place in a child's life. What does risk-taking mean to a child? How do children respond to risk? And how should we, as adults, respond to their taking risks? These are specific questions to consider as we look at children on the playground. A sensitive consideration of such questions helps us to realize that to expect all children to feel comfortable on swings, climbing frames and slides, without our being there at times, may be to expect too much of children and too little of ourselves. Such questions enable us to appreciate the inherent riskiness of children's playground activity, and at the same time, they help us to avoid the sort of adult indifference that makes the world seem all the more dangerous to children. From a position of responsiveness to such questions of risk we can try to adopt a child's perspective, which is to say, we can try to remember the child in the activities we are able to share and to cast these remembrances within a terminology of risk that might give direction to our everyday relations with children.

## Redefining Risk

Risk is a term which brings to mind our responsibility for the direction of children's activity. It is a pedagogically significant term to the extent that it defines some essential feature of adult conduct aimed at guiding young children towards a position of being responsible themselves for the consequences of their activity. This is not to say that risk is simply an adult formulation of children's activity. There is indeed a visibility of risk in playground activity—in its difficulty, danger, and challenge, in the observable fears it arouses, and especially in the obviously daring and audacious ways children respond to it. Nevertheless, it is only by being with the child as if returning to the landscape of our own childhood that the riskiness of children's activity becomes a disclosure of a shared and remembered world and a disclosure of our place in relation to the child. Only by being with the child in this interactive and self-reflective way do we appreciate the full meaning of the term risk.

There is an openness to the formulation of "risk as an aspect of the pedagogical relation" that defies more conventional notions of risk. It would appear to be at odds with the common assumption that risk is something like pain which we try to reduce and hopefully avoid rather than value for its significance for children's growth and development. It also distances us from those who deal in a calculus of risk avoidance and who seek to analyze, assess, manage, and communicate the extent of the threats and hazards posed by modernization. Such exposure to "risk factors," or being publically "at-risk," is of a different order of human significance to the taking of risks that are personally meaningful. The actuarial definition of risk upon which insurance tables, government legislations, and business practices are based precludes looking at risk "from the point of view of the person assessing the danger or potential loss" (Siegelman, 1983, p. 4). "Ordinary people, that is the vast bulk of humanity, probably use different criteria by which to assess their vulnerability to risks," being "influenced, not necessarily by the 'reality' of a risk, but by what they *perceive* that risk to be" (Plant and Plant, 1992, p. 114).

By the same token, risk is not simply a matter of individual perception. The fact that some unusual risks of living can be so magnified out of all proportion, distorting the actual probabilities of injury from these and more ordinary risks (cf. Laudan, 1994; Kluger, 1996), indicates a media construction of risk that influences individual perception. Indeed, certain authors have questioned defining risk solely in terms of individual perception, not only dismissing the idea of personalities disposed towards or averse to taking risks but also the assumption that individuals freely respond to risk without being influenced strongly by cultural biases with respect to a more generalized trust and confidence, or lack thereof, in social institutions (Douglas and Wildavsky, 1983; Wildavsky and Dake, 1990). Kirby (1990) maintains that the responses made to any quantifiable risk are not so much individually chosen as they are determined by "intervening social variables" (p. 284). Beck (1992), who has coined the notion of "risk society" to refer to the result of modernization where there exists a prevailing quest for safety, defines risks as the consequences of this modernization, which makes them distinguishable from other dangers. Individual perception is conditioned by the "new prominence" accorded the notion of risk in our highly technological societies (Douglas, 1990, p. 1). Risk replaces, to some extent, the older, socially constraining notions of danger, sin and taboo which served in past times to create moral community (p. 5).

But if risk is not simply a matter of individual perception, neither is it simply a matter of social definition. Though we live in a risk society where issues of public safety and individual responsibility determine our daily living, and though we also live in a society that glorifies risk of a certain kind and that venerates the publicly dramatic risk-taker (Adams, 1995, p. 17; Keyes, 1985, pp. 154, 255), individuals still remain free to *take* risks. Some element of choice is always involved, for risk is not some thing, either threatening or alluring, that determines action from the outside. Influenced from without, it is a consideration within the action itself, even if it is inaction in the face of overwhelming odds. Determinist notions, whether it be a perception of risk ascribed to the individual or the objective rendition of a risk society, begin to blur when we consider the intentionality of risk-taking.[2] Here we discover latitudes of freedom and choice in taking risks of different kinds and of differing degrees of private and public responsibility.

Risks taken may be *physical*, as in being exposed to injury in sports and adventurous recreations, jeopardizing your life in occupations like firefighting, policework, military service, and mining, or engaging in voluntary, public service, rescue work. They may be *emotional*, as in admitting fear or hurt, expressing anger, trusting another, falling in love, or being intimate with your partner. They may be more *social* in kind, as in the risks that go with being honest, trying your best, saying no, defending your rights, and being open to the ways of other people. They may be *intellectual*, as in the trepidations of asking questions, admitting error, or exploring new ideas. And they may be ostensibly *financial*, as, for example, when starting a business, playing the stockmarket, or loaning money (cf. Keyes, 1985; Siegelman, 1983; Viscott, 1977).

Any particular risk taken is not categorically physical, emotional, social, intellectual or financial. Risk-taking activity carries a mixture of different valencies; in fact, "it appears that there is considerable overlap between one kind of risk-taking and others. Risks are often interconnected" (Plant and Plant, 1992, p. 120). Recognizing this interconnectedness can direct our attention to a theoretical "risk construct" (Yates and Stone, 1992) that is common across a very wide range of behavioral contexts.

Such a construct is one that suggests a kind of risk-taking that is most physically, emotionally, socially, intellectually, and possibly even financially, worthwhile. In order to grasp such a construct, however, we need to deconstruct some commonly-held assumptions about the worth of different kinds of risk-taking. More important, we shall need to reconceptualize risk-taking along ethical lines by considering the intentionality of risk-taking in terms of levels of attentiveness to others. In the process we may begin to unravel the "inextricable tangle" of our involvement with others in a world of potential risks (cf. Merleau-Ponty, 1962, p. 454) and begin to see how risk is tied inextricably to a pedagogical responsibility for the lives of children.

**An Ethical Register**

Keyes (1985) distinguishes between two levels of risk-taking. At the first level are the audacious, adventurious, fearless, thrill-seeking individuals we find in motor racing, mountain climbing, hang gliding, cliff and bungee jumping, downhill mountain bike and ski racing, along with the high rollers at the casino blackjack and baccarat tables, and the commodity and stock market traders whose fortunes are made and lost in a day. These are the risk-takers who seem to have developed a "protective psychological frame" that instills a sense of safety even as they approach the "dangerous edge" of their respective pursuits (Apter, 1992). These are the risk "seekers" and "chasers" who seem more inclined than most to face danger, and who seem to crave that "incredibly exciting and vertiginous sensation" that Shapiro (1992) describes so well in considering the physical exploits of mogul and aerial snow skiers.

Level-two risks are far less noticeable and far more common. These are the risks that appear less physical and financial and much more emotional, social and intellectual, risks such as "creating ties to others. Building careers. Developing self-knowledge. Tolerating silence. Doing nothing. Not trying to control all outcomes. Being bored. Being boring" (Keyes, 1985, p. 154). While these risks may not seem like much when compared with the high excitement, level-one risks, they accentuate a different order of responsibility. Taking level-two risks brings a longer lasting calm, a deeper sense of oneself and a greater commitment to community (p. 156).

These levels of risk-taking point in the direction of what is perhaps "the hardest risk of all to take—the risk of letting your children take chances" (Keyes, 1985, p. 232). For, if genuine risk-taking implies change, growth, and the increasing acceptance of who we are (Anderson, 1988), then the most responsible thing we can do is to allow and encourage another person to take risks. In the case of our own children and the children entrusted to us, this responsibility becomes quite taxing as we struggle to let go, stand back, observe, listen, appreciate, and respond to their forays into the world. Our greatest fear, of losing the child, is one we must countenance as we learn to risk trusting the child to make his or her way in the world.

Our formulation of "risk as an aspect of the pedagogical relation" ascribes to risk something inclusive of, yet beyond, the first level macho, entertainment and escapist values of the risks we freely choose to take, and something inclusive of yet transcending the second level personal growth and maturation values of the risks we individually chose to take. It ascribes an ethic of responsibility for discerning the risks that children ought to take, which is an ethic that evolves out of an individual perception of risk tempered by social definitions of appropriate risk-taking, and that is expressed in one's concern for the physical, emotional, social, intellectual, and even financial well-being of one's children. Too often our talk of risk-taking falls short of this third level of responsibility. Too often the question of what makes a situation seem risky, especially situations involving children, is put aside for the sake of managing our fears (eg., Serafino, 1986) and instilling a "safety consciousness" in children (*Canada Safety Council*, 1984; Wishon and Oreskovich, 1986).

I am suggesting, in alluding to a third level of risk-taking, that we can derive a sense of pedagogical responsibility, a pedagogy of risk-taking, from our most common ways of experiencing risk. In order to do so we need, first of all, to be skeptical of those explanations which diminish the personal and relational significance of risk-taking behavior. Such explanations pertain to the physiology of enzyme production (Morell, 1986), the genetics of brain chemical stimulation (Benjamin et al., 1996; Dold, 1996; Ebstein et al., 1996), the psychologies of personality typing (Begley, 1986), risk tolerance (Sewell, 1986), "positive addition" (Glasser, 1976), "sensation seeking" (Zuckerman, 1979) and "flow" attainment (Czsikszentmihalyi, 1990), and to the sociology of job placement and economic aspiration (MacCrimmon and Wehrung, 1986, p. 36).[3]

Second, we need to look closely at various definitions of risk and the many interpretations of risk-taking behavior (Fishoff et al., 1984) in order to define that which is experientially significant. To take a risk, we are told, means to be open to danger, loss or hurt—"to navigate among cliffs" (Weekley, 1924, p. xii). A more recent interpretation goes: "To take a risk is to take a chance or a gamble; it implies a degree of uncertainty and inability to control fully the outcomes or consequences of such an action" (Moore, 1983, p. 1). Similarly, Roche (1980) notes that "Gambling as a movement represents an affirmation not of outcomes, per se, but rather their unpredictability; it thus represents the notion of taking a risk" (p. 79). But risk is experienced as more than navigating amongst cliffs, taking a chance or gambling; it is experienced in the uncertainty of a chosen task, in the responses made to a dare or a challenge, in seeking out adventure, and in the responsibilities of daily living. The complexity of the experience of risk depends upon the various ways it enters our lives and the significance of the risk depends very much upon not only the response that is called forth but also the meaning we make of that response in the conduct of our lives.

To take a risk is not simply "to face" a danger, nor to find ourselves without warning or conscious effort to be "at risk," nor "to run a risk" by acting in an oblivious way to inherent dangers (cf. Rescher, 1983, p. 6). To take a risk requires much more of us than this. It requires that the unknown be encountered, that we do indeed experience uncertainty. We are required to do more than that which feels comfortable, more than simply display those capabilities we possess. We must even at times dig deep within ourselves and test the limits of our resources. Taking a risk is the project of encountering the unknown wherein self-understanding occurs. "Risk-taking situations are occasions in which what kind of people we are is literally held open to question, indeed, in which we find out who we are in the midst of becoming who we are" (Hyland, 1984, p. 130).

The third thing we need to do in deriving a pedagogy of risk-taking is to determine that which in the experience of risk is relationally significant. Risks presented mainly as physical challenges carry some degree of social engagement and even if they are risks taken alone the experience still only has meaning to the extent that it bears upon one's sense of being part of a community (whether it be a fraternity of climbers, skateboarders, or extreme sports enthusiasts). While some risks to the soul, mind, and body have a noticeable relational focus insofar as they are risks that directly influence one's sense of being with other people, particularly significant are the risks that present themselves in the actions of children because these are not risks we take, seek, or chase, but rather risks taken by another for whom we are responsible and whose otherness we must risk facing. Such risks are not experienced vicariously; they are experienced bodily, empathetically, intersubjectively, and relationally. They call upon our ability to respond in ways that are helpful. Such risks essentially define our everyday relations with children and our pedagogical ways of being with them.

Bollnow (1971) helps articulate this pedagogical redefinition of risk by making clear distinctions between ordinary, self-referenced notions of risk, such as experimentation and gambling, and "true risk" that is referenced to the actions of another person. He says, "real risk always occurs because of genuine ethical responsibility." Real risk-taking has possible consequences which hit a person in his or her "innermost core" (p. 525). Real risk-taking occurs in the context of one's receptivity, commitment, and responsivity to the actions of children. It strikes an ethical register, not only in the concern shown for the well-being of the child and the quality of the child's relations with others, but also in the underlying concern for the manner in which the child comes to be at home in a world that is worth living in.

## Educational Relevance

A possible consequence of becoming receptive to this ethical register of risk-taking is that we begin to appreciate how an "ethic of risk" (Welch, 1990) redefines what is ordinarily understood as "responsible action," "grounding in community," and "strategic risk-taking" (p. 20). Our basic task becomes one of caring for children and the world they live in without any guarantees that we can ultimately make a difference. "Such action requires immense daring and enables deep joy. It is an ethos in sharp contrast to the ethos of cynicism that often accompanies the recognition of the depth and persistence of evil" (p. 68).

This response-ability for the risk-taking of children, drawing upon our own socially-determined experiences of risk, brings into focus two practical educational considerations. First, no matter what particular view of risk and risk-taking we adopt, from an educational perspective we must be mindful of the fact that for the most part ours is an adult view of risk and one which the child has yet to learn. For example, when we say a child is taking a risk, it may be one which the child cannot see. The child may need to learn about the hazards, difficulties, and dangers of an activity before we can actually say that a risk is being taken. And even when a child does appear to sense something of the riskiness of a situation, the question remains as to how much we can presume to know of the child's experience and how much of what we presume to understand of the child's experience is due to our adult interpretation of risk-taking. What constitutes a child's sense of risk other than that which we can understand from an adult point of view?

Which leads to the second educational consideration. As soon as the child comes into the picture then it would seem that we must consider most favorably that view of risk which is good for the child. There is an obligation placed upon us to consider risk in light of the child's growth towards maturity. For instance, in a business text on taking risks, the authors document a range of risks—financial, health-related, social, career, and so forth. They give the example of John deLorean who in the mid-seventies resigned from his executive positive at General Motors in order to start up his own car production company. The financial risks to such a venture were enormous not only because of the size of the investment needed but also because of the volatility of market conditions. Even with the backing of the British Government, deLorean soon found himself in major difficulties. Facing bankruptcy, deLorean apparently orchestrated a major drug deal to bail out his company. The actual transaction was recorded through videotaped surveillance, however deLorean was acquitted of all charges by reason of FBI entrapment. What is most interesting in this example, aside from the actual details of the case, is the authors' concluding comment that "John deLorean clearly fits our image of the entrepreneurial risk taker" (MacCrimmon and Wehrung, 1986, p. 7.) This individual may be considered an "entrepreneurial risk taker," however, this image of risk-taking appears hideously corrupt if it is to stand as an image guiding children's experiences of risk. Even if entrepreneurial risk does in fact lie within the paradigm of laudable risk-taking to which children are exposed, our task as adults in the presence of children is to see through our adult notions of risk in order to see the child more clearly.

This thinking about risk turns in an even more practical, pedagogical direction as we look at the playground and consider why it is problematic and why it calls for thought. We come to appreciate that, although an adult view of risk takes us far beyond the playground and seemingly beyond the sorts of physical risks to which children are exposed on the playground, the here and now concerns we have for what is good for children serve to bring our experiences of risk to bear upon the playground. In effect, to watch children take risks means our own experiences of risk already impinge upon the situation at hand. To then help children take risks means we should be critically aware of how our experiences influence our actions and how our experiences can inform right actions. Seeing the riskiness of the playground means holding open the question of what a sense of risk actually implies with respect to our ethical responsibility for the nurturance of the young. In playground situations of risk-taking it is our responsibility for seeing the risks children ought to take that is at issue.

Yet this ethical responsibility can very easily be regarded as an abstract principle of risk-taking, as an educational slogan that supplants concern for the exigencies of the playground, and as a pious remedy for chronic adult indifference to children, rather than as a way of pointing to an essential quality of risk-taking. In order to keep our feet on the playground it is necessary to see how this sense of responsibility might characterize our everyday dealings with children and how it might enjoin our experience with theirs. We need to see how this redefined notion of risk points to the primacy of an adult-child relation, which is not merely a relation that holds for the playground, but a relation which contextualizes an abiding interest in situations involving children on playgrounds and places farther afield.

## The Structure of the Study

If risk is indeed a term of our pedagogical relation to children, how shall we describe it beyond simply pointing to selected instances of playground activity? What language of risk shall we appeal to in describing this term of our relation to children? The answer lies in bringing a "pedagogical consciousness" (Hildebrandt, 1987) to bear upon selected instances of playground activity where risk is present, which in theoretical terms means, organizing our reflections on risk around such terms as the "place," "silence," "atmosphere," "challenge," "encounter," "practice" and "possibility" of risk, which already have pedagogical significance. These terms come from a tradition of pedagogical theorizing called the *Geisteswissenschaftliche Pädagogik* tradition (Danner, 1979) which is represented in this study in references to the work of Bollnow, the German pedagogue of the University of Tübingen (cf. Bollnow, 1966/1987), and that of Beets, Buytendijk, Langeveld, Van den Berg and more recently, Beekman, of the "Utrecht School" (van Manen, 1979). The task of this present series of reflections is to show that risk is implicated in these dimensions of "pedagogical consciousness" and to use this terminology of "place," "atmosphere," "silence," etc., in order to give a textual rendering of the relational view of risk which is our starting point.

Concerns regarding the structure of this study may arise as we think about this terminology. Will the playground stand up to such scrutiny? Will it be possible to stay within the confines of the playground as we think about the "place," "silence," "atmosphere," "challenge," "encounter," "practice" and "possibility" of risk? Such concerns over focus are not unfounded, however they do tend to be somewhat misleading. The playground is not so much an object of study (as would be the case in more positivistic forms of research), as it is the point of referral for our deliberations on the meaning of risk. The playground provides a reference point for what might be said about risk. Consequently there will be reference to events and situations outside the playground, although not to suggest that the playground is a limited and not so central example of the phenomenon, but rather to establish a context for making sense of the riskiness of playground activity. Examples of risk drawn from outside the playground will serve to contextualize this study, to situate its findings, and ultimately, to show the significance of a pedagogy of risk and the playground for bringing up children who inevitably leave the playground and its risks behind.

The divisions of this study have been made in keeping with this way of exploring the relational term risk. Chapter 2, The Place of Risk, explores a space for thinking about the meaning of risk. Through a review of pertinent literature, my intention is to show that the space called the playground derives from a concern for the safety of children and for their proper supervision, and that this concern points to a certain awareness of risk in children's lives. Chapter 3, The Silence of Risk, shows how we might become increasingly aware of this risk in children's lives and, in so doing, develops an interest in the meaning of risk into a methodology of educational inquiry. Taken together, these two chapters are a prologue to the next part of the study where a practical interest in children's risk-taking is explored in greater depth. Here the dimensions of risk, as they are disclosed through the adult's involvement with the child on the playground, are shown to characterize an interest that moves towards becoming pedagogically responsive. Chapter 4, The Atmosphere of Risk, considers the dynamics of the adult-child relation as a reflection of the texture of risk in everyday life. More particularly, it shows the mediation of this texture, or atmosphere, of risk to be a function of how children can be helped to meet the demands of playground activity. Chapter 5, The Challenge of Risk, presents the view that, although children respond to taunts and provocations, the response which brings the adult firmly into the situation has more to do with encouragement. Needless to say, there are limits to the encouragement of risk-taking. Fears arise and a sense of danger impinges upon playground activity. The concern for risk must therefore come to terms with how it is that the adult can lead the child in his or her risk-taking. This dimension of being responsive to risk is the subject of Chapter 6, The Encounter with Risk. The terms of a pedagogy of risk-taking are then developed in a more educationally obvious direction in the last part of the study. Chapter 7, entitled The Practice of Risk, gives evidence of a pattern to children's risk-taking, or rather, a logic that can be followed and even planned for. Chapter 8, The Possibility of Risk, then poses the question of how an awareness of this logic of risk-taking enables us to understand the nature of children's activity beyond the playground. Although somewhat explanatory, this last section of the study serves to show the importance of looking more closely at the quality of risks of the playground for education writ large.

Let us now consider very briefly how the fundamental questions underlying the above chapters are interpreted and pursued.

**The Place of Risk**

We begin with the question: how does the playground define risk in a child's life? Certainly the playground is not the only risky place for children. The home, too, is full of dangers; the street that borders the home is fraught with hazard; the shopping mall is a place where we must constantly keep a watchful eye on the young child. What distinguishes the playground is that it is a place designed for letting children take risks. It is a place where the adult need not see risk as danger or hazard, but more positively as challenge and adventure to which children can actively respond. Here risk can serve to highlight something that is being accomplished by the child, some intended activity that expands the child's sense of the world. To the extent that the playground is a circumscribed space, it is not just one arena for risk-taking among many equally significant arenas; it potentially represents the primary arena, the fundamental ground for understanding what risk-taking means.

Through a sociology of knowledge of the playground we can see how risk has become so essential to our appreciation of what happens there. We can account for the need to mark off a special place for children, as if they did not already have their own special places; and we can understand that the design of playgrounds has to do with a certain conception of childhood and the need to preserve its fragility. But we can see also that the separation of children from the mainstream of daily life had an effect which cannot be accounted for through a sociology of knowledge about the playground. Such an analysis cannot account for the lived experience of being caught up in the playground activity of children. In other words, an understanding of the social relations that led to the design of playgrounds makes sense of what happens there in general, but it does not necessarily account for the human significance of our involvements with particular children on particular playgrounds. More specifically, a concern for the safety of children and their proper supervision has led to the design of places where risk can become a theme of a lived relation to children.

This riskiness of the playground, this place designed for seeing risk positively, enables us to question our relation to children and to consider how through this relation we might enable children to take risks in relative safety. What makes the playground an important place of risk has much to do with how we might attend to the activity that takes place there. We have an ongoing role to play in securing this place, in making it safe, in creating the conditions whereby the child can test the confidence of what he or she knows. Our task is thus to see within playground situations, especially those situations that appear risky, a direction for the child's explorations and growth.

The playground is in this regard an exemplary place of risk. Through design and daily use, the playground exemplifies the relationality that makes risk a term of human significance. So, if risk can be defined as that which in part structures our relation to children, and if it can be shown that the playground reveals an underlying, deep-seated interest in risk-taking, then even playgrounds as we presently conceive them might evoke a sense of the domain in which pedagogical relatedness unfolds most clearly.

## The Silence of Risk

Since what is good for one child may not be good for another, what is the value of an analysis which ends up generalizing a situation-specific pedagogy of risk-taking? What is the good of an analysis that glosses over the tentativeness of decisions that are to be made in practice? The answer requires that we look more closely at playground situations where our responses to what we see taking place are problematic, and where we must question on what grounds we can even know how to respond at all. So when a child brings our attention to the riskiness of his or her activity, we ought to consider carefully what is the best thing to do for this particular child. What help should we give? What specific actions should we take? Our response will depend upon the particularities of the situation and upon our knowledge of the particular child. Even then, how can we be sure we have done the right thing? Of course, this is not to deny those general principles to which we can subscribe and by which we gain confidence in our dealings with children; however, the point of the present analysis is not just to define educational principles of being with children, but to show how these principles become meaningful in concrete pedagogical situations. In so doing we might come to see risk as both the topic of our inquiry and its orienting principle. We may come to see how any intervention on our part in risky playground situations is, at another level, a risk we must take.

So, as we try to talk about this relationality of risk we find that our engagement with children carries certain silences. We approach their activity with a questioning silence and often we must remain silent through our failure to see what is at stake in their activity. Such silences are the result of an inevitable distance between children and us, however this is not so much a lack as a means of redefining the nature of our relation. The silences of our approach lead to a deeper silence, a comprehending silence where we try to find our common ground. We remember taking risks ourselves in much the same way as the children before us do; and on the basis of these recollections we try to work out how to be in a position to help these children take the risks we see in their activity. These silences of our approach to children's playground activity thus serve to open us more deeply to the relational nature of risk. The silences of risk show the provisional status of any observational analysis. They show that our words make sense only when they serve to place us within the fluctuations, ambiguities, and uncertainties of playground life.

## The Atmosphere of Risk

If risk is a term of our relation to children and if we can see in the risks of the playground a positive account of this relation, then what are its constitutive features? What is the texture of risk we see manifested especially in playground situations? Perhaps the texture of risk is reflective of a generalized atmosphere of risk that is evident even in the normal course of everyday life. After all, children are often minded by people they hardly know; they are placed in the care of strangers; they are left on their own when adult activity makes their presence inconvenient. In the course of everyday life what we do with children and what constitutes the texture of our relation to them makes children aware of a certain atmosphere of risk. If left completely to themselves or if our actions are evidence of a complete disregard for them then we find children exposed unprotected in this atmosphere of risk—children who are at-risk. On the other hand, the playground, being a place that carries an adult regard for the child, is a place where this atmosphere, this texture, can be influenced in ways that bring a security to the child's explorations. Here we can see that risk comes down to how we might be present to the activities of children, that children can be helped to take risks in relative safety through the encouragements we are able to give them and through the way we encounter playground challenges with them. From this general atmosphere of risk might develop a pedagogical atmosphere in which risk signifies a way of staying in touch with the course of children's playground activity.

How can we be mindful of this texture of risk and so influence the direction of children's activity most positively? In response to this question we can be guided by the visibility of risk, or rather, by our observations of what children are already able to do. Their stepping onto the playground, their responding to the challenges of the things they find there, is evidence of their desire to see the world around them in an active way. The playground appeals to children because it allows them to step away from adult protectiveness and thus to feel somewhat responsible for what they do. To influence the direction of children's activity most positively requires, therefore, our looking at what children care to show us and our responding in ways that not only enhance their movement repertoire but also help them gain confidence in doing things for themselves. The visibility of this texture of risk thus enables us to see that atmosphere is determined in large part by the responses we care to make to children's activity. Through examples of risky playground situations we can even differentiate between these various responses and show that the texture of risk is disclosed in differing modes of adult presence, a classification of which might show how we can best instill confidence in children.

## The Challenge of Risk

As an adult, a parent, a teacher, how does this attunement to risk guide the responses we might make to playground activity? And how can we find within these responses certain embodied principles of pedagogical action? Our task is to work through these silences that seem so much a part of knowing how we should respond to the riskiness of children's activity. The task is to abide by these silences and yet still say something of consequence about the pedagogical significance of risk and how we might help children learn to take risks. This is our challenge to become reacquainted with the children we see on playgrounds as they are involved in their pursuits.

Taking up this subject, we begin to see the challenges that inhere in playground activity and that make risk visible. Just being with other children creates situations of daring, of children daring one another, taunting each other to try some activity that will test their mettle publicly. These are direct social challenges. There are also indirect, social challenges that arise from watching other children or from simply seeing the possibilities of movement that some piece of equipment allows. What is important for our understanding of risk, however, is not so much the social structure of challenge as the manner in which this particular visibility of risk allows us to construe a pedagogy. More important than an analysis of the general social challenges of the playground is the distinction that might be made between positive and negative challenges. For instance, when is challenge to be considered a positive encouragement of children's risk-taking? What form should such encouragement take? And what are the limits of this pedagogical response to challenge? Alternatively, when do our words and actions place undue pressure on the child? When do they ensnare the child in a situation where the risks seem much too great?

Our encouragements should enhance the child's independence of movement, especially since we are ultimately concerned with the child's growth and maturity. So we ask ourselves: what are the limits of a pedagogical response to risky playground situations? What is the point at which a child's independence of movement should be recognized? Perhaps we should look at how children find out for themselves how to meet a challenge and how our actions can be consistent with their learning to find their own way. Accordingly, we may then be attentive to the moment when a child no longer requests our help or even requires it—the moment when the child would just as soon try out the activity unassisted. We may indeed recognize in such situations of independence the limits of our involvement and the limits beyond which we must grant children the ability to take risks on their own.

## The Encounter with Risk

Having recognized a pattern in children's playground activity, are we now in a position to know what to do about risk and how to teach children to take risks? Have we seen the features of a pedagogy of risk clearly? Or have we stressed too much the visibility of risk and forgotten that risk is fundamentally a quality of the relation we have with children? When we talk about challenging children, encouraging their efforts, even letting them find their own way of doing things, we must remember that our responses are also expressions of our own experiences of risk and that a pedagogy of risk rests upon an acknowledgement of our own ability to take risks. These risky situations with which we are concerned, these shared encounters with risk, bring an adult's sense of risk to bear upon the child's activity and show the child a direction for his or her risk-taking.

The notion of an encounter with risk highlights the reflectivity that is at the heart of a pedagogy of risk. We want to trust the child to be eventually on his or her own, yet our greater awareness of risk leads to the prudence of intervening in the child's activity. Consequently we cast playground activity in terms of a series of challenges through which such trust in the child is made possible. Still, in this reflection on the risks of the child's activity we cannot be sure of what pertains to the activity itself and what is the product of our own way of considering the activity. It seems we must consider carefully whose interests are being served—the child's or ours. We must exercise a degree of vigilance in our thinking about the supposed riskiness of children's activity.

We see features of the encounter with risk in the manner in which we become apprehensive about the course of children's playground activity. Especially when playground things no longer seem so familiar to us, our apprehensions bring us in touch with the experience of a child who perhaps encounters such things for the very first time. We become mindful of the child, not so much out of fear as out of an attempt to stay in touch. There is, of course, always the risk of seeing too little of ourselves in the child's activity, which may lead to indifference or alternatively to a sense of danger which has no real basis to it. In such cases we bring a sense of danger to the activity when it is our understanding that is called for. The task, therefore, is to work through our apprehensiveness about children's playground activity, to understand how our feelings about the riskiness of what the child does can be the motive for helping the child learn to take risks.

The notion of an encounter with risk allows us to reconcile our need to lend security to the child's explorations with the child's need to test the security of his or her world. Encountering risk, we see that there are times when we ought to loosen our grasp of the child's activity. There is a point at which the encounter with risk obliges us to let the child go his or her own way. There is the point at which a pedagogy of risk comes down to our ability to trust the child to be on his or her own.

### The Practice of Risk

In our living with children, can we begin to see a direction to the course of their risk-taking? Do our challenges and our ways of encountering the playground with them conform to a type of sequence, a progression, even a development of movement competence? For instance, we may see how a certain playground activity becomes familiar to the child, then we may see how the child tries some variation that risks the certainty of what is known, until eventually quite difficult feats become possible. A child hangs on to the bars of a climbing frame. Later on she is able to swing from one bar to the next. Eventually she is able to travel from one end of this set of bars to the other. This child develops what are commonly called physical (sometimes motor) skills.

We might call this process skill development. The problem with the notion of skill development is that it denies the ongoing practice of taking risks. By attending to the visibility of playground activities we forget that it is fundamentally a relation of practice, a practical relation, that is being tested out in the child's explorations, and that what we are seeing of the child's activity is a consequence of the risks he or she has learned to take. Behind our talk of skill development we may find a child-oriented language of risk which may potentially give us a fuller sense of the meaning of young children's physical activity and of the continuity of the child's physical explorations. We may see how by learning to take risks the child learns to stay in practice. And we, in turn, can maintain a very practical relation to the child.

So we will speak of a practice of risk, or rather, an ordered exercise of a child's inclination to test out the relation that establishes his or her security. We will regard this practice as constituting a standard against which we can assess our responses to what we can see of the child's activity. Thus, when we see a child progressing in the difficulty of the things she can do we might consider how best to help that child achieve the potential that the playground apparatus holds. And this will require staying in practice with the child, or rather, attending to the riskiness of the child's activity over the course of successive playground encounters.

## The Possibility of Risk

What are the implications of this practice of risk? How might this practice apply to situations beyond the playground? To what extent is this practical interest in the riskiness of the playground constitutive of an educational view which extends beyond the domain of the playground? Here we can only consider some possible practical directions. Specifically, we will reflect upon what happens when the playground no longer holds such intense interest for children and when they begin to be pulled away from it. We will try to see in these new challenges and encounters an adumbration of the riskiness of the playground, or in other words, a further unfolding of the pedagogy of risk which was established in the context of playground activity.

We will speak of the possibility of risk in order to accent the broader pedagogical significance of the foregoing analysis. But this does not simply mean looking for points of application of a pedagogy of risk derived from the playground. If risk is a term of our pedagogical relation to children, then our reflections on the course of playground activity ought to reveal a *telos*, a highest possibility of the riskiness of the playground, and indeed, a natural fulfillment of the possibilities of the playground in activities that extend far beyond it. What we do with children on the playground might very well hold significance for a much broader domain of activity where risk is not so readily apparent.

But is risk itself a telos? Is it an end in itself? Or is it more a rite of passage, a test of life, or a means to other ends such as movement competence, self-knowledge, self-confidence, autonomy and self-direction? Again we can follow the lead which children provide, following them as they move on to activities beyond the playground, and considering these new activities in light of a pedagogy of risk and the playground. We can see, by moving on to these activities, if the significance of this pedagogy is confined to the playground activities we have attended to so far, or if it holds as well for a much broader domain of physical activity. And we can begin to formulate an answer to the question: in what longterm way is risk a function of the sense we bring to children's activity? How might this term of our pedagogical relation to children disclose possibilities for growth and development, even beyond the domain of physical activity?

## Pedagogical Considerations

Writing for educators and for anyone interested in the quality of children's lives, my intention is to provide critical ground for understanding how we might, as adults, bring up children. We are, as Langeveld insists, *"animal educandum-et educans:* the animal calling for education and the educating animal" (Langeveld, 1966, p. 91; see also Schmidt, 1973, esp. chapter 2). In this regard, I am not only making a certain anthropological claim as to the primacy of the playground in the lives of children, but I am saying that the thinking that led to the development of playgrounds and the thinking that is in evidence when adults interact with children on playgrounds also shows the fundamental responsibility that adults have for the growth of children. To talk about playgrounds and to become concerned about the risks that arise there is thus to talk about education in a very mundane yet critically important way.

Whatever we do with children on playgrounds has significance for the child's general growth towards maturity. But what we do pedagogically is distinguished by the level of reflectivity which we bring to these experiences with children. We must reflect, first of all, on whether playgrounds are good places for children and how they can be made better places. We must consider carefully our designs for children's learning. Furthermore, we must question the nature of our actions with children on playgrounds, and reflect especially upon how we might help children as they encounter the riskiness of the playground. From our playground reflections we may then be able to say something about how certain physical experiences should proceed for children in general.

From the present analysis might come some very practical recommendations regarding the learning experiences that are important for all children. All of which should not blind us to the fact that pedagogy remains a theory addressed to the individual child. After all, as Rilke (1910/1982) reminds us, it is possible that we say 'children,' without even suspecting that this word has "long since had no plural, but only countless singulars" (p. 24).[4] Pedagogy seeks to establish a relation to the child before us, and to bring a reflective sense of the Good to the actions we take on behalf of this child (cf. van Manen, 1982a). Pedagogy, as theory, should not be so speculative that it loses touch with particular children, but rather it should be "built up and formulated from the concrete situation of adult and child related to each other in an existential communication and encounter" (Nel, 1973, p. 204). Or, as van Manen put it: "Pedagogy is not found in philosophy, but like love or friendship, it is found in the experience of its presence—that is, in concrete, real life situations" (van Manen, 1982b, p. 284; 1991, p. 31).

Pedagogy connects us with the practice of being with children where there is the intention of guiding them towards "mature adulthood." It better enables us "to see the present situation and experiences of the child and value them for what they contain" and "to be able to anticipate the moment when the child can participate in the culture with fuller self-responsibility" (van Manen, 1991, p. 75). We reflect on the meaning and importance of the gestures, looks, tones of voice, and things said to children whereby the adult creates an atmosphere conducive to children's growth and development, establishes a relation of influence with particular children, and distinguishes certain risky situations as vital ones for this or that child's maturation.

Pedagogy brings a tact and thoughtfulness to the practice of being with children (van Manen, 1991, 1995). It engenders a practice of observing situations in which children find themselves and learning to distinguish a pedagogical situation from one that is not. It hones a sensitivity to children's concerns and predicaments, an attunement to their inner worlds, an interest in their interests, an inclination, in other words, to listen and watch children closely and become open to the possibilities of their growth and development. It prepares us to act by allowing us to assess situations with regard to our possible interventions and to then decide the best thing that can be done for a child in any particular situation. And finally, it brings a recognition of the restraint that is necessary as children become increasingly responsible for their own actions.

**Pedagogical Description**

I take the view that pedagogy will be most compellingly real if we speak of children directly. "Can you find the child?" asks Langeveld of most "educational research" (reported in Flitner, 1982, p. 66). The children of this study are Andrew, Carson, Christine, Cory, Denny, Dorian, Eduardo, Gerrard, James, Jamie, Jonathan, Kyler, Lewis, Lisa, Marc, Matthew, Paco, Rodrigo, Shayle, Sophie, Stephen, and Tyler. Their names are mostly fictitious, although behind the names I have given them there are certainly real children with real names. They are my own three children, my children's playmates, and my friends' children. They are children I see on playgrounds. In some cases they are children observed by others who have told me of risky events in these children's lives. There are also a few portrayals of children drawn from story books written for children. These children, whose ages range from four through ten years, are not subjects in any postivistic sense of the word, but mostly children I have lived with, listened to and followed around, for nigh on fifteen years.[5]

Far from being a random sample, these are children whose lives impinge upon my own, whose actions on the playground are influenced by my presence, and whose risk-taking preferences trigger a thoughtfulness about the nature and extent of my responsibility for them. Randomness applies only to the happenstances of the playground when certain risky events stand out as amusing, surprising, intriguing, breathtaking, unsettling, worrying, disturbing, or anxiety-provoking. These children provoke a range of responses that would not necessarily be elicited by a far more diverse and representative group of children selected with age, gender, ethnicity, and other demographic variables in mind; in fact, rather than accentuating any empirically visible differences between them, it is their individual and idiosyncratic perceptions of risk and varying risk-taking responses that are precisely the variables that matter in determining the nature of pedagogical reponsibility.

Of course age is not unimportant and in some examples of risk-taking we shall note the appreciable influence older children have on their younger siblings and playmates. Ethnicity has some bearing as well insofar as responses to children are influenced by culturally-defined norms for their care and nurturance. Gender is also an important consideration, and worthy of some comment, especially when we see that there are more boys than girls appearing in the examples given of playground risk-taking.

The predominance of boys may be related to the risk-taking activities traditionally enjoyed and defined by males (Trimpop, 1994, p. 200; Bromiley and Curley, 1992).[6] It may be attributable, furthermore, to the different uses that boys and girls traditionally make of the playground (Sutton-Smith, 1990) and their contrasting patterns of playground interaction (Finnan, 1982; Lever, 1976). But the predominance of boys in this study ought neither diminish the observation that gender differences are unnoticeable in the playground preferences of preschool children (Pellegrini, 1987, p. 4) nor the reasonable suggestion that the playground choices of older boys and girls are the result of teachers' discriminatory behavioral expectations (Evans, 1989, pp. 28–31) coupled with the persistence of "collective practices through which children and adults create and recreate gender in their daily interactions" (Thorne, 1993, p. 4). While there are cultural, social, and institutional reasons why there are more boys than girls represented in this study, there are no essential, pedagogical ones, even if we were to attribute something essentially male or female to the respective playground experiences of boys and girls (cf. Nabhan and Trimble, 1994, pp. 68, 69). The experiences of Christine, Kyler, Lisa, Shayle, and Sophie are as different from one another as they are from the experiences of Andrew, Carson, Cory,

Denny, Dorian, Eduardo, Gerrard, James, Jamie, Jonathan, Lewis, Marc, Matthew, Paco, Rodrigo, Stephen, and Tyler.[7]

I describe what these children do in actual situations on actual playgrounds. My intention is to base this study on an awareness of the concrete situations in which risk appears. And yet I do not want to be totally bound by the situations in which these children are to be found. I want to take some distance from the clutter of each situation, not so much to leave the child behind as to see the situation more clearly. Consequently, I "write up" these situations (which is quite a different matter altogether than writing things down), going beyond the written record of what children do in order to explore in narrative form the value of what they do and of what our responses might be. Composing rather than simply recording the situations in which we find ourselves with children on playgrounds, my intention is to disclose a "narrative knowledge" (Denske, 1988) of what the pedagogical relation might be.[8]

The form of the anecdote is used to help define the meaning of these playground situations and to find within each particular situation the point from which pedagogical reflection should proceed. Anecdotes of children on playgrounds thus become a means of deliberating on the point of the concrete situation to which they refer. Anecdotes serve to keep the child in view while obliging us to reflect upon not only what a situation holds for this particular child, but also what similar situations might hold for other children. In other words, the anecdote stands between the particularity of being with children we know and the more general truth, or the pedagogical theory, which we wish to formulate on the basis of these encounters. It could therefore be said that anecdote underlies the method of this study. It is the methodological device for providing points of attachment, lifeworld attachments,[9] for the somewhat abstract pedagogical theorizing by means of which we will give structure to our deliberations on the riskiness of the playground. So when we talk about the place, atmosphere, silence, etc., of risk and tend to become immersed in a fairly weighty tradition of pedagogical theorizing, the anecdote will serve to keep our feet firmly placed on the playground.

**Pedagogical Method**

The use of anecdote in this study conforms to the guidelines for lifeworld description which van Manen (1984; 1990) has developed. Here the emphasis is placed on writing as the *modus operandi* of the research endeavor. Writing is the "measure of our thoughtfulness" says van Manen (1990, p. 127). It is a reflexive activity whereby we take distance from the events in question, whether taking notes while sitting on the margins of children's activity or noting certain phrases, bits of dialogue, expressions, gestures, and bodily motions which we will translate into text later on, all for the sake of becoming more thoughtfully immersed in the events, "reuniting us with what we know, drawing us more closely to living relations and situations of the lifeworld, turning thought to a more tactful praxis, and concretizing and subjectifying our deepened understanding in practical action" (p. 129).

Writing is the task of seeing, hearing, and feeling more deeply one's responsibility for children. "Writing exercises us in the sense that it empowers us with embodied knowledge which can now be brought to play or realized in the performance of the drama of everyday life" (p. 130). Through the narration of risky events in children's lives, there can be a respite from the practical demand these events impose on us, for the sake of returning to them with a clearer vision of what is needed. Through the reflective distancing that writing allows, the full extent of our implication in creating meaning out of these risky events can be discerned. Through simplifying the sequence and scope of actual risky events, omitting extraneous details, we can better focus on what is of paramount importance in being most helpful to the children concerned. The resulting text is one that can be read in different ways (cf. Geertz, 1973; Ricoeur, 1971, 1982; Silverman, 1986), being open to analyses and interpretations beyond those I provide, yet it remains a text that raises the fundamental question: how might one see oneself connected pedagogically to the risky actions of children on and beyond playgrounds? In other words, the anecdotal quality of the writing up of this study situates us within a "dialogic textuality" (van Manen, 1986, p. 90) of the riskiness that permeates children's lives.

The application of anecdotal writing to the particular matter of the riskiness of the playground is something that will unfold as this study progresses. Besides, method should not be discussed totally apart from the contextualized pedagogical questions we want to raise. At a technical level, such a division of method and substance tends to result in a "reconstructed logic" of the investigation which bears little resemblance to the actual conduct of the inquiry (Soltis, 1984). At a phenomenological level, method is as much a way of speaking about our orientation, commitment and presence of mind as it is about procedures by which we come to understand what children do on playgrounds. Researching the riskiness of the playground aims at answering the question: how might we establish and maintain a relation to children which would attest to the significance of risk-taking for their growth and maturity? Our method of inquiry thus stems from an understanding of what it might mean to lead children into the wider world via the playground. So, although the anecdote stands out as an important methodological device within a broader phenomenological method of lifeworld description, we will follow such a phenomenological method only so long as it allows us to see the point of being with these children on playgrounds. More importantly, we will develop our own phenomenologically oriented, pedagogical method as we seek to address the questions that arise when risk is seen to be a term of our relation to children on playgrounds with which we are familiar.

Nel (1973) wrote that "pedagogy should evolve it own approach, its own method starting from the pedagogical situation as point of departure" and that " the pedagogical situation, as an existential situation, will itself indicate how it should be analysed and interpreted" (p. 209). Our immediate task, then, is to define the situations that are of interest and that require our involvement in the actions of children. Our task will be to map out a space for our investigation in such a way that we are situated in the midst of children's activity. Hence, the starting point for pedagogical consideration will be the risky playground situations in which we find ourselves with children. From this starting point we shall hope to see the nature of our particular method of pedagogical inquiry. This means that any further explication of the pedagogical method underlying the study shall have to wait until we have defined more clearly the nature of these pedagogical situations and our stake within them.

**Pedagogical Theory**

A final consideration for this study pertains to the place of this phenomenological style of pedagogical theorizing in the North American context. To be sure, we should acknowledge the European tradition of inquiry from which many of the insights of this study are derived. In particular, the claim made by representatives of the *Geisteswissenchaftliche Pädagogik* tradition to the effect that pedagogy is an autonomus discipline (van Manen, 1987) is one which I make for the purposes of the present study. According to Weniger, who was one of the more influential proponents of the idea of pedagogical autonomy, there is a distinctiveness to pedagogical activity, which is to say, to activity serving the interests of children. This distinctiveness then suggests a need for places designed specifically to serve children's interests. In order to ensure what these interests are, however, there is a necessity for a science of pedagogy which would understand the distinctiveness of pedagogical activity and provide a knowledge of how the conditions of the world for children can be improved (Beugelsdijk and Miedema, 1984). But even though this claim has not been widely considered in the

North American context, except by way of calls for the autonomy of educational theory (eg. McMurray, 1955; Kneller, 1984) and for seeing the importance of a "phenomenology of education" for establishing a North American philosophy "of education" (Vandenberg, 1974, 1979, 1987), the claim of the present study goes beyond an ostensibly theoretical justification of the place of pedagogical thinking. The claim I shall make throughout this study is that our theorizing should be grounded by a practical understanding of how a pedagogical life ought to be lived.

Van Manen (1986b) has been especially critical of the ethical slippage between what educational theorists say and do, maintaining that "few educational theorists have addressed the question of how to apply the measure of pedagogy to the standard of one's own work" (p. 79). We seem interminably caught up in intellectual yet disembodied discussions of the connectedness of theory and practice and forget "that all [educational] theory and research were meant to orient us to pedagogy in our relations with children" (p. 79). Accordingly, the more important task to which the principle of the autonomy of pedagogy lays claim is that our theorizing should be a way of orienting ourselves to the world we share with children, and that it should be a way of principling the everyday actions we take on behalf of children for the sake of their maturity.

The present analysis of risk and our pedagogical relation to children on and beyond playgrounds is intended to be a North American example, or let us say, a locally familiar example, of the practicality of pedagogical theory. Playgrounds are, after all, a common feature of our cultural landscape, and thinking about playground activity does resonate with the conditions of North American life. So, if there is to be a place for thinking pedagogically, then the phenomenological style of analysis adopted in this study of the riskiness of the playground should serve to remind us of how we should live in the everyday world with children. It ought to direct us back to the lived experience of being with children on playgrounds with a deepened interest in doing the right thing by them.[10] This is the acid-test of the value of the following account of children's risk-taking.

# II

## An Awareness of Risk

# 2

# The
# Place of
# Risk

The notion of the playground opens up at least two lines of inquiry. First, it contains the suggestion that one ought to consider that physical locale where children behave in a "free, spontaneous, non-serious, and joyful manner" (cf. Ellis, 1973, p. 14). The playground, that area where children play, becomes of interest because of the distinctive type of activity that occurs there. And it is a place of psychological, sociological, anthropological, philosophical, even philanthropic and antiquarian interest, to the extent that play is held up as being of value psychologically, sociologically, anthropologically, and so forth (cf. Pellegrini, 1995).

Certainly these interests are apparent as one looks to the literature on playgrounds which, for the most part, deals implicitly with enhancing the values of play activity by paying explict attention to the nature and design of the grounds where such activity might take place. Four fairly distinct types of playground stand out. Traditional playgrounds are comprised of jungle gyms, see-saws, slides, swings of various types ranging from trapeze bars to metal rings on chains to wooden or, more recently, rubber seats, as well as revolving platforms and the occasional sets of parallel bars and horizontal bars—each piece of equipment standing separately and anchored firmly in a terrain of gravel or asphalt. Designer playgrounds link together apparatuses which, instead of being metal, are now made of wood, rubber and plastic—playgrounds where one finds tire swings, plastic tunnels, variously shaped climbing frames, slides of differing shapes and widths, all connected together by means of platforms, ladders, and even landscaped terraces. Adventure or junk playgrounds are established on vacant lots where children may come and actually construct their own play area using building materials and tools supplied by a playground supervisor who also directs the activities in a specifically built indoor play area. And then there are creative playgrounds where heavy construction materials such as cable spools, water pipes, large tires and telephone poles are fashioned into a variety of play shapes, and where children may either play on this equipment or in some of the other areas with sand, water, or with smaller pieces of lumber (cf. Frost, 1985, p. 168; also Brett et al., 1993).

Various studies have been undertaken to show the benefits of one type of playground over another (eg. Frost and Klein, 1979; Hart and Sheehan, 1986; Rothenberg and Beasley, 1974); nevertheless, "children themselves do not discriminate strongly, and sometimes not at all, between such areas and a multitude of other places in the environment that they find attractive—or places that they are obliged to use simply because there are no other options available" (Moore, 1986, xiii). These many and varied places where children play show that perhaps the design of playgrounds alone is not as important as adults may think. In fact, through their play space preferences children challenge the wisdom of an adult-constructed, self-contained, play space. They call into question the motives adults may have for being so preoccupied with playground design.

The preference shown in the playground literature for certain types of playgrounds over others would seem to reflect more an interest, on the part of adults, in defining "the perfect play experience" for children (Hill, 1980). One notable example of such interest is the advocacy of adventure playgrounds as places where children can learn to take risks. Perhaps the best-known proponent of adventure playgrounds spoke of children's "love of freedom to take calculated risks" and how this freedom " is recognized and welcomed in adventure playgrounds for these qualities bring their own exhilarating sense of independence and adventure." Adventure playgrounds provide a corrective to the confinement and regulation of children "in crowded cities or in over-regulated and over-tidy estates" and "are placed where they can learn to come to terms with the responsibilities of freedom" (Lady Allen of Hurtwood, in Bengtsson, 1972, p. 8, see also Hurtwood, 1968, p. 17).

It is interesting to note in passing that play is thought to be related etymologically to the Old English *pleoh* meaning "danger or risk," to *pleon* meaning "to expose to danger or risk," and to the Dutch *plegen* meaning "to care for, and be accustomed to" (Klein, 1971, p. 568).[1] These meanings, when taken together, resonate with the thinking behind the development of adventure playgrounds. Yet even here, in this admirable attempt to expand the traditional boundaries of play by appealing to certain risk-related qualities of children's playground activity, a playground design and an existing design rationale appear to be the dominant considerations. The direction of inquiry that this interest spawns could thus be considered as one of developing alternative playground structures and environments which may, through increased usage, attest to the importance of play in a child's life.

Now I do not want to disregard this line of thinking about playgrounds, although, no matter how well intentioned, it seems to me always in danger of misunderstanding the rationale behind playgrounds. Playgrounds are not just places to play, regardless of how broadly or specifically the idea of play is defined; they are presumably also good places for children. Playgrounds represent, in fact, an implicit connection, and one which is borne out etymologically, between play and children.

> For the Greeks, play, *paizo*, is what a child, *pais*, does. . . . Children play with playthings or toys, *paignion*, or play at a game or sport, *paigma*, or play an instrument, dance, and sing. . . . Anything suited to children is described as *paideos*, whether it be a game, paidia, or their education, *paideia* or *paideusis*. . . . Play, education, music, athletics, and the religious festival, are all bound to the same root-syllable, which sounds the vocative for Greek children: *Pai*. (Krell, 1972, p. 77)

This etymology betrays as well a "common cultural meaning" (cf. Taylor, 1979) of being a child. Ontologically speaking, "playing brings a fullness to the child's being that is otherwise lacking and forms the fundamental world that will otherwise be taken for granted. In childhood play the fundamental and primordial relation to being is formed and remains rooted . . ." (Vandenberg, 1971, p. 46; cf. Vandenberg, 1990, p. 201). Play, "that ontological mode essential to the development of human culture and, even more, to the development of the evolving child" (Suransky, 1982, p. 21), stands out as that which best characterizes what it means to be child-like.[2] Accordingly, when we look at playgrounds we not only look at children at play, we also look at that which the idea of play signifies and symbolizes. The playground, provided it is a good place to play, lets us look at the meaning of childhood.

Playgrounds represent a space for thinking about children. Perez and Hart (1980) make a similar point when considering what they regard as a narrow interest in enhancing the design of playgrounds so as to maximize their use. Their point is that "children—not playgrounds— should be the basis for planning" (p. 253). They ask: "What can be said from present knowledge of the development of children and from the behaviour of their caregivers, about the environmental opportunities which need to be created for children?" (p. 253). Now while I am sympathetic to the design project in which those like Perez and Hart are engaged, my point is that thinking about children on playgrounds requires a greater measure of self-reflection than that which is needed for planning and designing playgrounds. There remains something to the notion of the playground that needs to be addressed. There is the question of the nature of this space that begs understanding—the question of what makes the playground, or any other place for that matter, seem a place for children. And there is the supplementary question of why we should, as adults, even be interested in such places and how it is that we are in a position to observe their "specialness" (cf. Langeveld, 1983; Polakow and Sherif, 1987).

"What is 'place?'" asks Moore (1980), another playground designer. "To me, it is a means for integrating knowledge of the world into human relationships. It is a currency of belonging—a hierarchy of intersecting social and physical geographies" (p. 59). Playground places provide, in other words, a "landscape" of childhood—landscape as "a construct of the mind as well as a physical and measurable entity" (Tuan, 1979, p. 6). The playground, as a landscape of childhood, not only provides a place for thinking about children, it also symbolizes how we think about children. It is our special place maybe as much as it is the child's. Accordingly the behavior of children and their caregivers in that particular physical location defined as a playground cannot be viewed solely in terms of the design of that play space, because the question remains as to what makes that space interesting, which is to say, a child's place and a place where childhood can be recalled. The second line of inquiry into the notion of the playground thus requires not only considering the design aspect that distinguishes playgrounds from other human spaces, but also examining our own sense of a child's place in the world that a playground affords. It requires considering the grounds for thinking about children.

My contention is that playgrounds provide a clearing, a *topos*, a multi-dimensional space where seemingly disparate events can be gathered together to connote a network of interaction between adults and children. The notion of play has served to denote this interaction and mask it at the same time (cf. Sutton-Smith and Kelly-Byrne, 1984a). Certain activities have been shown to be of interest without the basis for our interest in them having been disclosed, and some activities have been ear-marked as being of more value than others, again without it having been made clear upon what basis a preference might be given.[3] Consequently I prefer to stay with the notion of the playground with its topographical orientation, its implication of an expressive and interrogative space which might provide clarification of childhood existence, and ask: what is the nature of this place? What view of life does it allow? And how might the adult be present for the development of such a view? Clues to answering these questions may be found in a review of the playground-related literature where it is possible to show how the notion of risk serves better than the notion of play in capturing this potentially pedagogical nature of playground activity. Here I shall attempt to show that risk is actually a more important notion than play in understanding the playground. And by implication, I will be showing how risk is also more important than play in understanding all pedagogy.

## The Safety of the Playground

From an historical perspective, an interest in children coupled with a concern for their safety led to the development of playgrounds as places set apart from the traffic of adult life. Curtis (1917), referring to the proliferation of what we now regard as traditional playgrounds, wrote that they "provide a place for play where the children can go during their leisure time, and be off the street and away from the evil influences which they might encounter there, and under the constructive leadership of trained directors" (p. 19). Playgrounds would keep children out of harm's way, whether it be "evil influences" or the injuries that might incur when playing in the midst of city traffic.

But we should be wary about inferring that this relatively recent interest in the safety of children can be equated directly with an interest in children themselves. Wood (1977) denounces the very idea of a playground and dismisses outright the notion that playgrounds became popular due to an increasing sensitivity to children that was reflected in adults' concerns for the safety of children. He refers to what the Opies had to say about past attitudes to children playing too near adults.

> Children always do seem to have been in trouble about the places where they played. In the nineteenth century there were repeated complaints that the pavements of London were made impassable by children's shuttlecock and tipcat. In Stuart times, Richard Steele reported, the vicinity of the Royal Exchange was infested with uninvited sportsmen, and a beadle was employed to whip away the "unlucky Boys with Toys and Balls." Even in the Middle Ages, when it might be supposed a meadow was within reach of every Jack and Jill in Britain, the young had a way of gravitating to unsuitable places. In 1332 it was found necessary to prohibit boys and others from playing in the precincts of the Palace of Westminster while parliament was sitting. In 1385 the Bishop of London was forced to declaim against the ball-play about St. Paul's; and in 1447, away in Devonshire, the Bishop of Exeter was complaining of "yong peple" playing in the cloister, even during divine service, such games as "the toppe, queke, penny prykke, and most atte tenys, by which the walles of the saide Cloistre have be defowled and the glas wyndowes all to brost." (Opie and Opie, 1969, p. 11)

Wood concludes that the idea of the playground is actually a convenient way of not being bothered by children and that, by confining children to playgrounds rather than having to look out for them on streets and in busy thoroughfares, adults are thinking much less of children and much more of themselves. "It was the automobile that made it possible, for the first time, to disguise this selfishness under the sanctimonious skirts of pretended concern for the safety of children" (Wood, 1977, p. 235).

Woods' denouncement of playgrounds rings harshly in our ears.[4] Perhaps his criticism is too strident, especially when the concern for safety does not stop at the idea of a playground *per se*. There is still a measure of concern for the design of "safe" playgrounds. For instance, the leader to Lady Allen of Hurtwood's article extolling the virtues of the Danish experiment in Adventure Playgrounds, which appeared in the November 1946 edition of *Picture Post*, referred to the dangers of bombed-out play sites. Readers were asked, "Why not make them safe places to play in?" (Bengtsson, 1972, p. 25). If concern for the safety of children were simply a disguise for adult indifference to children then why would adults be so concerned about the safety of playgrounds and the safety of children on playgrounds?[5]

Literature on the historical and social context of childhood is important at this point since it shows the conditions that give rise to an interest in the safety of children. We see that childhood is at least in part an historical invention (Aries, 1962; Boas, 1980; De Mause, 1974; Lee, 1982), that childhood can be easily eroded (Suransky, 1982), and that it might even disappear (Postman, 1982). The safety of children in general is tied to a rather precarious notion of what it means to be a child (Aptekar, 1988). We also learn that there is today an absence of "public love" for children (Grubb and Lazerson, 1982) and that far too many children continue to live in a state of "vulnerability" (Konner, 1991). In fact, the preferred attitude towards children at large seems to be one of antipathy in view of the pressures to which parenting is subject, especially in Western countries (Greer, 1984, pp. 26–29).[6]

There are, however, subtleties to this public indifference to children. These become apparent on one very traditional playground located within a tourist attraction where, on busy days, we can observe large gatherings of people at this particular site. Children, and some adults too, queue up to try the slides, the carousels, the horizontal bars, the see-saws, and the assortment of swings. On this playground the question of which child goes with which adult/s is not too hard to answer since we can watch as the children are shepherded around the playground, enticed down the slides, and photographed on the swings. What we notice is that, for the most part, the adults only have eyes for their own children. We hear one adult say to a child on the slippery slide: "Wow, look at you. . . . Come on Jessica. Come to Grandma. . . . Sure, you can do it!" Jessica falters for a moment and then, with children backing up behind her, she lets the slide have its way. "Hey, Mom," says the grandmother, "did you see your little girl?" Jessica runs to her mother, gets a cuddle, and then hurries over to her father who stands near the ladder to ensure that Jessica can find a place in the queue. Another adult carries his child up the ladder of the slide. He holds the toddler in front of him and both adult and child come down the slide together, watched by the rest of the family standing nearby. They are greeted by applause from these family members, which is a bit distracting, for as they move away from the end of the slide they stumble over a small child who dawdles in the sand. Holding his own child close to him, this adult does not notice the child underfoot. He does not mean any harm to that child. It is just that he, like the other adults on the playground, does not see children other than his own.

It is strange that so much delight can be taken in the cuteness of our own child and yet we can be so indifferent to other children. It is strange that we can be so protective of our own child and yet seem so oblivious to the safety of other children. But is it all that strange? One might object to my interpretation by arguing that in the concrete situation we would not be indifferent to the children of others if they were in distress. The point of the example, however, has not to do with indifference to children who are at-risk, but with an oversight of children that makes the normal course of their playground activity unsafe. A general indifference to the safety of children is what is at issue. On the other hand, can we be genuinely caring about all children who come within our purview? That would seem to extend the range of our concern and our responsibility for the safety of children beyond all reasonableness.[7]

This contrast between the personal and the public view of children, or rather the narrowness of the parental view, is disturbing. And it is all the more disturbing when we question to what extent present notions of parenting even allow us to see our own child. Perhaps even this seemingly well-intentioned interest in my child's safety requires closer scrutiny, for as Miller (1983) argues, child-rearing practices testify to a "poisonous pedagogy" where parents inflict cruelty upon their children under the pretext of parental care and concern. She claims that an interest in children is actually an interest in taking vengeance for the poisoning of one's own childhood. In this context, an interest in children, especially an interest that takes the form of a concern for their safety, cannot be taken at face value.

An interest in the safety of children expresses a cultural valuation of childhood that is reflected in the development of playgrounds. For instance, Zelizer (1985) argues that the disappearance of "the street hearth of play" (Zerner, 1977) actually indicates an increasingly sentimentalized view, a "sacralizing" of children's lives. The establishment of supervised playgrounds and the subsequent limitations that were imposed upon the so-called spontaneous children's games that existed in the past did not so much stifle childhood as bring the notion of childhood to prominence. That is, getting children off the streets was based upon concern for the physical and social dangers that threatened their safety (Zelizer, 1985, pp. 33–36), and this concern, Zelizer says, was part of a more pervasive cultural change in the way children have come to be valued. Consider, in this regard, the nostalgia sometimes expressed for the games that once existed beyond adult control and were presumably "played for no other reason than pleasure" (Postman, 1982, p. 4). Zelizer would say that this nostalgia is itself part of the sentimentalizing of childhood, and reflects an attitude to the supposed innocence of childhood that now allows for an *investment* in the lives of children, and for the high degree of adult control and supervision of children's play that is reflected in the present-day concern for playground safety.[8]

Nowadays school playgrounds, home backyards, rumpus rooms, community pools, playing fields, ice arenas, gymnasia, even water parks and thrill centres, are preferred by parents as places for their children to play over more traditional, and perhaps more alluring, places such as streets, vacant lots, woodland areas, streams and other water courses, and "such dangerous and forbidden places as sandpiles and quarries" (Hart, 1979, p. 334). Safe playgrounds, even playgrounds *per se*, are increasingly defined as those areas that are limited spatially and that allow the adult's view—that lie within the adult's purview. They are places designed with children in mind, which is to say, according to the view that childhood needs to be protected and secured. In effect, the design of the contemporary playground becomes a self-fulfilling prophecy of the nature of childhood to the extent that safety is the lens through which we look at children.

Of course, it would be unreasonable to argue against the safety of children; nevertheless, this does not mean that concern for the safety of children need be accepted unquestioningly. It may be that this concern, and the adult view from which it draws, places unnecessary limitations upon the child's experience of the world.[9] It may be that the concern for the safety of children, expressed in the provision of playgrounds, actually makes us increasingly insensitive to the child's place in a risky world. In fact, Van den Berg provides real cause for concern when he claims that the safety of the playground attests to the exile of children from an adult world. He says there is no better place than the playground to observe the separateness of the child's world. It is there that the child is not only separated from the adult world but also "put down" in a seemingly loving way. The observant adult will notice "certain peculiarities" there.

> Or rather, he must take off the glasses which make all inevitabilities seem acts of love. What he will then observe is . . . a fenced-in space, an island in the middle of the mature world, an island of comparative safety in a fatal maturity, an island of (necessary) exile. (Van den Berg, 1961/1975, pp. 94, 95)

Yet, lest we feel secure in what we have provided for children in terms of well-designed playgrounds, Van den Berg goes on to indicate the damage that occurs under the weight of such gestures of benevolence.

> When the child ventures on the street—he must go to school and home again—he has to be armed against the dangers he will meet. The grownups have given him a crossing guard. The children wait on the pavement until their little group has grown big enough, then the guard puts up his hand, the traffic stops, and the group of exiles hurry to the other side of the street. No sooner is the last child off the street than the waiting traffic accelerates and hurries on.
>
> A group of exiles? The thought that we are good for the children is more agreeable; so good are we that we lend them the attributes of

maturity to defend themselves. Look, there they go; everybody stops; the business man whose time is money, the large truck, whose delay can be expressed in hard cash—everybody stops for the children. Are we not good to them? Doubtless we are, but it is the least we can do; we are obliged to be good to them, because of the great amount of irreparable evil we have done. Our goodness pays for a great injustice. (Van den Berg, 1961/1975, p. 95)

Seen in this light, the safety of the playground becomes a troublesome notion, especially when we are reminded by Slukin (1981, 1987) that "growing up in the playground" often entails subjection to the threats and intimidations of older children and, in general, submission to a brutal order that overrides the design of playgrounds as places where children can safely be by themselves. A fairly common situation is that of one child being threatened by another and then having to find a way out of being drawn into a fight. For example, one child grabs another, and says "I'm going to smash your face in (and knees him in the stomach)." The other child merely smiles, and replies "I'm going to let you off this time" (Slukin, 1981, p. 38). For this second child, no physical design can make the playground safe.

An initiative designed to make playgrounds safe from bullying and victimization involves teaching "playground etiquette" as a "subject" in elementary school classrooms (Davidson and Seligman, 1987).[10] Here we have an attempt to ensure the playground's safety by telling children how to behave there, an attempt which would seem to express an adult longing for the type of playground Van Den Berg describes as "an island of comparative safety in a fatal maturity." Such an attempt should certainly give us cause for concern as we wonder about the need to "lend them [children] the attributes of maturity" so as to ensure their safety on the playground. One wonders if, under the guise of playground safety, we have not merely substituted one rigid order, albeit an adult-sanctioned one, for another. Still we must ask: what has this concern for safety achieved for the child?

## The Supervision of Children

In order for there to be a real measure of safety in what children do on playgrounds it is necessary that their playground activity be properly understood. The safety of playground activity is not the absence of risk, nor is it simply a matter of the successful design and management of risk. The designers of playgrounds have been quick to point out that playgrounds can be made totally safe by minimizing those features that provide challenge, variety, adaptability, and complexity, and that by reducing the risk-taking opportunities the safety of these playgrounds is guaranteed in that they would hardly be used at all. "Indeed, this is the case with many of the traditional playgrounds now in existence. They are not being heavily used because children do not like them; they are neither fun nor challenging" (Wilkinson and Lockhart, 1980, p. 87). This is also the case with many of the newer designer playgrounds designed more out of fear of litigation than in response to children's desires to take risks. The safety of the playground hinges on more than just playground design and teaching children how to behave there (eg. Chlad, 1987). It is largely a function of our view of things that happen when the playground is in use. While ensuring safety requires checking equipment, it also means overseeing children's activity and inspecting what it is that they are doing. Safety is the requirement of ensuring adequate supervision of children's playground activity.

Supervision is a defining of children's activity, a bounded way of observing children, a framing of one's thoughts about them. Supervision is the practical, parental measure of the safety of the playground. Perhaps it is not totally out of hand to say that "[p]laygrounds themselves are really nothing other than places that have been set aside for children. They're not safe; they're not special; they're just marked out areas that it's okay to be in" (Beckworth and Hewes, 1974, p. 64). What makes a playground safe, although not necessarily special, is the presence of an adult who supervises the child's activity.

Early playgrounds had adult play supervisors, adventure playgrounds were conceived as requiring playground leaders, and now, paid monitors and supervisors supervise the recess and lunch-time play of elementary school children while community playgrounds yield to summer playground programs under the direction of trained recreation workers. Supervision has become the watchword for children. The point to recognize about playground supervision, however, is that in spite of defining playground activity quite narrowly and confining children's activity within an adult view, it holds out the possibility of truly seeing the child.

To see the child rather than simply to view his or her activity according to preconceived categories of adult interest means bringing to light that which makes the events of a playground of interest and that which cuts deeper than the verdict that children are "playing in safety." We need to look at playground activity, not with any preconceived framework which would make our looking into a set view, but rather with a certain attitude that is mindful of our involvement, even as observers, in the situation at hand. In effect, it is necessary to suspend certain theoretical as well as practical interests in playground spaces and explicate what motivates our urge to supervise playground activity. Some time ago Herbart wrote:

> Perhaps it has been my misfortune to witness too many examples of the effect of strict supervision in public institutions, and perhaps, having due regard to the safety of life and strength of limb, I am much too possessed with the idea that boys must be allowed to run risks if they are to become men. Suffice it briefly to remember that punctilious and constant supervision is burdensome alike to the supervisor and those he watches over, and is apt therefore to be associated on both sides with deceit, and thrown off at every opportunity—and also that the need for it grows with the degree in which it is used, and that at last every moment of its intermittance is fraught with danger. Further, it prevents children from knowing and testing themselves, and learning a thousand things which are not included in any pedagogic system, but can only be found by self-search. (Herbart, 1806/1896, pp. 97, 98)

Here, it seems to me, is the crux of the matter. The safety of children that is bought through a preoccupation with their strict supervision may eventually put them at-risk, because this single-minded concern would deny the risks that are a natural and inevitable part of their activity. The strictness of this supervisory concern would also deny the adult's part in helping the child take risks in relative safety.

Strict supervision means that the child is far too conscious of the adult's approval of "safe" action. Consider your own remembrances of how a feeling of being supervised and hence being only a "kid" outweighed any benefit from being seen by the adult in attendance. In fact, recollections of favorite times on the playground tend to revolve around those times when we "had it to ourselves" and could try things that might not necessarily meet the approval of adults. But did we really have it to ourselves? Or was this sense of being in charge of our destiny really a result of a much less overbearing, far more subtle, adult presence? After all, children will invite adults to join their playground activity provided that the adults are kindly disposed towards them and prepared to enter the spirit of their activity (e.g. Corsaro, 1981). Or, as Lindsay (1984) concluded from his study of playground activity, "teachers who show an interest in the games [of children] are welcomed even though they are adults. This is one very effective way for teachers to achieve rapport with a class, and the thrill of acceptance by being invited to join a game can be as satisfying for the teacher or visitor as it is for the 'new kid on the block'" (p. 11). Strict supervision suggests a disinclination to understand the nature of the risks of the playground, yet the idea of interested, engaged supervision allows for the possibility of seeing this riskiness in a more pedagogical way.

There is in fact a riskiness to the playground that undercuts our attempts, through the design of the playground apparatus and the formal, detached supervision of activities allowed on this apparatus, to ensure the safety of children. This riskiness is not antithetical to the child's safety, rather, we need to look at the child on the playground in such a way that our concern for playground safety might disclose the risk-taking that seems to be so much a part of the child's coming to terms with playground things and the things that the playground represents. We need to consider supervision for the sake of a child's safety in light of the more fundamental aspect of that child's propensity for taking risks.

## The Observation of Children

If we really want to assess the riskiness of the playground perhaps we should at least sit close by, watching what children do there. "Perhaps we have only enough energy and interest to sit on a park bench in the sunlight. But a world may be discovered there that has been screened off from our previous high-strung and overambitious consciousness," says Barrett (1972, p. 275) in words that apply nicely to this study. By the same token, we should be mindful also of what our proximity to the child implies. Walt Disney also sat on a park bench watching his children at play and in the process dreamed up "Disneyland." "It all started when my daughters were very young and I took them to amusement parks on Sunday. . . . I sat on a bench eating peanuts and looking all around me. I said to myself, dammit, why can't there be a better place to take your children, where you can have fun together?" (Thomas, 1976, p. 11). His watching led to a design for children and adults that overlooked the riskiness of the playground altogether. Of course we, too, have designs for children. The question is: to what extent might our designs open up the possibility of a relation to children that goes beyond the supervisory concern for safety? More specifically, how might our concern for the riskiness of the playground bring us closer to an understanding of how we should stand, or sit, in relation to them?

Consider, for a moment, the ubiquitous park bench: brightly-painted seats set into concrete slabs that border the traditional playgrounds, or lower benches and forms that tend to blend in with the construction materials used in the newer creative and designer playgrounds. No matter how unobtrusive the design and placement, the park bench signifies a certain relation of the adult to the child. The bench is a place for sitting down and taking a relaxed view of what the child is doing. The well-placed bench is meant to give the adult a sense of security, not only about the safety of the child, but also in making him or her feel comfortable in a place that is ostensibly for children. This latter aspect is not so much a feeling of physical comfort (although who would deny the need for that?) as it is a feeling of correctness about one's place on the playground. It may well be that sitting with the child on one of the platforms of the playground apparatus is just as physically comfortable as reclining on the park bench, while standing on the platform at the top of the slide area is possibly more comforting safety-wise; nevertheless there is a strong tendency for the adult to move away from these positions as if it is not proper to be seen there. At a community swimming pool, for example, the sign on the slide clearly states that only children under eight years of age can use this equipment. And the unwary adult who climbs up the ladder behind her young child is soon made aware of this rule by the attendant with the megaphone on the far side of the pool. Likewise, some outdoor playgrounds have signs that ensure that adults stay in their designated place on the park bench.

The park bench is also something upon which children do not generally play, something which they approach only when wishing to break away from the activity at hand to seek consolation, reassurance, or some other contact with the adult sitting there. The child rushes over from the swings, pulling and tugging at the coat that now seems too hot to be worn, and as he comes near he flings the coat in the direction of the bench, turns on his heels, and races back to the swings. He knows the bench is not there to be played upon; it is simply placed there to ensure the comfort of his activity. Another child approaches in tears, having been treated roughly by one of her playmates. She sits for a while beside the adult on the bench and finds some solace in the detachment of this place from those who caused her injury; but before too long she becomes restless, hearing once again the noises of those on the playground. She pauses a moment longer, unsure whether or not to leave this protective place, until she hears her name called by one of the children. All is forgiven, the bench has served its purpose, and the child re-enters the playground.

The park bench thus signifies more than a physical proximity to the child. It signifies the nature of the adult's relation to the child without necessarily foreclosing the possibilities of this relation. From a design perspective, the important consideration will be that of the proper placement of park benches. Let me cite one exaggerated example of the designer's concern.

When a mother arrives at a playground with her child, she is usually already footweary. She has no doubt pushed or pulled or carried a carriage, a stroller, a large bundle of toys, something to drink or eat for Junior, her knitting or a book—perhaps for part of the way she has even had to carry the child. And she has juggled these various difficulties while making her way across busy streets, keeping hand and eye on the child, and watching out for traffic. If this young mother has two young children with her, the problems are fourfold.

It is no harder for this mother to let down her guard against potential danger once ensconced on a playground bench than it is for the long-haul automobile driver to be inclined to doze off while driving. It is a reflex which one cannot completely control. Many accidents happen because she is such a long way away from her child that the imminent danger is not apparent until too late. (Aaron and Winawer, 1965, p. 68)

For these writers, the design concern is that children should be supervised "at a range close enough for control" (p. 68). To be open to the possibilities of the adult-child relation on the playground, however, it is necessary to look beyond supervision, which means questioning the meaning of the park bench and that which is intended in its design.

Like the seating of a theatre, it is possible to choose where one sits in relation to children on the playground, to see the things they do in a many-sided way, as in theatre-in-the-round, and even to take part in the drama which unfolds. But beyond the issues of control and supervision, the deeper issue of the park bench is that it brings to the fore the significance of the adult's presence on the playground and the question of how he or she should be present to the child's activity. The adult is not a mere supervisor of children's playground activity, but rather a keen observer of what children can and cannot do, of their fears and difficulties, of the danger and challenge of their activities. The adult can come to see risk in the context of the playground with a mindfulness of the child. Although the playground, as an adult construction, gives certain visible evidence of the adult's presence, still there is a need to have the child feel this presence in a way that makes the playground a place of responsible risk-taking. So, although one needs to be in a position to see the child, the more important issue pertains to how one tries to observe fully the question of how it is that the child can learn to take risks in safety.

The task is not only to look at the child, but also to take note of how the child is placed. Observing means looking with care. "The word 'observing' has etymological connections to 'preserving, saving, regarding, protecting.' The teacher serves the child by observing from very close proximity while still maintaining distance" (van Manen, 1986, p. 19). This is what the park bench allows. And yet, to appreciate fully the significance of the park bench, it is necessary to see it as a means of observing children in a particular manner.

Beets (1952/1975) outlines the ways this significance might be appreciated. He describes various situations of watching young children playing soccer and highlights the different ways in which we might observe what is going on. In the first case, Beets writes about the adult who just happens to be passing by a soccer field. This person can become interested for a while in what is happening there, yet he or she can just as easily leave the situation behind without having had any real effect upon the children's play. In the second case, Beets refers to the adult observer who is known to the children in more than a passing sort of way. As a coach perhaps, or as mother or father of one of the children, the adult is in a position to observe the children in a far more engaged and responsible manner. Even so, this kind of observation still leaves room for a deeper pedagogical stance. So Beets goes on to talk about a third case where the adult who watches the soccer game has special responsibility for the education of the children involved. He says:

> They know me and I know them. When I stand still and watch while they are playing, I am an outsider in a certain sense, since now I observe them from a scientific or an educational vantage point of "pedagogue" or "diagnosticus." But I am also involved, since I am and feel that I am responsible for their education. I stand beside the parent—on the side of the educators. Now I observe in a special manner, however. I have learned to adopt a scientific vantage point and my observing is observation from that "vision." (Beets, 1952/1975, p. 16, translated by van Manen, 1979, p. 8.)

Each of these cases not only reflect different stances taken up by the passer-by, the father/coach or the pedagogue, they also express different forms of interaction between children and their observers. They are different ways of responding to the children's activity. Accordingly, the significance of the well-placed bench is that it not only enables the child on the playground to be seen, but it also places the adult in the midst of the child's activity and calls upon his or her ability to respond to what is seen to be happening there. Borrowing from a more technicist language, it allows for "skillful" handling of the child, where "[a] skillful observer develops sensitivity to the uniqueness of personality and becomes increasingly able to interpret the language of behavior" (Dowley, 1969, p. 517). Such "skillful" observation is a function of attending to the child's gestures, body language, and facial expressions as well as the tone of voice and force of expression. It is the observation, not of distanced appraisal, but of proximal bodily register.

The well-placed bench puts the adult into a situation where he or she can sense the significance of the child's activity on the playground. One can feel the child's apprehension, taste the child's fears, palpably follow the course of the child's activity. The well-placed bench allows empathic understanding of what a particular child is experiencing here and now while "being a child-watcher who keeps in view the total existence of the developing child" (van Manen, 1986, p. 18).[11]

## Risky Situations

Let me give a more concrete illustration of this form of observation. Consider watching some young children at play. From the park bench I see two small girls on a circular slippery slide. One stands at the top while the other straddles the raised edge of the slide, and starting at the bottom, she begins to pull herself up the slide by gripping under the edge and allowing her outside leg to dangle freely. "This is fun," she says to her friend at the top. "Why don't you try it?" Now half-way up, she decides to try something new. "Hey, watch what I can do!" Standing on the edge and then bracing herself with her arms against the pillar around which the slide curves, she edges up further. But her friend at the top becomes perturbed by what she sees. Her concern shows even more as the adventurous one reaches the casing that covers the top of the slide, the curved plastic casing that offers no purchase for this girl and that has no guard rail to stop her from slipping over the edge and falling down onto the packed sand below, the casing that this girl is presently trying to climb over.

I have been watching what these girls are doing and now I, too, am concerned for the child who is at this moment precariously situated on the top of the slide. In fact, I am concerned for them both, because both of them find the situation risky, albeit in decidedly different ways. The little girl standing at the top is scared by the antics of her friend, while the latter child finds herself in a danger that she had not been able to anticipate nor one over which she can now exert some control. Her bravado, her attempt to impress her friend and I suspect, myself, has prevented her from appreciating the inevitable consequence of what she does.

As I watch these two little girls I feel responsible for what has now transpired. I have not shown either of them "what is the nature of mature adulthood toward which she is striving" (van Manen, 1979, p. 14). I have not helped them see a risk that is not necessarily a likely danger. An action component is missing from this situation, quite apart from the action of stopping the child from climbing up the slide. Unfortunately it is too late to act in any way. The child falls off the slide. My heart stops as I see her sprawled on the ground. A slight relief—she starts crying as I rush over to where she lays. I am further relieved—although she has fallen heavily, fortunately the little girl has suffered only some minor bruising. I help her up, allowing her to hobble around for a little while before she and her friend head off to the swings. But as I return to the park bench, having done my job of consoling her after the fall, I feel more than a little responsible for what has happened and for what may well have been a more serious injury. I should have stepped in before the child put herself in danger, before a fall became imminent, although I am not at all sure, even now, that preventing the child from going further up the slide would have been the best action to take. What would my concern for danger do for the child who watches from the top in a state of concern? How would she be helped by my pointing out the danger that lurks in the playground? On the other hand, the vitality has gone from the little girls' movements. I watch them now on the swings and I cannot help but think that something has been lost for these girls as a result of the fall and the lack of observance of that which led up to it. The children have gained an awareness of safety at the expense of an awareness of risk. A potential opportunity to teach them the life-affirming consequences of taking a risk has been lost.

This situation shows that, while the park bench provides a measure of security for the child, at times it obscures the difference between watching and truly observing the child's activity. At times it is necessary to step onto the playground and address face-to-face the question of risk, the question which defines the boundaries of the playground, the question which makes the playground interesting, and the question which asks how we might observe what children do there. The young children on the slide need not so much to appreciate the potential (and in this case, actual) danger in the situation at hand, as to see the risk involved in what they are doing. Well before the likelihood of mishap, the adult must not only be able to assist the child and be in a position to do so, but in addition, there must be something about the adult's positioning on the playground that enables the riskiness of the activity to become clearer to the child. In other words, the adult who has the ability to see the riskiness of a young child climbing up the slide, who sees the fear this strikes in the heart of the little girl watching from the top, who sees that the motivation for this risky activity depends very much upon the responses of those who stand nearest, this adult must acknowledge the decisive moment of his of her positioning on the playground.

Are we there simply to watch the child, to dare the child, or does the fact that we are in attendance mean the situation is potentially a pedagogical one? Can we "convert by way of a pedagogical intention some incidental subject or problem situation into a situation where a certain question or problem becomes a critical one for the young person?" (van Manen, 1987, p. 22). Can we act in such a way that both children can see in the risks of the activity an opportunity for safe movement exploration? To be sure, there will remain a risk in the situation involving the girl climbing up the slide, yet it is the observer's awareness of this risk that can create an upswing in their being together on the playground. These children on the slide look to the adult who sits on the park bench. And now that this vantage point is sighted it creates a site for their explorations. The adult is caught in a situation where he or she can either stay seated and leave the children to their own devices, or where their glances can be acknowledged and the movement possibilities of the situation drawn out. Either way a decision has been made.

Bollnow (1972) makes a useful distinction between the "position" we find ourselves in and "situation" for which we are responsible. The former refers to "the living environment of man [sic], the totality of all the circumstances that influence him in a stimulating as well as restraining way" (p. 376). Positioning is a function of external pressures, including social obligations, professional expectations and culturally inscribed norms for proper behavior. To take up a position on the playground is thus to comply with what it generally means to be an adult who is responsible in varying degrees, depending upon one's assumed role, for the safety of children and for their proper supervision. To be situated on the playground and to find oneself in particular, ever-changing situations of responsibility for what children are observed to be doing there is, however, to acknowledge "a determinate critical position, namely a position that places man [sic] before the necessity of making a decision" (p. 376). Being in a situation with children on the playground has a stronger sense of personal immediacy. It requires that choices be made between standing back and stepping in and between the kinds of interventions that might be made. Risky situations, especially, require decisions that determine the quality of a child's life and the kind of influence that we have over the direction that life might take.

Of course not every risky situation requires that something decisive happen on our part. One must be sensitive to the difference between critical instances and those which are not, since pedagogy fails as much at the extreme of investing absolutely everything with momentous significance as it does at the other extreme of seeing nothing at all as decisive. The truth of the matter may be that the most important decision is the one to be there for the sake of the child's explorations. This decision potentially circumscribes not only a position, a posture towards playground activity, but also a situation that gives meaning to the particular decisions one might make regarding what to do with the children one faces. This decision to observe children's playground activity creates a situation in which one is implicated no matter what one decides to do in specific instances. This decision creates a situation of moral responsibility for children.[12]

We are somehow responsible for the child's falling off the circular slide, although not necessarily in any culpable way. Like many other playground incidents, this incident could have been avoided. From the sidelines we see that slides as well as climbing frames, swings, ladders, beams, and bars, each pose a challenge for children and require them to take risks. We see dares, challenges, contests, and games take place around these playground things and become part of the awareness of risk. And we see this happen on all sorts of playgrounds, even playgrounds where things appear to be quite safe. Yet as we observe more closely we see that "safe playgrounds" only make sense in light of the question of risk. The consideration of the riskiness of the playground is thus not so much a matter of watching particular situations as a matter of seeing our place within those situations and ensuring that this place holds out the possibility of bringing a sense of security to the child's explorations.

How do we do this? How are we to take up such a position of responsibility? We need to be aware that the riskiness of the playground points beyond the situation at hand. The incident of the two young children on the circular slide, for instance, says something about children's experience of risk and something about an adult's response, however it attests to a more pervasive meaning of risk that is compressed within this particular situation. In the words of Buytendijk (1958), the "analysis of human relations must be part of the more extensive analysis of the meaningful structure which we call a 'situation'" (p. 109). We see, for instance, that the child is fearful and that at a certain moment she becomes distressed. We can experience her fears and trepidations ourselves but we do not yet know their fully situated meaning. In order to understand "the meaningful structure which we call a 'situation'" we must delve more deeply into the "dialogue" that sustains it (p. 109). What is the nature of this resonance we feel when observing children? What is the basis for our empathy with the child? What is the motive for this gestural communication that occurs most decidedly in risky situations? Questions such as these require interrogating the meaning of the adult-child "dialogue" and, in Buytendik's words, coming to "understand this dialogue as an 'historical idea' in a situation that has become its own" (p. 109).

We should reconsider playground situations where risk appears, discerning within these situations important questions pertaining to children's fears and difficulties, and questions pertaining to the place of danger, challenge, and adventure in children's lives. We should raise questions that have to do with what we should or should not do for children when a sense of risk pervades their activity. How can children be taught to take risks in safety? How can parents and teachers enable children to become responsible risk-takers? These are important questions to ask in specific instances. But ultimately this questioning of the riskiness of children's activity is a questioning of our relation to children within the context of a precarious social-historical world. It is a questioning of what we should do for and with children for the sake of their continued movement towards becoming responsible themselves for the risky texture of life itself.

The playground is a unique place for addressing the meaning of risk in a child's life, but it is not the only place. It is designed to shield children from the risks that lie beyond it; yet, not surprisingly, we cannot totally minimize the risks of the playground without losing children's interest. So we create playgrounds which, to a greater or lesser extent, allow children to take risks in a sheltered environment. Instead of children climbing trees and rooftops or balancing on the tops of fences, they can now climb ladders, frames, and cargo nets, and walk along wooden beams set only a short distance from the ground; instead of exploring tunnels and caverns, they can now play in concrete pipes and plastic tubes installed on playgrounds. The designed playground allows for some control over the risks a child might otherwise take when left to his or her devices. Nevertheless, children will invariably test the design of the safest playground. They will take risks which even the best of playground designers could not anticipate. Hence, in order to avoid adversity, it is necessary for us to be present to the activity of children and to stand close by at least in a supervisory relation to them. Now we can observe children from close quarters. Now we can begin to see what is at stake when we are present on the playground. We can see that risky situations are occasions for interacting with children and for helping them gain confidence in their range of movement. But risky playground situations not only have a bearing on the particular physical activities in which children are engaged, they also influence children's confidence in a world which the playground represents for the moment. The playground, we shall find, is not such an isolated place after all. This place where risk can become a term of a relation to children allows us to consider how we can help children find their place in a precarious and sometimes all too risky world.

# 3

# The
# Silence of
# Risk

How shall we investigate the risky situations in which we find ourselves with children? What method will give us access to the risk-taking experiences of children? What set of procedures shall we use for observing children's playground activity while acknowledging the potential influence we have on the course which that activity takes? To ask questions such as these runs the risk of putting up research barriers between adult and child and ignoring the very thing we are trying to tease out in this study, namely the relation between adult and child that is somehow defined by the notion of risk. Listen to Beekman (1983) as he tells how procedures can get in the way.

> I would be like the observers of a playground in Holland, counting their
> own made up categories but not understanding. This is described very

clearly in *Kinderen buiten spel (The Play of Children Out-of-Doors)* where so-called objective observers went inside an unobtrusive workman's shack, made a peeping hole, and made coded observations. In their protocols we find scores of "activities" numerically coded. The meaning of the experience is missing. For instance, if you were really "in" the park, you would see girls hanging around on bikes. Doing nothing? Or being social? How do you know, until you are really out there, interacting with the children? (p. 39)

How do you know children are taking risks, and how do you know what risk-taking might mean, "until you are really out there, interacting with children?" Procedures that deny the adult's place on the playground also deny the point of observing children in the first place. They deny the point of being on the playground and of seeing how our presence mediates its risks.

This emphasis on situated, interactive experience does not mean there is no method to this study. On the contrary, I prefer to make a distinction between general procedures and techniques which can be followed by almost any researcher, and pedagogical method which first requires an attunement to the field, a committed stance to the researched, a certain moral sensitivity. Procedural recommendations alone do not necessarily have this orientation. Too often they serve as devices to keep us at a distance from that which is truly important. They do not necessarily connect with an educative interest in the riskiness of the playground. By the same token, understanding the meaning of risk in playground activity does not require the denial of any procedures whatsoever, but more an acknowledgement that the procedures being followed only make sense in terms of a deep-seated, interactive understanding of how certain situations first stand out as being risky. The question of procedure is really a second-order question determined, in the first instance, by the experience we have of the risks children encounter on the playground.

Perhaps the distinction that ought to be made is that between procedure and methodology, the latter referring to the reflective stance that makes sense of any particular procedure of inquiry. Methodology, in the present context, expresses a standpoint in relation to the playground, a decision to stand in a particular relation to those situations where risk is apparent, and a desire to make one's presence felt. "But is that not more an ethical imperative than a methodological prescription?" asks Beekman (1983, p. 38). He adds: "The question presupposes a gap between methodology and value realization. Is that gap justified?"

My task in the present chapter is to show that any gap between the methodology of understanding the riskiness of the playground and a pedagogical interest in the value of children's risk-taking is simply untenable. Here I shall explicate the methodological principles that are at work when such an interest thematizes one's relation to children.

## An Approach of Silence

"The child," says Smith (1986), "is always beyond our understanding because he is always beyond us" (p. 4). But this difference is not so much an impediment, as a formative principle of understanding playground activity. That is to say, the aim of this understanding is not to conceptualize children's activity, as if somehow taking hold of their experiences, but rather to make explicit the nature of those interactions that occur when a child's sense of playground activity touches us. When children show fear, or even when they are oblivious to danger, when their risk-taking demands our attention, this is when the difference between adult and child is played out. This is when pedagogical understanding arises, which is to say, understanding which is not "of the child" *per se*, but between the child and adult, and encompasses both. And this is when "the question must be asked how the constitution of such understanding can be conceived and made feasible in the pedagogical context and how the specific interaction structure of an act of pedagogical understanding can be ideally represented" (Scarbath, 1985, p. 94). This is the methodological question I shall now address as I look to certain inquiry approaches that potentially show a child orientation, that allow for an interrogation of the ways and means we have of acting in the best interests of the child, and that in turn hold promise for representing the interactional structure of our attempts to understand the riskiness of the playground.

To begin, Zerner (1977), in his admirable study of the "dwelling places" of children in the city, outlines an approach which shows a degree of deference to children. Instead of the grandiose title of "fieldwork" he prefers the term "Alley Work." Instead of observational categories, interview questions, rating scales, and so forth, his procedure was to observe children with as little interference as possible.

> Alley work occasionally had the contours of silence, the mantle of near invisibility. It meant being absolutely still and silent, sitting on a sunwashed step in Fresno Street while a moon exploration was occurring before my eyes. I sat for two hours on this modest perch, barely looking up for fear of disturbing the incredible drama of alley astronaut and Mr. Mission Control—writing down verbatim the details of a conversation transpiring between earth and moon. At these unexpected

moments there are no questions to be asked. A question during these rare moments is as jarring as a thunderclap during a holy ceremony. At these times one writes, one listens, one pretends he is doing his homework on a sunwarmed step in the city's springtime alley. (p. 19)

Zerner adopts an attitude of silence while observing children. He sits close by, listening intently, yet keeping quiet for fear of intruding upon the children's activity. What he has to say he keeps to himself; what he has to ask is confined to a realm of silence. To a certain extent, he finds himself in a situation that seems to require that he maintain a position of silent detachment.

Can such a position of silence be taken in a study that acknowledges the reflexively interactive constitution of childhood experience?[1] Is what Zerner does sufficient for understanding and being responsible for the riskiness of the playground? Will "being absolutely still and silent" allow for a pedagogical response to risk? In comparison with the present study of children's risk-taking, Zerner's detachment would seem to derive more from curiosity about the dwelling places of children than from deep-seated interest in dwelling with children. He shows disdain for the "spells of excruciatingly dull times" and asks: "How many replays of a common game of tag, football, or Chinese jump rope can one watch before succumbing to the pall of tedium?" (p. 26). And in his preference for the "rare moments of the exotic and surprising" over "the lion's share of the commonplace" (p. 26), a position of silent detachment is legitimized as method. The question of how risk thematizes our pedagogical relation to children, on the other hand, has to do with engagement and with how it is that we can stand in a relation to children that directly influences the nature of their activity. This question does not deny the importance of being silent at times; rather, it requires questioning the strictures of silent detachment in order to disclose an approach that allows for thoughtful, helpful relatedness.

Consider, by way of contrast, a much less silent posture. Consider observing children as they dare each other, as they find themselves in difficulties, and as they look to us for some measure of assistance. Here it is not possible to simply observe in silent detachment. Some guidance is required lest children are actually put at risk. Our silence must be broken. But does this mean that our research interest in these children must also be put aside as we engage in activity with them? On the contrary, I suggest that sometimes remaining silent while being present where children are playing (and thus nevertheless breaking another silence, that of children's privacy, for example) is being less attuned to a relation of pedagogy than it would be to involve ourselves in the children's activity. Here we may be guilty of trading one kind of silence, the silence of pedagogical intentionality, for another more trivial kind of silence. We may, in effect, be confusing the need at times for being silent, a literal silence, with the more important project of addressing the tension between our understanding and the child's understanding of risky playground activity, which is an epistemological silence.

How might we gain access to this deeper sense of silence? Certainly we can encounter the silences left behind by those who would make pat formulations out of the question of risk. In fact, no sooner are silences of understanding encountered than the explicit meanings, such as those defined in the theories, explanations, and conceptualizations of risk-taking, lose their hold and the lived meanings come into view. Still, what would silence be without the attempt to establish meaning? It would be a muteness, a silence that does not speak, an ignorance. So, perhaps it is better to think of understanding risk and our pedagogical relation to children in terms of the way silence and explicit meaning augment and deepen each other. "For where are words which are meant to be said, ever entirely said? Where does meaning end? In the unity of the sentence? Rather in the unity of the utterance which ends in silence." And in that silence the meaning of the words finds a deeper comprehension—"meaning spreads outwards only in the stillness of it having been said" (Gadamer, 1982, pp. 181, 182).

Silvers (1983) illustrates how one can access this epistemological silence when describing a situation of young children swinging on a tire. While watching this activity he notices a group of younger children standing off to the side, content, it seems, to simply watch what is going on. He asks one of them, a little girl named Sylvia: "Why don't you join in?" Sylvia responds: "They're the big people." Silvers thinks to himself that perhaps the younger children do not want to be bullied by the older ones, or perhaps they only want to play amongst themselves. His interpretations of Sylvia's response do not, however, account for the force of her remark that "They're the big people." Within this remark Silvers discerns "a thickness of history, of conflicts, of judgment, ways of relating to those older boys" along with "special meanings held within it that Sylvia and her friends would talk about" (Silvers, 1983, p. 92). For Silvers, these hidden meanings disclose the limits of an adult way of understanding.

> There are subtleties of meaning in what the big people are for her that I cannot know: neither do I know what to say to her nor do I know what to ask; the way I understand the big people allows me no access in comment or question, no way to address the depth of Sylvia's remark. In my failure to ask about the big people, I recognize a silence as a limit of my understanding. (p. 92)

Of course we are not confined to the silences that come upon us as if there is a point at which understanding ceases. While "silence is a failure borne out of difference" (Silvers, p. 96), it is in the awareness of difference that silence becomes truly meaningful and pedagogical understanding opens up. "Self and other with their respective interpretive domains stand together in the context of silence in a tensive relationship, the self and other are constituted as a dialectic" (Silvers, p. 105).

The situation involving Sylvia, her friends and "the big people" requires an understanding which not only recognizes this difference between adult observer and the child on the playground but also acknowledges that difference as the condition for a particular kind of understanding, namely pedagogical understanding, that is engaged, committed and continues to question its own meaning-making. The silences that fall upon us due to an acknowledged failure to fully understand the children's experiences also draw us forward to that which is of interest. So, it may be that "these interpretive occasions [cases where it is particularly difficult to understand] would provide better clues to the process whereby comprehension is achieved" (Polkinghorne, 1983, p. 226). But in the case of observing children while maintaining responsibility for the quality of their experiences, being brought to silence is not just of epistemological interest but fundamentally of pedagogical significance. Silence signifies the recognition of that difference which makes a pedagogical difference. It is the lived expression of sensitivity to the child and the thoughtful posture of response-ability for his or her actions.

Let me illustrate the nature of this way of understanding playground activity by referring to a situation in which silence can so easily go unnoticed unless one is mindful of pedagogical difference, a situation which thus shows pedagogical understanding to be more than a way of passively attending to the silences of playground activity.

"You're It" says Terry as he scampers away to join David on the blocks at the opposite side of the playground. "Not fair" cries Wayne, "I'm always It...Why don't you get David for a change?" He mutters to himself while keeping an eye on the other two. Next moment Wayne tears off after Terry. Wayne, it seems, has one last chase left in him. Twice around the playground they run until Terry leaps onto the platform of the main frame, leaving Wayne gasping for breath on the ground below.

As some new rules are being formulated in a last-ditch effort to save the game, Lewis and his friends arrive—ten of them altogether. David listens as Lewis tells his friends: "I'm It. You've got twenty seconds." "Are you allowed on the boards"? asks David, referring to the sleepers that serve as a border to the playground and form a circular path around it. Lewis nods, not only in agreement, but also in acknowledgement of the admission of the three boys to the larger game of It. Meanwhile the children are each finding their own space away from Lewis. Some have launched themselves onto the tire swings, some stand poised on the stumps and pillars ready to jump to a new vantage point, others hide beneath the playframe watching for signs of Lewis' approach, while a few of the little ones group together on the platform at the far end of the suspended bridge perhaps sensing that Lewis will give them time to escape if perchance he decides to come after them.

Lewis understands this game. Being a little older than the others he knows he can catch whomever he chooses. So he moves steadily towards no one in particular and creates, as a consequence, an excitement among all the children. He sends them scurrying in all directions, each child feeling that perhaps he or she is the one that Lewis has in mind. Lewis orchestrates this game. He is sensitive to its internal structure.

The game runs its course. It falters as some children find swinging on the tires to be more interesting, while others start to dig around in the sandy base of the playground, until eventually no one cares about "It" anymore. The game has broken down. Even Lewis has lost all interest. This seems to be an opportune moment to move onto something else, or maybe to intervene, for just as Lewis and his friends brought the earlier game to life so might some addition revive the present game.

As I observe this scene unfold I become attentive to the nuances of the game of "It." In so doing I encounter a silence that questions the ready interpretation. I recognize a silence as signifying my stepping into the game, as the limit of my understanding the game from a distance. Being drawn into the game I feel a certain responsibility for the children who are gathered there. I sense a loss in seeing the game disintegrate. Yet my interest in the activity of these children requires that I do not act solely on the basis of my impression of what has transpired, rather that I look even more closely at this activity so as to enter a playful relation with the children. Although a specific response may be called for, such as a suggestion of a new activity or even the cessation of play for the child who is in my charge, this response ideally comes from my interest in the children themselves, out of a respect for the integrity of the activity at hand and not out of a subordination of this activity to my categorization of it. I must literally bite my tongue for fear of adulterating the children's activity. Silence mediates and augments my understanding (cf. Dauenhauer, 1980, p. 154).

## A Silent Procedure

What does it mean, in practical terms, to understand the activities of children? Such understanding is much more than a method or a protocol. It is communicative action that tells the child "I care for you; what you say and feel is important" (Snyder et al., 1980, p. 149). I see what the child is up to and seek to understand the actions I observe and the expressions I hear as constitutive of who the child is and who she or he might become. My "understanding does not know and judge as one who stands apart unaffected; but rather, as one united by the specific bond with the other, [who] thinks with the other and undergoes the situation with him" (Gadamer, 1975, p. 288).

I understand the child from within the relation established with him or her. This is no mean feat; moreover, the control we can have over children's activity means that too often such a level of understanding is simply assumed to exist. Smith (1957) compares the parental attitudes of an earlier era when there appeared to be a stricter division between the things children did and the interests of adults. "My fear now is that all of us grownups have become so childish that we don't leave the kids much room to move around, that we foolishly believe that we understand them so well because we share things with them" (p. 123). It may very well be the case that we understand children best when "the most precious gift we can give the young" is the "privacy" of their own play spaces (Opie and Opie, 1969, p. 14). But even this "gift" requires an understanding of how we stand in relation to children. It requires seeing and hearing what matters to the children who are already in our view and deciding, at times, to remain silent.

This procedure of silence could therefore be defined as listening to children, observing them closely, and taking care in approaching their activity. In the first approximation of the object of my interest I must be cognizant of "the couple *hearing/keeping silent*" (Ricoeur, 1982, p. 59). I must see where I stand as a place for interpretation and as a place for hearing what calls forth my interpretation. It is a place to be silent, especially when the situation lends itself to silence.[2] But it is also a place from which to act in response to a child's predicament. In the second approximation of the object of my interest I cannot remain unmoved by what I see, rather I must act in response to the fact of my being an adult in the presence of a child in need.

Recall the situation of Sylvia and her friends standing near the tire swing. "They're the big people," she says, referring to the older children who monopolize this part of the playground. Hearing this, should I step in and insist that all children have their turn? Or should I not attend more closely to the tone of her remark about "the big people" in order to get some inkling of what is really at stake here? Perhaps if I had observed the situation more closely I might have seen the older children wrap one of the tire swings, the swing that Sylvia and her friends were using, around the side support so that it would be out of their way. I might have noticed these children taking turns to jump onto the swing from a platform just off to the side, and being grabbed by their partners whose job it is to keep kranking the swing up high and steer it towards the platform. I might have noticed how Sylvia and her friends watch this activity, how they are enthralled by it and more than a little in awe of what "the big people" can do on the swing. So when I (or Silvers) ask Sylvia: "Why don't you join in?" I might have realized that this question accents the activity in a particular way. My question is more than a means of understanding. It is a way of defining this playground situation for Sylvia. It is a type of challenge, perhaps even a dare. My question is a way of acting in response to what I see as being the child's predicament.

Similarly, when I watch Lewis chase the children around the playground I am taken in by what I see happening there. Because of Lewis' maturity I am able to sit still and watch the children jump from one thing to another, scale the higher sections of the playground, shimmy down poles and chains, or just jump to the ground when Lewis comes near them. I can sit and watch the children taking risks. And I can feel a sense of loss when the game disintegrates, especially when I see that Lewis has lost all interest. I want to show Lewis what the game is good for. I want to take over where Lewis has left off. Even when I am silently watching these children on the playground I am nonetheless attending to what I think matters to them.

This way of understanding playground activity requires an admission of our involvement in the activity of children. Although we need to take sufficient distance to question how the activity at hand is to be understood, still we must step close enough that no one interpretation satisfies. The task is to silence the ready interpretation and then, within this silencing, encounter playground things with children in mind. The matter of silence in understanding playground activity is not, therefore, simply the inaccessibility of the child's experience but rather the meaning of that which matters both to children and to us as observers of children, or participants with them, on the playground. The matter of silence is, on the far side, the otherness that is evident in our inability to fully account for the child's activity, and on the near side, the concealedness of that which is the motive for our interest in the playground.

Bollnow (1974) says: "we realize we are on the right track when the subject-matter resists our interpretation, when it remains independent of our expectations and forces us to correct our original starting point again and again" (p. 11). This is what I mean by the farther side of silence. The near side attests to our complicity in the actions of children. We identify ourselves when taking an interest in playground activity for this interest is only possible because of a prior complicity in such child-like activity. Hence there is a tension in our understanding playground activity pedagogically—a tension of self and other which, because of a common interest, continually questions the one-sidedness of my view of things. And this questioning, to the extent that it discloses common ground, allows us to see how we might be with children in a very understanding, caring manner.

I wish now to develop further this way of grounding an understanding of children's action—to elevate the discussion from a concern with procedural issues to a concern for a way of knowing about playground activity that might sustain a methodological orientation. At the same time, I want to show how the consideration of method is inextricably bound up with the very notion of risk. Already it should be apparent that to see risk we must be attentive to the silences of playground activity; now I would like to show that how we might respond to the risky situations in which we find ourselves with children, that is, what mode of presence we bring to bear upon the child's explorations, is contingent upon our ability to stand in the midst of the activity at hand, to take a risk ourselves, even to risk the ground upon which we stand.

## The Unspoken Ground

Bollnow (1982) says that of the many kinds of silences "there is also a comprehending silence, a well-intentioned silence, for all kindness takes place in silence." There is, first of all, "a forgiving silence" that excuses the child's impetuosity, allowing for mistakes, false starts, even willful actions. "This is not merely silence, but a mode of behavior that consists in not intervening straightaway, but of simply standing to one side with a certain understanding smile" (p. 43). A deeper kind of silence is the possibility of "wordless agreement" where "no words are necessary" and where "in this mutual silence [one can have] the sensation of belonging together" (p. 44).

This deeper kind of silence would seem to point beyond the realm of adult-child interactions. It is the possibility of being with the other person and for the other person, mutually and reciprocally. It would seem on this account to apply less to understanding children's activity than does the possibility of a "comprehending silence" where one acknowledges the child's relative immaturity and is content to be with him or her in a far more one-sided, child-oriented way. Nevertheless this formulation of "wordless agreement" indicates a direction for understanding the nature of our relation to children in situations even where a fully "comprehending silence" is not easily achieved. It discloses certain possibilities of our being in the midst of children's activity and having a sense of "belonging together" through the access that one's own maturity provides.

I think, for example, of four small girls on one of the tire swings at Alice's Playground. One is seated while the other three stand up by holding on to the long chains attaching the tire to its supporting beam. Higher and higher they swing. "I'm scared," says the one seated on the tire. "*I'm* not scared," responds one of the others hovering over her. It seems that the first child is not to be taken literally, for in the next instant she gives a squeal of delight and calls out "Higher! Higher!" Meanwhile a third child, finding the pitch of the swing a little too much, sits down to face the first child. The extra space between the chains now allows for greater mobility on the part of the two girls who remain standing on the tire. One reaches out with her foot to touch the platform towards which the swing now revolves. She misses. Next time she manages to make contact with it. On the third attempt she finds the edge of the platform and, pushing against it, sends the swing into a much wider orbit than before. "Stop! I'm scared!" pleads the girl who registered her fear only a short while ago. "I want to get off!" The swing slows down, and for the present the girls seem content to sit on the tire and talk amongst themselves.

Their talk drifts away from this activity. They see a boy from their school ride past. "Jeffrey, Jeffrey," they call out, until the boy spots them and then self-consciously proceeds upon his way. Inevitably, though, their thoughts return to the tire swing. And now, as if rested enough, the swing must once again be set in motion. But who shall they ask to give them a push? Of course I am standing close by watching Tyler on the adjacent tire swing. I glance over at the group of girls thinking they might request my assistance. Instead, one of the girls calls for her older sister, Lisa, to come and give them a push. She calls again, and again. It seems strange to be standing only a pace or two away and yet not be asked. True, they don't know me very well. They have seen me before at the playground, but they don't recognize me as part of their activity. In a sense they don't see me. They only see Lisa who must leave the game she plays with her friends on the far side of the playground in order to give assistance to this little group on the swing. They see Lisa as she wanders over to them while muttering something about "little brats that can't do anything for themselves"; yet they sense that hers is only a mock annoyance. Lisa is happy enough to come and help them.

So why don't they call upon me for help? Apart from the obvious reasons, ones that are not necessarily so obvious to the children on the swing, it seems that Lisa is better disposed to give assistance. She knows what the children want. She understands what is required of her by these girls. Lisa is called from a distance, while I who am standing closeby get ignored, because Lisa will know how much to push the swing. On the other hand, perhaps I might have offered my help. "Can I give you a push?" I might have asked. Such an offer might even have been accepted; and yet the situation that would then unfold would differ, possibly dramatically, from the situation in which Lisa found herself. Would this adult know how hard to push? Would he know when to stop? In this regard, perhaps there is a time, not so much to mind one's business, but rather to view an activity in what Bollnow calls "comprehending silence, a well-intentioned silence" (Bollnow, 1982, pp. 43, 44). My reluctance to offer help until asked holds out the possibility of seeing the activity at hand even more clearly than Lisa can. In relation to the potential fearfulness of this activity on the swing, this "well-intentioned silence" holds out the possibility of helping the child in a way that even Lisa is not yet able to understand.

Such silence, seeking a fuller comprehension of the situation at hand than the simple immediacy of pushing four children on a swing, brings an attentiveness to how the activity is meaningful to them in ways they do not fully know. This is not to diminish the sense of risk felt by the children, nor to suggest there is a comprehensibility to children's experiences that denies children their ultimate uniqueness and otherness. On the contrary, a comprehending, well-intentioned silence prevents me imposing my will on the children and allows space and time for me to better understand the meaning and importance of the situation at hand in the broader context of these children's lives. I see how they respond to Lisa pushing them higher and higher. They sit a little differently on the swing. The daredevil from before urges Lisa on, but she seems less inclined than before to extend her reach beyond the other three girls, while they, in turn, seem a tad more adventurous, moving their bodies rhythmically and synchronously with Lisa's heaving pushes. I smile, realizing that the situation is not as it first appears and that my ready intervention might have precluded the possibilities of being with the children in the manner I now discern and would like to encourage further.

**Reminiscence**

Here we have an active questioning of what matters to children on the playground. Watching Lisa push these children on the swing, we can remember how to play on swings ourselves. We recall the effort of getting the swing started, how far back we must lean in order to thrust the seat forwards, how, by standing on the wooden seat an even greater thrust is possible, and how after a while it seems safer to sit down again.

Someone starts pushing us and we go even higher—too high! The supports seem to move in the ground. At the peak of the swing we feel the chains go slack and we drop into a downward arc. Will the swing break? Will we do a complete loop over the bar at the top? Stop pushing, we want to get off!

We see "the child within us as a way to the child before us" (Lippitz, 1986, p. 58). That which is remembered is not so much the children we once were as the child who stands before us. Our memories of being pushed on swings are caught within an interest in what Lisa is doing with these children on this tire swing.

Such memories afford access to a wide range of situations. Even fictional situations draw upon a memoric disposition towards the events that are described as being formative in the characters' lives and relationships. Memories of the playground fall sway to character understanding, for example, in an episode of D. H. Lawrence's *Sons and Lovers* where we read of Paul pushing Miriam on a rope swing in an old cowshed.

> She felt the accuracy with which he caught her, exactly at the right moment, and the exactly proportionate strength of his thrust, and she was afraid. Down in her bowels went the hot wave of fear. She was in his hands. Again, firm and inevitable came the thrust at the right moment. She gripped the rope, almost swooning.
>
> "Ha!" she laughed in fear. "No higher."
>
> "But you're not a *bit* high," he remonstrated.
>
> "But no higher."
>
> He heard the fear in her voice, and desisted. Her heart melted in hot pain when the moment came for him to thrust her forward again. But he left her alone. She began to breathe.
>
> "Won't you really go any farther?" he asked. "Should I keep you there?"
>
> "No, let me go by myself," she answered.
>
> He moved aside and watched her.
>
> "Why, you're scarcely moving," he said.
>
> She laughed slightly with shame, and in a moment got down.
>
> (Lawrence, 1913/1981, pp. 200, 201)

The episode is meaningful in large measure because of the reminiscence it evokes of being pushed on swings when one is fearful of going too high. We can identify with what Miriam might have experienced in that moment just as Paul's enthusiasm needed tempering. The anxious feeling that is evoked then allows us to better understand the themes of Miriam's life. We see so vividly in her timidity on the swing what it is like, more generally, to be so "physically afraid" (p. 203). Such fictional meaning-making is the author playing on one's own reminiscences. By contrast, in real-life encounters with children in risky playground situations meaning-making is a little more difficult since the "text" of the encounter is being "read" in the process of being "written." While the meaning these situations hold is intimated in reminiscence as we try to imagine what it is like for the child or children before us, it is only grasped concretely in a deliberate movement of interest into the space and time of presently unfolding events.

There is an empathic quality to such situations. And it registers with what Barritt et al. (1985) say is the purpose of educational research, which is to understand situations "from the point of view of those living through them" (p. 84). In reference to the game of hide-and-seek they ask: "Is there anyone who does not recognize this experience? Who has either played this game or watched it being played" (Barritt et al., 1983, p. 143). And who in watching it does not feel the urge to become part of the situation? Ton Beekman certainly does. He describes being away at camp in the summer and, after dinner, playing a game of hide-and-seek with a group of children. Although an adult at the time, his description of going off to hide with an eight-year-old boy called John is strongly evocative of the enthusiasm and excitement of playing this game as a child.

Together they find a hiding place "on the side of a large field, under a bush where there is a kind of shallow hole in the ground" (Beekman, 1986, p. 40). It is the kind of hiding place one comes upon, reveling in the good fortune of finding it and chuckling at the prospects of not being found.

> As we work our way inside, we are under the cover of leaves in filtered light. I really have to dig myself in, in order not to make a bulk; John, with his slender small body, fits exactly in place. As we lie there together, he covers my back with dry leaves and twigs. We hear the voices of the searching team coming nearer. We hardly dare to breathe, push ourselves to the ground. Time seems an eternity. They pass, and their voices fade away. We breathe more freely and we look at each other with glittering eyes. John tells me "we stay put. They will never find us." He laughs softly. As time passes we hear the voices of the others far away. We look around us and see the ants working to restore the damage we did to their work. We enjoy the cozy lazy togetherness, and wait till we hear the chorus of voices calling out. The game is over, and we were not found. Proudly we come out of hiding. (p. 40)

Beekman empathizes very closely with the child, becoming child-like in his appreciation of the nature of John's experience. He draws upon personal memories of playing hide-and-seek. "The child in us often seems dead," he says, "but is always alive, waiting to be reawakened" (p. 41).

Beekman's words, which are not to be taken literally, speak to an empathic manner of relating to children. The inner child does not really exist as some being that has fallen asleep and can be awakened, nor is there any child-dimension that is not at least filtered through adult consciousness.[3] These words, suggesting a recovery of "the child in us," indicate the difficulty in describing how, by simply joining in with the games children play, empathic understanding can be achieved. Strangely enough, what is so difficult to imagine without recourse to disengaging and overly self-consciousness memory constructs seems so easy to do. Certainly Beekman's engagement in the activity at hand seems preferable by far to the "method of investigation" where one reconstructs a childhood game experience without even playing the game in question and where it is claimed that a certain engagement with children's experience can be understood within the realm of imaginative recollection (Eifermann, 1987). Such reminiscence, in contrast with Beekman's bodily recollection, seems not to lead to any practically informed "understanding of the experiencing child" (Eifermann, 1987, p. 143). The value of Beekman's method is that it shows the memory of childhood existence to be a bodily memory that comes to life in the context of our present activity with children. Its virtue is that the method cannot remain separate from the intention the adult has in interacting with children to better understand the nature of their activity.

"My memories need a material and social support so that they do not remain just products of the mind" (Lippitz, 1986, p. 58). For instance, Van den Berg tells the story of how Jean Cocteau visits the neighborhood where he grew up. He describes Cocteau visiting the house in which he once lived. And then he describes how Cocteau finds himself wandering the streets of this familiar neighborhood being led on by a desire to find that metaphorical child within. How does Cocteau recover his childhood? He does what many of us have done when we have gone back to the haunts of yesteryear. We reach out and touch the tree that now seems to have shrunk or peer over the railing of an overpass that now appears so much closer to the ground. We touch these landmarks of childhood, feeling for a past that is tantalizingly out there, just as Cocteau reached out to feel the texture of the familiar wall beside him. And as he walked he let his hand follow the shape of the wall.

But the result was not very satisfying. Still he could not grasp a sense of the past. Then he realized that, of course, he was much smaller as a child. The tracings he knew were lower down the wall. This time

Cocteau crouches over to the height of a child and, with his eyes shut, he runs his fingers along the wall at exactly the same height as when he was a small boy on his way to school.

> And immediately appeared what he had vaguely been expecting. "Just as the needle picks up the melody from the record, I obtained the melody of the past with my hand. I found everything: my cape, the leather of my satchel, the names of my friends, and of my teachers, certain expressions I had used, the sound of my grandfather's voice, the smell of his beard, the smell of my sister's dresses and of my mother's gown." (Van den Berg, 1961/75, p. 212)

"The forgotten experience is revived by the occurrence of a sensation that has left a record, a trace, behind; or it is revived by the understanding and reliving of the bodily attitudes, muscular and vegetative, that the forgotten experience produced" (Schactel, 1959, cited in Ross, 1991, p. 55). One can remember the sounds, sights, and delights of childhood provided a certain posture is adopted, provided one has a feeling for the pavement underfoot, provided one's hands trace the contours of the wall, provided the paths of childhood are taken with the light, lithe spring of youth.

Through Van den Berg's description we can empathize with Cocteau's search for his childhood, but at the same time we can wonder about the way he reawakens the child within him. To be sure, his intent was not so much to reawaken the child within as it was to remember his actual childhood in the light of adulthood. Cocteau simply wanted to rekindle the memories associated with this particular street. But in terms of the present study, what can we make of such reminiscence? Is it necessary to adopt such a childish posture? And what of the remembered child? Perhaps Cocteau's child is too much a child of nostalgia, a sentimental child, even worse, an embalmed child, or only the remains of a child. Might not a better reawakening be achieved by actually watching children doing such things as tracing their hands along walls, by having children of the here and now, actual children, make our past seem vividly present?

Reminiscence can be an occasion for nostalgia and sentimentality; it can also bring us in touch with the present and help us appreciate what children in front of us are up to. Azarov (1981) says "Look around with the eyes of your own childhood. Visit the places where you lived as a child" (p. 26). See what is happening there.

> Here is the steep bank from which you first jumped, so that you would not be called a coward. This steep bank did not give you any peace for

a long time. You dreamt about it. And even now you look at other small
children that are romping around jumping . . . you look and you are
filled with excitement, mixed with sorrow, for the childhood years that
have irrevocably gone into the past. (Azarov, 1981/1983, p. 26)

But look closer still. Attend to the children who can be seen jumping
from this embankment. Look at their faces. The timid ones. The daredevils. Look at their crazy antics. Hear how they taunt each other. Very
soon nostalgia gives way to our own excitement over the quality of these
children's experiences.

**Good Memories**

Perhaps we do not even need to try to recall the past ourselves. All
we need do is watch a child like Lisa pushing children on a tire swing
for certain memories to stir in us of being pushed ourselves. But let us
not be content to dwell upon these memories; let us watch how Lisa
pushes the swing, how she moves to catch the tire and then propels it
forward. Let us watch while pushing a child on an adjacent swing. Now
we can be drawn fully into the situation, and paraphrasing Cocteau,
hear the melody of the past with our hands upon the tire. Our remembering is at this point a kind of "body memory." We draw upon "the
body as a memorial container—as itself a 'place' of memories—[as that
which] furnishes an unmediated access to the remembered past"
(Casey, 1987, p. 179). "And it is as a body that one inhabits the past and
it inhabits one's body. . . ." (Mairs, 1989, p. 8).

I think of Tyler who likes to lie on the swings on his stomach. Each
time we go to the playground he resists my suggestion that he sit on the
swing and let me push him; instead, he takes hold of the seat, pushes it
forwards until it rises up to his chest, then dives onto it. Too big a jump
and he will tip over, too small a jump and he will fall underneath. It is
amusing to watch as he holds tightly to the seat, balancing there, letting
himself glide to and fro. Nevertheless, it is not totally satisfying to feel so
distant from his swinging. I would like to show him how to really use the
swing, not that there is anything wrong with how he is already using it,
nor can there be any doubting the pleasure he gains from his preferred
position; yet, to sit on the swing going higher and higher—then he would
really know what swinging is all about. So I wait. I wait until some time
later he sits on the swing of his own volition and asks: "Can you push
me?" I comply with his request, being careful at first not to betray his
trust. But I am soon caught up in the activity, remembering the joy this
brought me as a child, yet hearing also the excitement at this moment in

Tyler's voice, an excitement that cancels out all the swings that made me feel nauseous and all the swings I fell off. Before too long he will want to swing himself, but for the moment it is good to be pushed higher and higher than he has been before.

Van Manen (1991) writes: "The past may have been forgotten, but it may also confront us again when the past becomes relevant to the present" (p. 22). Through such encounters as pushing a child on a swing we can bring back childhood memories, not only to better understand the child, but also to deepen our own view of things. Specific recollections which, admittedly, differ from the actual experiences we had as children may, in fact, provide greatest access to the shared meanings held within these present encounters (Barritt et al., 1985, p. 66). Such recollections, "gathering together" and "binding" our experiences (Casey, 1987, pp. 283, 303), make us sensitive to the situation of Lisa being called over to lend a hand, sensitive, that is, to what seems best for these children. Just as we remember what it is like to be pushed too hard, so can we now appreciate the children's reluctance to ask us to push their swing; and yet it is this memory which discloses what is best for children, whether it be our silent watching or our offering help. Here we have the advantage over Lisa—the advantage of a maturity which allows us to ask: What is best for these children?

You see, imbedded in these memories is a sense of the good of playground activity. In spite of being pushed too high at times, in spite of being fearful and afraid, still we retain a sense of the enjoyment of swinging and a feeling for the good of it. Perhaps it would not be too out of hand to refer to the words of Dostoevsky who, through Alyosha Karamazov, said:

> You must know that there is nothing higher and stronger and more wholesome and good for life in the future than some good memory, especially a memory of childhood, of home. People talk to you a great deal about your education, but some good, sacred memory, preserved from childhood, is perhaps the best education. (Dostoevsky, 1912, p. 819)

It would seem that far too much of what we do with children stems from our attempts either to live out personal hopes and desires or to ameliorate the unfortunate aspects of our own childhoods. By speaking of good memories it may be that we can avoid imposing our own conceits, defects, and defeats on children. In fact, good memories are not projected recollections at all. They are memories of a past childhood that create an interest in being with children here and now. They are not necessarily "those moments" from childhood that Woolf (1976) said "can still be more real than the present moment" (p. 67); rather, they are presently memorable moments. We might speak more precisely of the *good* of a childhood memory. For the memories we have in mind are those that carry some essential truths about the present.

Accordingly, what makes the situation of Lisa and the children on the tire swing so interesting is that it appeals to us as a "good memory" of childhood. Through Lisa's presence we can question how these children might learn best how to enjoy the activity. We can even question Lisa's ability to help them. And in this questioning, which is much more ours than Lisa's, we can be drawn into the situation in an adult sort of way. Watching Lisa push the swing is not mere recollection, since the question that gave moment for pause—the question of how these children should be helped—is not a remembered one, but rather it is a question of how we, as adults, should help these children on the swing. The remembered experience is more a "standing-with-oneself, a self-identification with oneself, a process not of introspection but of self-becoming in the action itself" (Bollnow, 1974, p. 17).

Adult recollection signifies, on the one hand, an attempt to address the child's view of things and, on the other hand, the inevitable distance separating adult and child yet a distance that lends significance to what the child does. Merleau-Ponty (1968) asked: "Do we have the right to comprehend the time, the space of the child as an undifferentiation of *our* time, or *our* space, etc. . . .? This is to reduce the child's experience to our own, at the very moment one is trying to respect the phomena" (p. 203). As soon as we face the child, his or her experience is in danger of being reduced to our own. As soon as we utter some words of encouragement and direction, we speak as if the space and time of the child is coextensive and synchronous with our own. Our task is to question this reduction, not to contribute to it, yet to be mindful that whatever we do with children is inevitably a mediation of their experience. Our presence is of itself mediational. Meyer-Drawe (1986) says in reference to the task Merleau-Ponty has laid before us, "We can only thematize childlike possibilities as specific deviations [of our adult conceptions], and this means that we cannot avoid implicating our own point of view" (p. 50). We are there with the child on the playground. With Sylvia, Lewis and Lisa we can "thematize childlike possibilities" which belong neither wholly to them nor to us. They are, if you will, cointentional possibilities.

The point we should consider is whether this standing *vis-à-vis* the child, this methodology, implies a distortion of the child's experience. For Meyer-Drawe the test lies in our capability to be surprised. For me I would prefer to stay with the notion of silence to the extent that surprise also ushers in silence. Thus, we ought to take pains to listen carefully to what the child is saying when she says "They're the big people," when he asks "Can you push me?" or when we are surprised that some young children do not want to ask us to give them a push. We should be silent, if only for a moment, as we try to work out more fully what is the best thing to do for the child who is now before us. And in working out what is best for this child, what can be better than attempting to define this present activity as the stuff of good memories. Such a procedure, I believe, stands a good chance of "respecting the child's experience" of the playground and of "thinking it *positively*" (Merleau-Ponty, 1968, p. 203).

## A Silent Trust

Should we risk reducing the child's experiences on the playground to our own? By now we can appreciate that risk is involved in a most profound way in our attentiveness to the silences of playground activity. As well as the risk that gives occasion to help the child, the effort to be mindful of what the child does requires that we are ourselves open to risk. For instance, it is always possible that the expectation we have of children exceeds their ability, that they do not measure up, and that our efforts may only serve to discourage them. Asking Sylvia "Why don't you join in?" may actually make her acutely aware not so much of "the big people" but of the activity that she and her friends find so intriguing. The question we ask so matter-of-factly risks formulating their interest in the swinging activity for them. Our question may even turn them away from the activity and from us. This is the risk we take. This is the riskiness of the playground for which we are responsible when we attend to the silences that separate us from children. This is the motive for our taking care in attempting to understand children's playground activity.

How can we properly respond to the child's experience? It seems at times we must trust children even though there remains a chance of mishap. Many things can happen, for instance, as Lewis chases the children around the playground. He shows a certain maturity and still the children do hair-raising things in their attempts to avoid being caught. To what extent, then, can these children be entrusted to Lewis? To what extent can we stand back and say nothing? It is worth recalling the words of Bollow in this regard when he said:

> The risk of trust shown to the child may succeed, and if so, then the educational involvement was worthwhile. But at the same time, there may also be failure, and then the educator appears as one who lacked necessary precaution, one who had acted with irresponsible credulity and stupidity. The educator then must bear ridicule as well as experience failure in his work. (Bollnow, 1971, p. 530)

Our trust in Lewis, and the fact that through him the children are allowed to take risks without being deliberately exposed to danger, depends upon our ability to commit ourselves to trusting Lewis. We lay ourselves open in a willingness "to risk being human in students eyes," which is a different order of self-disclosure altogether than the "personal disclosures" and "private information" one might share (cf. Appelbaum, 1995). The risk of trusting children and courting failure in one's expectations of them is the pedagogic risk we take, "and he is only a good teacher if he can definitely accept this risk which is inherent in his profession" (Bollnow, 1979, p. 77).

We should not be too surprised at how well Lewis orchestrates the game, nor, for that matter, at how well Lisa ministers to the fears of the girls on the tire swing, since by their presence they have inspired confidence in the children with whom they are playing. We should see what Lewis and Lisa do as giving notice on how we ought to approach playground activity ourselves. We, too, ought to have confidence in what children can do on the playground.

> Only when I believe the child to be capable of something does it also believe itself to be capable of it and is it prepared to overcome its hesitancy and its timidity. Hence the great significance of encouragement in education. . . . Conversely, when from the start one does not believe a child capable of doing something, when one says to it as it were: leave it alone, you really can't do that, then one robs the child of its power and the result is that it actually does not do it. There is, in fact, no worse poison than mistrust. (Bollnow, 1979, pp. 75, 76).

Where might this silent trust lead us? In subsequent chapters I shall show how it enables us to say more about how risk is implicated in the manner in which we approach playground activity. Here I shall follow the silences of risk in order to explore the ways in which we might address the child's experience of the playground. I shall follow these epistemological, ontological, and ultimately, pedagogical silences of playground activity in order to reveal the nature of a pedagogical response to the perceived riskiness of the playground. That is to say, by utilizing an approach of silence, by addressing the unspoken ground as the basis for our understanding what the child might be attempting to do, and by acknowledging a silent trust as our way of respecting the integrity of the child's experience, I shall outline the conditions of a pedagogical response to children on the playground. In particular, I shall use this "method"[4] to explore how we might approach the riskiness of children's playground activity.

# III

## A Responsiveness to Risk

# 4

# The
# Atmosphere of
# Risk

There are risks that lie beyond the playground, risks to which children are exposed even in the normal run of everyday events. One might say the child lives in an atmosphere of risk which influences all that he or she does, including what happens on the playground. This is especially the case with latch-key children, sexually abused children, children from physically abusive homes, abducted children, children of homeless families, street children, and children for whom the world is a risky and all too dangerous place to be. But it is also the case with children who may find themselves at times unnecessarily exposed to risk by being left alone, by having little sense of protection in situations they find threatening, or even by having their fears and difficulties disregarded in situations that are familiar and comfortable to us.

What are we to do about the riskiness that encroaches upon the lives of all children? How might those responsible for the care of children ensure they grow up sensing the security that is necessary for their growth and maturation? Must the child simply learn to cope in a general and pervasive atmosphere of risk or is the pervasiveness of this atmosphere a function in the first instance of parental concerns and attitudes, or the lack thereof? More importantly, how does our sense of it define the nature of our responsibility for children and the ways we might treat them, especially in playground situations? In other words, is there a certain texture of risk which, although evident in everyday life, is susceptible to influence on the playground?

Bollnow writes, in this regard, of a "pedagogical atmosphere" characterized by the sense of security that is brought to the child's explorations. He says:

> Only in an atmosphere of security can the child grow in the right direction and only in this medium does the world reveal itself to the child in all its reasonable order. Should this security be missing, then the world remains a shocking, threatening power. And if this sense of security is not guaranteed elsewhere then the child is refused the will to life and hopelessly he or she withers emotionally.   (Bollnow, 1970/1989, p. 7)

The child needs to feel the security that comes from being cared for by the mother or the father, the security that the home ideally represents, and the feeling of security which, in the normal run of events, allows other adults to take the place of the parent and other places to draw the child beyond the safety of the home.[1] The child needs to explore the world with a sense of security, or as the term originally implied, in a way that is "free of care," where "care" meant grief, a burdened state of mind, or to be troubled.

It is impossible, however, for parents or educators to take all trouble away from children. Indeed, many parents ask themselves whether they are overprotective of their children in attending so closely to their "cares." It follows that, rather than shielding children from the riskiness of everyday life, they should be made aware of clear and distinct instances of risk in a general context of security. Children are often at risk precisely because they have so little awareness of the atmosphere of risk and because they recognize dangers only after it is too late. Still, the more precise point of this qualification is that a totally pervasive atmosphere of risk is apedagogical, furthermore, that genuine pedagogy does not proceed wholly blind to risks nor neurotically exaggerate risks beyond all coping, but carefully meets and transcends risks in a context of security. Practically speaking, between the home and the world are places like playgrounds where the child can feel secure and from where he or she can, in due course, venture into the more threatening world beyond the playground. Pedagogically speaking, it means responding to children's difficulties, becoming sensitive to their fears, building upon the trust earlier "invested in a single person [and] now . . . become a more generalized trust in the world" (p. 17; cf. van Manen, 1991, pp. 6, 55–58).

The question we take up is in part a question of how the risky texture of life in general can be softened by what we do with children on the playground; but it is in greater part a question of how what we do with children on the playground can actually create a clearing in this grey atmosphere of risk. It is a question of how our responses to the riskiness of children's playground activity can constitute an atmosphere of security sustaining their movement toward greater independence.

## The Texture of Risk

Let us first consider some everyday occurrences, events of daily life, "small events that are likely to happen in any child's day and that need to be handled as they occur" (Bettelheim, 1962, p. 27). They may be events in the child's life to which we are largely indifferent, perhaps distracted by our own concerns, regarding them to be of small consequence and feeling little sympathy for the trifling concerns, fears, or anxieties the child may show; or they may be events that, while small, mundane, scarcely surprising, and hardly worrisome, draw a response that acknowledges the child's predicament and seeks to alleviate it. The difference lies not in any circumstantial features of the events in question, but rather in our inclination to be mindful of the child and to be sensitive in our interactions with him or her. The difference it makes to the child is that "these—the many small experiences that form the essence of our lives—are, added up, what form the child's personality and our relations between him and ourselves" (p. 28). Taken together, such events, though hardly momentous at face value, add up to "a good life or a pretty miserable one" (p. 28).[2]

I think at this juncture of a three year old boy I see wandering the streets near my house. He seems happy enough to join the children in our communal play area, however I am concerned that his parents may not know his whereabouts. I feel I need to have him take me to his home so that I might reassure them of his safety. "Don't worry," Stephen's parents tell me, "he knows his way around." I feel a little foolish, not so much for interfering as for being unnecessarily concerned. And yet the response of these parents, who greet me as reasonable people, does not put to rest my concern. After all, is it simply a question of a three-year-old knowing his way around? Their faith in the little boy's capacity to look after himself actually increases my concern, especially when they come knocking on my door long after dark, asking if I have seen their son of late, or if I see him, would I please send him home.

Of course, it would be easy to become indignant at these parents' lack of care, and if they paid no heed, to advise those deemed to be the authorities of childcare. But wait a moment. Stephen and his family are new to this neighborhood. They have moved recently from a country where the events of daily life carry very real and obvious dangers. Perhaps the parents have been lulled into a sense of the security of Stephen's explorations by the relative peace of this new neighborhood. They need to be warned. And yet, although such a course of action may very well be needed, the presence of this child also requires a personal response. By being in my neighborhood, by knocking on my door seeking a playmate, Stephen asks me to look out for him. He asks not only for a response that is mindful of the dangers to which he is exposed, but for a response that is mindful of his being a child and of the obligation that this fact places on me as an adult. How should I respond? Whatever I do, I am responsible in some way for the risky texture of Stephen's life.

Vandenberg (1971) reminds us of the responsibility we share as adults to ensure the safety of children. This is not a mere matter of designing the world as a safe place for children nor simply a matter of keeping children safe from the world. Design and protection have limited safety value within the confines of playgrounds and even less value in ensuring the safety of children in the wider world. Children's safety is not guaranteed by the provisions we make for them so much as it is achieved by what we do with them, how we respond to their relative helplessness, what measure of support we provide for their explorations, and how we encourage them and help them feel at home in the world. Simply allowing Stephen to roam around the neighborhood is a total abnegation of this responsibility. It is, at best, a blind trust in the world's safety that puts him at-risk. It also denies him the risk-taking that is possible and desirable when we acknowledge "his helplessness" and make provisions that "free him to explore an inviting world" (p. 64).

Now you might think that this situation is a little on the extremely lacking side of adult concern. Consider, then, a situation closer to home—a common household scene such as that of parents leaving their children with a babysitter for the evening. Let me describe how it might be for two children, Marc and Matthew.

Marc comes softly to the door to see his parents off. "What time will you be coming home?" he asks. "We won't be too late—we should be home by 9:30," they reply. A look of mild relief shows on Marc's face. He then says: "Papa, Mama, you make sure you put on your seatbelts." And with an assurance from them that they will certainly buckle-up, Marc again seems content. His mother and father give Marc a kiss goodbye and some instructions for the evening, and then make their way towards the car. Marc comes out a few moments later with the same soft approach they only half-noticed before, a softness that makes the departure seem all the more busy and blustery. He asks: "You promise you won't be late?" "No, Marc, we won't be late. Now off you go inside." Marc saunters back to the house, is met at the door by the babysitter, and disappears inside as the car pulls out of the driveway.

"Marc," says his father, "is very aware of consequences. He worries a lot about things that might happen to him. And he worries about us when he is not with us. He's even made me concerned about this seatbelt thing. I find I always buckle-up now. I figure that if I ever have an accident and didn't have my seatbelt on, Marc would never forgive me. Even worse, he'd agonize over whether or not he told me to wear it. I am sure he would feel personally responsible if anything happened and I wasn't wearing it." "Matthew is just the opposite," says the boys' mother. "He doesn't seem to mind if we are there or not. When you say goodbye to Matthew you have to drag him away from what he is doing. I guess he's what you might call a pretty well-adjusted little guy. But, you know, I am glad we have a Marc as well as a Matthew."

Marc brings the question of risk to the fore by showing a certain insecurity in spite of the safety of the place that is provided for him (or perhaps, precisely as a consequence of it and the preoccupation with it). He has a sense of what is at stake when his parents leave. He is concerned since he knows that their departure not only puts his relation to them at risk, but it also jeopardizes the trust he has in the world they bring to him. Also, in showing such concern, Marc allows us to question his brother Matthew's nonchalance at the departure of the parents. Whereas at first sight Marc seems a little neurotic in comparison with Matthew's adjustment to the impending situation of parental absence, his concern starts to have us wonder how it is that most children can, like Matthew, accept absence so matter-of-factly. After all, it is a little disappointing to know that you will not be missed, and somewhat disconcerting to think that absence may mean so little. Matthew, however, is not unaware of his parents' departure. He looks forward to the babysitter coming over, so when the moment comes for his parents to leave already this expectancy has suffused his actions. In order to say goodbye to Matthew it is necessary to contain him physically for a moment, to interrupt him as he rummages around for something he wants to show the babysitter, to bring him to look at us so an instruction can be given. We must bring him physically face to face with a situation of our absence—a situation he has already understood on his own and in his own way.

The difference between Marc and Matthew in this situation would seem to lie more in the realities they perceive as a result of their parent's departure than in the form of their responses. Certainly for Marc who is anxious about the separation, the reality is different than for Matthew who enjoys the opportunity of a break from his parents' attention and for whom the attention of a babysitter is welcome. While Matthew is off about his business, Marc continues to fret about the imminent departure. He feels this separation and plays out the feeling by imagining all kinds of scenarios which might prolong it further. Thus, on the surface of it, Matthew's matter-of-factness can be regarded as a sign of independence, while Marc's exaggerated sense of responsibility may be viewed as an inextricably rooted insecurity. At a deeper level, however, Marc shows a greater maturity than Matthew as he contemplates the possibilities of the present situation and senses the fragility of his and his younger bother's relation to their parents. He can envision the relation as subject to certain risks. Nevertheless one cannot help but think that if maturity requires such a fearful sense of responsibility, maybe it is too much for one so young as Marc.[3] It is best to hope that Marc will grow out of this "phase," which is a strange hope since what we are hoping is that Marc will abandon something of those feelings we think he should acquire as he grows towards maturity.

This situation involving Marc and Matthew seems to disclose something of the nature of risk that gets lost when the question of risk is removed from the context of adult-child interaction. There is a texture of risky situations to which Marc and Matthew respond in differing ways and to which their parents knowingly or unknowingly contribute; and this texture increasingly defines children's relations to the world these adults care to represent. Conversely, adults are primarily responsible for the texture of risk by the manner in which they treat children in the context of an impending separation, which is to say, by the way they observe the significance of their presence for children and the ways they respond to what children may do when faced with the thought of their absence.[4]

This texture of risk is apparent when we stop to consider even the most common of family practices. Tyler asks one evening: "How come Shayle sleeps in your room and you get to sleep with Mommy, but I don't have anyone to sleep with?" Is it any wonder that fears arise when, in our efforts to do something for children (such as providing them with space of their own), we overlook what we do to them and to their sense of security in the world as they understand it? We take our children to so-called "parent-free" classes for swimming and gymnastics, and we sign them up for "day camp" programs as soon as their daycare and kindergarten programs go into recess. It seems the life of the young child is structured around a series of well-intentioned provisions which inevitably run the risk of placing the child at-risk. In such situations of parental absence, the risks of everyday life become dangers that threaten the child's safety; and to compound the situation even further, we give over to others the job of educating our children about such dangers and teaching them how to defend themselves. Through the rationalization of children's lives we deny our own place within this atmosphere of risk.

We must be clear in what is at stake here. I do not wish to conclude from these examples that we do children great harm by leaving them alone. In fact, Bettelheim shows how sometimes the apparent "abandonment" of children is a means to their gaining a sense of independence and personal responsibility for their lives. Bettelheim says:

> The child of school age cannot yet believe that he ever will be able to meet the world without his parents; that is why he wishes to hold on to them beyond the necessary point. He needs to learn that someday he will master the dangers of the world, even in the exaggerated form in which his fears depict them, and be enriched by it. (Bettelheim, 1975, p. 166)

More importantly, there comes a time when the child will want to be left alone, when he will want to sleep by himself, and when he will need to be trusted to explore the neighborhood unaccompanied by his parents. Before this time it may be appropriate to speak of abandoning the child, but when the child expresses a desire to venture out on his or her own, a much greater disservice may be done by keeping the child in protective custody. If we ignore the moment, rather than bringing a sense of security to the child's activity, our presence confines it and taints it with a distrust of the world. The lesson given the child is that the world is to be feared except when the adult is present. By drawing the child's attention to the atmosphere of risk in this manner, we deny the very movement towards maturity which prefigures our pedagogical relation to the child.

Let us look more closely at how this atmosphere of risk, this texture, is modulated not only by the extremes of presence or absence, but more particularly, by certain modes of presence of the adult to the child. After all, we must keep in mind that atmosphere is not only "the way in which space is lived and experienced. But atmosphere is also the way a teacher [or parent] is present to children, and the way children are present to themselves and to the teacher" (Bollnow, 1989, p. 36).

Atmosphere is affected by the way in which the adult is present for the sake of the child's explorations.

## Modes of Presence

A risky situation that stays with me involves taking children on a climbing expedition. We are preparing to climb a mountain. For the past few days we, along with forty or so children, have been doing environmental studies, rock climbing, orienteering, canoeing, and bushcraft; and throughout each activity we have spoken of the early explorers in the area, the routes they had taken, and the settlements they had established. Ours is to be one such settlement for we are also explorers of this land. And all the while Mount Maroon stares down on us. Some sketch it, some photograph it, others find faces and forms within it, each anticipating in his or her own way the climb we are about to make.

The climb up Mount Maroon is not particularly difficult. Some sections require ropes, but for the most part it is a five hour hike and scramble to the top. Nevertheless we experience a peculiar discomfort. The children, except perhaps the "leaders," seem nervous. One of them, Chris, is scared by this mountain. Her determination to reach the top is threatened by the fear she has for her safety. Each step pulls her away from where she feels comfortable. The glazed look in her eyes indicates that the mountain evokes a fear that prevents any attachment to the here and now. She does not see risk, but is overpowered by a sense of danger which prevents her from seeing very much at all. Her sense is that of being dominated by the mountain.[5] Even on the descent, when generally the worst is behind, she still sees danger. Still she winds her way down in a crab-like position, unaware of the terrain levelling out, unaware of the others who stay with her, talking all the while about school, home, and familiar things (and afraid that the seat of her pants will soon wear out). "Not far to go now, Chris. . . . I wonder what the others are doing. . . . Do you think they might have reached the bottom already?" "You're doing really well. This will certainly be something to tell the folks at home about. . . . Hang in there, there's not much farther to go." Chris maintains her posture of fear in spite of, and perhaps, because of the advances of those around her. Their words provide little comfort for, in a way, they continue to address the thought she has of danger and the fear she has for her safety.

It may not be too hard to find all sorts of reasons for this child's fearfulness on the mountain—prior experiences, a complete lack of self-confidence, inability to trust others—yet the inescapable fact is that this child is cut off from us. Though we intend to be there for her, Chris feels marooned. The actions of those around her do not help Chris to take a risk. Our support only exacerbates the situation. We simply try to make Chris feel better instead of addressing head-on the fears and trepidations that this hike creates for her. Our support for her "tries to substitute 'good' feelings for unacceptable ones, to deny the reality of them, or to distract the child. The message the child receives is, 'You shouldn't feel the way you do'" (Snyder, Snyder and Snyder, 1980, p. 171).

Chris is not the only one who does not see the risk. In our attempts to support her, we, too, fail to observe her activity in a way that would enable us to offer her genuine help.

How could this child be helped? I am playing with a much younger Chris at Lansdowne Playground. She spends her time clambering over the decks, climbing the ladders and bars, and coming down the small slides; however she avoids the larger spiralling slide at the farther end of the playground. "I bet you can't come down that one," I say, thinking that the slide's location explains why she has left it alone so far. But my words come as a challenge—as a dare which shows in the cautious way she climbs the steps to the top. Chris calls from the top: "You come down with me!" And having played on the other equipment with her it seems natural to do as she asks. Yet somewhat surprisingly this child still does not want to come down the slide; instead she proceeds to come back down the staircase. "What's the matter?" I ask, thinking of slides twice as high from which I can't keep her away. My question is also tinged with a sense of guilt at having put her in a situation where she had to back down. So I press harder: "Why don't you want to come down the slide with me?" to which Chris answers, "I'll be upside down." I look again at the slide, noticing how the protective casing makes it appear to be a tunnel in which one might conceivably turn upside down. Still, I am not satisfied. I have understood the reason Chris gave me but the question of why she would not come down with me remains. Was I wrong to dare her? How might I have encouraged her efforts? Perhaps my guidance left too little room for Chris to make her own way. Maybe her response is meant as something for me to think about, a response that might stop me from bothering her as she tries to come to terms with the challenge of the slide.

Another occasion in another playground: three children of differing ages are mounting the ladder that leads to the top of an unusually high slide, one which is probably twice as high as they are used to seeing. These three chatter among themselves, although from a distance it is not possible to get the gist of their talk. Perhaps they express some concern regarding the activity, for their mother soon appears in an agitated state. "Now, how do you think you're going to get down?" She moves even closer so that the children appear to hang directly over her. "I told you not to go up there." The three children stand rigid. The youngest one starts calling for his mother to come up and get him, at which point she reluctantly begins to climb the ladder. As she moves closer she sees that this youngest child is quite fearful. She says, in an attempt to reassure him, "Just stay still—mommy's scared too." She climbs up to grasp this youngest child and then all four come back down the ladder, quite relieved it seems to be safely on the ground. "I don't want to see any of you going near that slide again," she cautions the children as they run off to the nearby swings. And as they run off I wonder about the risk of climbing this slippery slide. Where was the danger and what was the source of the children's fear? What was the nature of this parent's concern? In effect, how were these children helped by their mother being there on the playground?

The situation obviously changes for the worse as soon as the mother arrives on the scene and starts berating her three children. They evidently feel her concern since, with her there, the slide seems a dangerous thing as well. This situation is not unlike many others where adults impose a sense of normative order on children's activity. Instructing children, adults tell them what to do and what to feel about their activity. Children learn not to think for themselves and to become increasingly dependent upon adults whenever challenges are faced. "Instructing makes the adult feel important, but it robs the child of her independence" (Snyder et al, 1980, p. 171). Perhaps the mother of these three children on the slide might stop to reflect upon her own sense of risk and the manner in which she projects her fears on the three children, thereby denying them their own capacity for making sense of the situation.

I am reminded now of a little boy, Cory, who acts just the opposite of these children. Cory is a dare-devil. At the aquatic center there are a number of swimming pools, each designed with a different group in mind. One of the pools seems ideally suited to five-year-old Cory. It has slides of differing heights at one end, and inflated inner tubes and large plastic saucers for him to play in. But Cory soon becomes restless in this pool. He much prefers to go with his father to the large swimming pool with the high diving board.

Cory has been on this diving board before. He shows little hesitation in running out onto the board, and although he has still to master fully the take-off from the end, already he is trying somersaults into the water. So we watch as Cory puts on a show for us. We watch him follow his father and try to perform the dive he has just seen. We watch him go it alone. We hear his father tell him to keep his legs together, and we watch with admiration as Cory manages to hold his legs partially together during the next dive. Then, as our attention starts to wane,

Cory calls out, "Watch this one. . . . Are you watching?" "Enough, Cory. We've seen enough. Let's try something different. Let's see if you can still swim across the pool," says Cory's father as they both hold on to the side of the pool at the deep end. Suprisingly though, Cory appears quite reluctant. "I'll swim beside you; and if you get tired you can hold onto the lane rope," says his father. Cory still clings to the edge of the pool. Some more cajoling and Cory agrees to the plan. With gritted teeth he dogpaddles to the other side, grabbing the lane rope every so often in order to take gulps of air and water. It is clear Cory does not enjoy this activity, because as soon as he reaches the other side he asks, "Can I go on the diving board now?"

Cory prefers the diving board. That is clear. What is not so clear is why he is so fearful when it comes to swimming with his father across the pool. Swimming across the pool is certainly a lot of effort for someone who dogpaddles. But the effort Cory expends is even greater in diving. Perhaps Cory's fearfulness is due more to the fact that he cannot feel his father's presence. Or perhaps this presence is usually a matter of being watched rather than being watched over. Again I refer to Snyder et al. (1980) in attempting to draw a lesson from this example. They talk in terms of a way of evaluating the child that is also a way of not understanding the nature of the child's activity. Judging what the child does "attempts to coerce behavior" by making the child's sense of activity dependent upon adult approval (p. 171). In Cory's case, he obviously enjoys diving, but to what extent this enjoyment can be distinguished from his attempts to win his father's approval is questionable. We get the impression as we watch him perform his dives that his risk-taking depends too much upon the gestures and words of approval that follow each dive. We are drawn further towards this conclusion as we note that he is quite reluctant to take a risk at something he feels he can barely do, like swimming across the deep end of the pool. Perhaps Cory's dare-devilishness on the diving board is, like his fearfulness in the water, too much a case of being denied genuine help.

Children need help in order to help themselves. I see my child is afraid to climb the jungle gym. What do I do? Do I let him work it out for himself? Do I cajole him to come down? I may be tempted to say "Look at Jamie. See, he can do it. You can do it too." But I know this dare may not work. It may not be appropriate. I know how high this frame stands for a child. The world looks so far below. And the metal bars are only a precarious connection between the high platform and the safe ground below. I have been a child and I know this fear. So what do I do?

There is, in this questioning of what I should do, an admonition to be with the child as he or she ventures out into the world. I may very well support, guide, instruct, and even evaluate the child's activity, however I should realize there are degrees of consideration to each of these types of adult-child interaction. No matter what I say or do, genuine help requires my being present, being in the present, living presently with the child. Genuine help can be characterized, beyond these terms of interaction, as a committed presence.

I help the child by being with him or her in such a way that risks are seen where, without my help, danger might lurk. I help, not so much by looking out for the child's safety, as by caring sufficiently that his or her explorations can be carried out with an underlying sense of security. Within this perspective we are, for instance, up there on the climbing frame with the child, for that child is like us. Though we stand below with outstretched arms and request the child to "be careful," in the spirit of the moment we revel with the child in the activity at hand. The child takes us up there with him or her, and in knowing we are there, climbing feels secure. "Watch me, Dad! Watch me!" the child says as he shimmies up the climbing frame, drawn like a magnet into the throng of children gathered there. Over the bars he moves, threading himself in and out of this wrought-iron maze. Extricating himself momentarily he cries "Are you watching?" Is this a question or a plea? There is a degree of apprehension in this child's voice. He calls again with greater urgency. "Are you watching?" And with our reassuring nod he finds his place among the children. This child has nothing to show off but himself. He does not necessarily ask that we watch what he can do as if intent on giving us a performance. No, the child may want only to be watched, to feel the security of our protective gaze, to know that he is not alone. This cold metal frame full of unfamiliar faces needs a parental warmth.

If the child then becomes a little anxious on the climbing frame maybe we ought not be unduly concerned since this anxiety is part of the child's coming to know the world in his or her own way. The child finds distance between the present context of activity and the world he or she knows. A risk is seen in shadowy outline. Our adult obligation, however, is to ensure that this anxiety does not separate the child from the things that are known, and in particular, from us. For example, we recall the same child on the slippery slide refusing to come down on the seat of his pants, and we remember his plea that we come down with him. And on occasion we would climb that ladder behind him, and then, with him nestling against us we would plummet down that slide. "Do it again" he pleads, but no, we think it is time he tried it by himself, after all, aren't we standing at the bottom ready to catch him? Similarly, we think of the child who will not go upstairs by himself—we must come with him. Do we help this child by laughing at his anxiety? Or does our help require us to go with him, to be with him as he comes to find the upstairs region increasingly familiar?

Langeveld (1975) tells us that what matters most in our interactions with children is "the intention" to be helpful. An "appeal" for help issues from the "child's helplessness. . . . What will our answer be? It need not be given in words. It may suffice that we are there; our presence may be a guarantee of security" (p. 7). Our response may also threaten the child's security, especially when the child's appeal for help goes unheeded and the child is then left alone to his or her own devices. "The outcome depends on the common experiences of the child and the adult or with other adults" (p. 7). It depends upon what we share in common and the common meaning that we intentionally create.

How should we be helpful to the child? Does it not depend on the child and on the occasion and on all sorts of factors that cannot be clearly specified and which, when discussed generally, sound like romantic platitudes? Listen to what the child says. "Help me up" he cries out, not even looking for ways he could pull himself up onto the climbing frame. He wants a boost, a reassuring hand, in order to get started.

## Pedagogical Presence

Too often it seems risky situations put children at-risk. Even well-intentioned efforts at times deny children that mode of adult presence which would lend security to their explorations. There is a children's story called *Michael is Brave* (Buckley, 1971). In this story we follow Michael as he is enticed up the ladder of a playground slide by a teacher who thought he could assist a little girl who was already stuck at the top. The teacher's plan works, although it could just as easily fail, since what the teacher fails to recognize is that Michael is probably just as scared as the little girl he is summoned to help.

As Micheal mounts the ladder of the slide he becomes increasingly afraid. He climbs warily, focusing his attention on each rung, not wanting to look down to see how high up he is getting. He hears the pleas of the little girl for help. This only increases his apprehensiveness. Climbing still higher, Michael wants to back down. But the story involves Michael being "brave." There can be no backing down. Michael must grit his teeth and summon the courage to go the last few steps to the top of the slide.

Now, with Michael behind her, the little girl is no longer so frightened. She looks around at Michael, then down at the teacher below. She is reassured by Michael's presence. She relaxes her grip on the rails and plummets into the teacher's embrace. "That was fun," she cries. "And now it's Michael's turn!"

Meanwhile Michael remains petrified at the top. He surveys the playground, eyeing his friend over on the jungle gym. But this sight provides cold comfort. It is at best a momentary distraction from the impending activity, the thought of which is so frightful. Michael regrets being up there on the slide and dreads the thought of coming down.

He looks down to the teacher who smiles and waves to him. Is this a signal that his time is up? Michael breathes deeply and moves into action. Dismissing further concerns for his safety, he plunks himself onto the slide and skims to the bottom. Way to go, Michael. Well done. "Good for you!" the teacher exclaims.

The particular questions this story raises have to do with how the teacher can be as sensitive to Michael as she is to the little girl whose helplessness is more noticeable. To what extent does it show the teacher being of help to Michael? Is it really a matter of Michael being brave, or is there a pedagogical task that the teacher's benevolent smile overlooks? Where, in other words, can we see evidence of the intention to be helpful to Michael? In praise that fails to appraise his fearful state of mind?

I suggest that being present pedagogically has to do with *challenging* the child with a mindfulness of how the child encounters the world. It has to do with seeing risk as the child may come to see it. For example, I see Carson standing above me on the platform at Alice's Playground. I see that, whereas before Carson was content to come down the slide attached to this platform, the "fireman's pole" situated off to the side has now caught his eye. I ask if he wants to try sliding down it. "No," he replies rather unconvincingly, thereby convincing me he must really want to try it. "Oh, I bet you could do that," I say as I move underneath him. "Reach out and grab the pole." Carson leans forward and commits himself. "Now jump onto the bar and I'll catch you at the bottom." This he does. He clings momentarily to the pole, then drops clumsily into my arms. "Do you think you can do it again?" I ask. No, once is enough. Carson wants to do other things, although I feel sure he will return before too long to the challenge of the "fireman's pole."

Jago (1970), a playground worker, provides a similar example. He watches as a young boy climbs up a set of tires that form a ladder on the side of a tree. When he reaches the top, he becomes scared and too afraid to come back down by himself. So Jago climbs up to meet him, suggesting to the young boy that the two of them come down together. Jago encircles the child with his body, creating a buffer between the child and his fears of falling. Jago writes: "We backed down the tree rather like a circus act with two bears. He could have fallen out through my arms but he felt he would not. Two tires down and he dismissed me"

(p. 2). The challenge of climbing down the ladder was lessened by the playground worker's presence, by not only his physical proximity to the child but also by his engagement with the child in the activity. This same child who appeared so fearful a moment ago is now confident enough to go up and down the tires all by himself.

That children return to activities about which they were quite apprehensive, that they will repeat an activity until it seems easy, means something has been gained by these children. They have been helped to see the worth of taking certain risks on the playground.

Some time later I am with Carson at Malmo Playground. He has been following some older boys around, hoping to join their chasing game. But now, as these boys leave the area, he turns to other matters. I see him climb up to the platform from which a "fireman's pole" is anchored on either side. He moves to the one closest to where I sit on the concrete border of this playground, and says: "Watch me go down the pole—with nobody helping me!" He leans forward and tentatively grasps the pole, falls against it with his body, hooks his legs around and drops to the ground. "Did you see me?" he asks. I nod. "I'll show you again." A short while later, even before I realize that Carson is again on the platform, I hear him calling: "Come and stand over here. "Why?" I ask. "Because I want you to. I want you to watch me." "But can't I see you from here?" I reply. Carson does not respond directly; he simply requests once again, "Come and stand over here." So I move closer and watch him slide down the pole in one motion. "Do you want to see me do it again?" he asks.

I wonder why I must stand so close. Is this another instance of a child being dependent upon adult signs of approval, or is it an occasion for further reflection on the difference between pedagogical and non-pedagogical modes of presence? Perhaps it is an occasion for self-reflection on our relatedness to the child before us, of where we stand with this child, and on what basis, what common experiences, it is possible to stand close by. After all, as Crowe (1984) remarks: "If we never feel even a twinge of apprehension at the unknown, or if we conveniently overlook the fact or have never faced up to it, the chances are that we shall be unreasonably hard on our children" (p. 128). Denying our own fears, we expect more of children than of ourselves, "wanting them not only to be more confident than we are, but more confident than is reasonable or even possible" (p. 128). This is the corollary of the mother who projects her conscious fears on her children and makes them more apprehensive than they ought to be. To be most helpful to children is neither to project fearfulness nor to repress it. Instead, we might be of greatest help to children if we were to recall our own fears on the playground and the manner in which they were addressed.

From childhood we recall a newly painted climbing frame, a jungle gym, over in the park. It shares a space with the see-saw, the slide, and a few lesser pieces; a space which is defined not only by the ant-bed dirt which has been spread over the worn out ground, but also by the contrast it provides with the rest of the park. This play equipment presides over a large parkland that stretches over a bank to the river on one side and down to the duck pond on the other. To climb this frame is to be king of the castle and indeed the estate.

This climbing frame is what we run to first. Hanging on to the lowest bars is not enough. We have to climb it. Dad stands underneath, arms up watching for the sudden slip while we, through effort, concentration and the occasional assist are soon standing atop the frame. The raised centerpiece then allows for movement around the top. "Be careful, be careful," we hear, but already we are beyond the grasp of the outstretched arms below, and do not want it otherwise. Sometime later the climbing frame loses its attraction. The slide takes our fancy, but now we refuse to come down in a seated position. We prefer to lie on our stomach and hold the sides so that we can brake the slide at will, and so that we can feel the loss and then the regaining of our attachment to the slide. Though they tempt us to come down seated as we used to, it is to no avail, unless they come down with us and even then we are not so sure. So what has changed that we no longer unwittingly climb so high? No longer do we stand on top peering down as if without a care. No longer do we send a shudder through that adult standing below.

We must come to terms with these playthings in the park. Though they beckon us, it is in a way that might very well pull us away from the adult and that secure place where the adult stands. The climbing frame and the slippery slide look over this place. They afford a view of the one who would otherwise be looking over us—a view which can create a profound sense of distance between us and them. The higher we climb the more distant we become from the familiar world. And the higher we climb the more we feel the concern, the pull, of the adult below. The climbing frame and the slide must be treated carefully.

On the basis of these recollections we see children on the playground become aware of the risks of their activity. We look at the hesitancy that attends their movements. We see them become fearful, perhaps even afraid. Children are done a grave disservice if we left the matter there, for their fearfulness is related to our efforts to become mindful of them. In other words, it is not sufficient to say that children become fearful if our observation explains away their actions and avoids the question of our responsibility for their state-of-mind; on the contrary, we imagine ourselves taking a risk when we look at fearful children. We watch as they navigate between the familiar and the unknown, we share in their discoveries, and we regret their failures. Their apprehension strikes at the heart of our concern for them. Becoming fearful signifies our relation to children, our fearing for them, as well as our becoming mindful of how the world appears to them.

We see the child as he or she courts fear. The fearsome object, that which is disclosed as the object of fear, can be approached in various ways. A young boy responds in his own way. He swings on the low bars of the climbing frame and controls his fall on the slippery slide. Either way a sense of security comes with these more tentative responses to this playground equipment. And with use the equipment becomes less distant and increasingly familiar. The child's fear of the distant and unknown becomes a questioning of both the world and his place within it. If we close our eyes to this child's fear then there is the danger of his becoming truly afraid and incapable of taking a risk at all. We remember this from the slide where any admonishment serves only as a provocation to which the child is even less likely to respond. This dare to come down the slide only accentuates fear, making him afraid of the slide. We must simply wait for the child to see for himself what the slide involves. To do otherwise is to jeopardize this possibility of self-disclosure and turn attention to those possibilities that encapsulate a fearful state-of-mind and put the child at-risk.

Being present for the sake of the child's explorations thus requires not merely helping nor even just encouraging the child's activity; it also requires responding as if through the child's activity we encounter the playground together. This should not be too hard, for in a very real sense seeing children on playgrounds rekindles the fears and trepidations along with the joy, spontaneity, and trust in the world which we remember from childhood. Being present pedagogically joins adult and child in a relation that encounters the riskiness of the playground. Consider, in this regard, the young child on the other end of the teeter-totter. She giggles each time we bounce her into the air and delights us with her happiness. She allows us to see things afresh and shows us a joy in being alive. So we bounce her higher and higher, ever mindful of the limits of her trust. Yet this same child cries and clings to us when we put her on a mechanical donkey at the local shopping mall. This child asks us to attend to the lived meaning of her activity and to observe the relation that ameliorates the activity's potential for causing distress. This child asks for something which I think all children ask for in some way or another: that we care for the risky nature of their activity, their playground activity in particular, by re-awakening to the world which the child sees.

## Playground Atmosphere

There are probably as many ways of being with children as there are adults and children, and even then it would vary according to time and circumstance. We ignore the child one moment, next moment we allow something he or she does to catch our eye and make us forget what seemed so important such a short while ago. Or we chastise the child one instant and then, realizing that we have jumped to too hasty a conclusion, we take him or her in an apologetic embrace the next. The adult-child relation is in constant flux and riddled with misunderstandings. For heuristic purposes, as well as for the purpose of sketching a relation that is especially mindful of children's risk-taking, it has been useful to talk of certain ways of being with children, certain modes of presence such as supporting, guiding, instructing and evaluating, and to distinguish them from challenging and encountering the child as modes of pedagogical relatedness. In this way it has been possible to see not only that the nuances of the adult-child relation influence the riskiness of the playground, but also that the way the adult responds to the child's playground activity is a reflection of the texture of risk. The particular responses an adult gives have direct bearing on the atmosphere of risk to which playground activity is exposed.

Through reflective awareness of the responses we make and how it is that such responses are possible, we can bring a sense of security to the child's activity and thus create a "pedgogical atmosphere." Rephrasing Vandenberg's (1975) usage of this notion, the "pedagogical atmosphere" is determined by the dispositions which children and adults show towards playground activity. These dispositions furnish the medium within which it is possible for adult and child to be open to each other and for them to be attuned towards each other and to the possibilities of risk-taking that the playground affords. The pedagogical atmosphere is felt, therefore, when the child's and the adult's presence together is "ontologically founded in a particular mode of genuine being with (that is, the pedagogic relation)" (p. 38). It is felt when they enjoy the playground together. Challenging the child, becoming mindful of how the playground appears to the child, and seeking to make this playground activity a common encounter, are the determinants of this pedagogical atmosphere. These are the atmospheric conditions of our responsibility for children on playgrounds and the dimensions of our thinking about how children can learn to become responsible themselves for the riskiness of everyday life.

These suggestions as to how we might best help children learn to take risks require more detailed exploration. We need to describe the various forms of challenge and the types of encounter that define our playground interactions with children; moreover, we need to see this adult responsiveness to the riskiness of the playground not just in an heuristic way, but in a motivating, guiding, orienting, and principling way. Our description should compel us to act pedagogically. Hence, we should ask: How can we be committed to certain courses of action? What is the basis to a pedagogical interest in playground activity? What underlies the approach we take to helping children learn to take risks? How may we be drawn to children's experiences of risk and how may we know what course of action is best to take in particular risky playground situations? Such questions as these lead to a fuller understanding of how risk can become a practical term of our pedagogical relation to children.

# 5

# The
# Challenge of
# Risk

Children like to be with others on the playground. "Do you want to go to Alice's Playground?" I ask my child. "Yes. But can I go and see if Dorian can come?" He always wants to go with a friend, be it Dorian, Matthew, Paco, or some other child who is currently his best friend. More so than most other places, the playground is regarded by this child and by children in general as a place of shared experience. This does not mean that children do not act out their own plans when on playgrounds. They co-opt each other into doing things which they would perhaps not try if left alone. They are sometimes obliged to stretch the limits of their abilities. Yet the presence of others does not necessarily signify the loss of self-direction. On the contrary, being with others creates a context in which self-direction is essentially possible. That is to say, the presence of other children calls the actions

101

CARL A. RUDISILL LIBRARY
LENOIR-RHYNE COLLEGE

of a particular child into account. Through the involvement of others the child can be defiant, the child can stand up for himself or herself, the child can make a claim to personhood. And thus it makes sense to take a friend, to have a friend to play with, someone the child can trust, someone who understands that the playground presents inescapable, personal challenges that should not be faced alone.

If the child understands the risks of the playground better when in the presence of a trusted friend, then what might be achieved in the company of say, a Lisa or a Lewis, or better still, in the presence of an adult whom the child trusts? How might the risks of playground activity be responded to when the child gains confidence by being with a trusted adult? To answer these questions we need to look more closely than before at the social construction of playground risks, that is, at how children dare each other and at how the playground itself poses challenges which children articulate for themselves and for others. But most importantly, we need to consider the ways children can be encouraged to respond to risk and the limits to which they can be pushed. We need to show not only that the perception of risk is socially constructed, but also that a positive sense of risk, a sense of challenge, can be brought about through the tactful encouragement that comes from a trusted adult.

## The Dare

"I dare you to. Go on. Go on. I dare you to. Bet you can't. You're too afraid! Go on—I dare you to." Such taunts are common on the playground as children take great delight in daring each other to respond to challenges. And once a dare is made, how can the challenge be ignored? To not accept the challenge contained within the dare is to court possible ridicule, yet to respond to the dare is to risk failure as well as the chance of getting hurt. Either way there is risk involved when a dare has been made.

Sometimes the dare is made the focus of children's playground activity. Children often play a game of "dares" or some variant of it such as follow-the-leader. "Can you do this?" Kyler asks Sophie before jumping up onto the narrow beam beside them. In order for Sophie to stay in the game she must do as Kyler has done. Then it is her turn to try something adventurous which Kyler must follow. She moves over to the swings, climbs on the nearest one, and rocks back and forth into a higher and higher arc. "I bet you can't go this high!" she yells to Kyler who has already moved around to the adjacent swing. "See if you can get as high as me!"

It is apparent from even the most casual of playground observations that daring, adventurousness, and audacity are common properties of playground activity. Two of the best known chroniclers of children's playground games made an observation familiar to many of us, that "children do not merely sit on the seats and see who can swing the highest, but try [to see] who can climb furthest up the chains while swinging, and who can best twizzle the swing while swinging, and who can jump off his seat from the greatest height, and who, by swinging hard, can leap the furthest off the swing" (Opie and Opie, 1969, pp. 272, 273). Risk is actively sought, and when an activity seems too staid, children will invariably challenge one another to make it more interesting. It is the dare that gives specific shape and direction to the challenge that is sought.

Acts of daring may suggest foolhardiness, however a dare also implies a degree of common sense. What one child is dared to do the others must do sooner or later. Daring a child to try some new trick on the swing inevitably requires that those who are watching for now also have their turn. There is, in other words, a common sense of the activity at hand, a sense of sharing in the excitement and being prepared to take up the challenge when called upon.

There is, as well, a different kind of daring, the purpose of which is more to single out a child from the group and to make of him or her an example of that which is only more darkly held in common. For instance, while on a swing a child is pushed as high as possible before those around cry out: "Now! Jump!" And if the child waits too long, a torrent of abuse flows in his or her direction. "James is a scaredy-cat!" they chant in unison. The child is now compelled to jump or face the prospect of being totally ostracized by the group. So he jumps, not when they dare him to, but after they have stopped pushing and the swing has subsided a little. He picks himself up from the ground and says with a sneer to Eduardo who just happens to be the one standing closest to him, "Well let's see you do it. See how good you are." But his words have little effect other than fueling the jeers of those standing close by and increasing the misery of James' isolation. These children are now far more interested in picking on James than in allowing him into their circle and thus risk being dared themselves. Yet even here, in spite of the unfairness of the situation, there is an underlying distinction between daring and foolhardiness. The children sense that James will not jump when they dare him to; and even if he did, the best he can do is to show that the activity is not quite as dangerous as they thought it to be. James serves to highlight the common sense they have of the danger of this particular activity. Daring him reflects a sense held in common of how difficult the activity really is.

At a certain point, the dare is not only unfair but irresponsible. This is the point where children overstep the bounds of common sense when their dares becomes malevolent and not simply mischievous. Here we may speak of the foolish dare and of the type of daring that is fraught with danger. Of the many so-called "daring games" described by the Opies and by Slukin (1981), for example, many actually seem to be based upon the very real possibility of physical harm. Some are mainly threatening, as in the game of falling forwards towards another child whose outstretched arms and fingers risk poking out the eyes of the falling child. The threat of being blinded is removed only in the final instant before contact. For the child who accepts the dare, the challenge is neither to flinch nor even blink for fear of being a "scarebaby" (Slukin, 1981, p. 25). But other "daring games," particularly those that spill over from the playground into traffic areas, carry the distinct possibility of physical injury and possibly death. Such games, in stepping over the bounds of the playground, also overstep the bounds of common sense. In fact, overstepping the bounds of common sense would appear to be their very rationale, and would suggest that they are pursued only by children who are old enough to know what that common sense is and who dare to defy it.[1]

It behoves us to question very seriously the idea of risk-taking that is being invoked in this kind of dare-devilishness. Is it true to say that "these games by their very emphasis on daring, help the majority of children to understand the nature of risk-taking" (Opie and Opie, 1969, p. 263)? To be sure, they show that risk-taking has a daring quality to it, but what they do not show is how a positive sense of risk can be invoked when children specifically dare one another. Although a dare is not the only way a child encounters risk, it is significant primarily because it draws attention to risk and exposes the child to the possibilities of experiencing it. The dare provokes a response. It provokes by suggesting limitations, but it also admonishes the child not to accept limits, or at least to test them out. The dare instructs the child to look more closely at what he or she might be capable of. At the same time, it is possible for a dare to be informed by an understanding of how children might relate to each other. Thus we can see in James' case that his being taunted has a lot to do with his dubious relation to the children, his already being an outsider and someone to pick on. The question to consider is: Can the dare express a more positive relation?

This is how it might be for Ben:

> Hi. My name is Ben. I am six years old. That means I'm almost grown up. But sometimes things still scare me.
> I took my first swimming lessons this summer.

On the first day, I was afraid to go into the water. I just stood on the edge of the pool. The water looked awfully deep.

My brother Tim was already in the pool.

"Hey, Ben," he called. "What's the matter? You scared?"

I didn't say anything. I just sat down. I was afraid all right. The water was deep. It was cold too. I didn't want to go in at all. But I was afraid Tim would laugh at me if I stayed out. So I made myself get in the water. (Conaway, 1977, pp. 5, 6.)

There is in this situation a type of dare resulting from Tim having taken the plunge already and his now being in a position to sense his brother's predicament. His words and indeed his reproachful presence make sense in the context of a brotherly relation; nevertheless, the writer of this story has not really shown how this relation might prefigure a sensible dare. The writer has not shown what form a dare might take when it is premised by a brotherly sense of responsibility for the other child.

Consider, then, the following situation. Paco and Eduardo sit astride the beam from which a cargo net is suspended to the ground. They are content for the moment just to perch up there and rest upon their accomplishment. Meanwhile Paco's younger brother, Denny, has come over. "How did you get up there?" asks Denny, seeing no other way up than the steep climb up the cargo net. "It's easy," says Paco. He pauses, perhaps reflecting upon how hard it really was. "Do you think you can come up?" he says, now daring his younger brother. But it is soon clear that the challenge is just too great for Denny. "You're too little. Ha, ha, you can't come up," chants Eduardo. The two older boys enjoy their superiority, although it seems to mean more to Eduardo than to Paco. A moment later Paco tells Denny, as if to explain his superiority, "You're only four, and I'm six. I'm bigger than you." He then asks Denny, "Do you want me to help you up?" Of course, it is important not to be mislead in understanding Paco's intention in daring Denny to climb up the cargo net; nevertheless, in contrast to Eduardo's taunts, there is a benevolent tone to Paco's words that intimates a way of daring another child which acknowledges a relation to that other child (in this case, a brotherly relation) and a sense of responsibility for him or her.

I do not mean to imply that a good dare is only possible within a brotherly relation—a relation of fraternity—rather that it is a good dare to the extent that it is based upon a genuine interest in the ability of the other and of the limits to which he or she can be challenged. So the question is: how can this good sense of a dare prevail? How can a dare show an even greater measure of empathy for the child? How might a dare show a degree of sympathy for what the child might achieve?

"Jump! Jump!" Jamie calls out to Cory. We look up to see Cory balancing on the railing of one of the high platforms three meters above the ground. He hesitates momentarily then leaps high into the air and successfully clears the ladders and poles anchored alongside the platform. Unfortunately he lands awkwardly and hobbles around for a minute or two, rubbing his leg until the pain of the landing subsides. Jonathan has been watching all this time, and now he looks on with some concern as he sees Cory attempting to cope with his injury. He chastises Cory, telling him: "You don't have to do what he [Jamie] tells you to." Cory turns to look at Jonathan. With a whimsical expression he answers: "I do. He's my conscience!" Cory seems even to surprise himself with this retort. He laughs at what he has said and heads off after Jamie.

Cory has been dared. Seeing the other child perched above him, daring him to jump off the railing, means there can be no backing down, no way of ignoring the dare. One might even conclude that his blindness to the situation and to the dangers lurking there yields a blind trust in this other child. Through the dare Cory is subject to the will of the other child. So he jumps and hopes for the best. But is he really blind to the situation, spellbound, as it were, by Jamie's dare? After all, Cory can still laugh at the idea of Jamie daring him to jump. It seems almost as if he wants to be dared, to be challenged to the limit of his physical ability. Besides, Jamie's dare to jump from the railing would fall on deaf ears if it did not in some way already impinge upon Cory's inclination to try this activity. If not for Jamie's words to make Cory conscious of this activity, and if not for the relation upon which this dare is premised, then Cory may not even be challenged at all. Like Denny, he wants an articulation of his inclinations. He wants someone to be his "conscience." The dare is, in this regard, neither thoughtless nor malicious. We watch as Cory follows Jamie up the ladder of the large spiralling slide. He hesitates at the top, but having seen Jamie disappear down the shute so effortlessly and now hearing him call from below, daring him to catch up, he seems reassured. Down he goes. "I did it!" he cries gleefully. "I did it! Did you see me? I'm going to do it again." This is the first time he has dared to go down this particular slide, and it took a boy his own age to get him to have such a feeling of accomplishment.

The dare is not always articulated in so many words. The child is often dared in other less obvious ways, ways in which the child must be his or her own conscience, ways in which the child must find his or her own way. We need to consider these more subtle dares, provocations, and excitements. We need to consider the dare within a broader context of how the challenges of the playground are articulated. Also, in seeing a pedagogy beyond daring the child, we need to say more about what sorts of risks are worth taking and how pedagogically we can bring children to decide. How can we encourage children to take risks that are considered worthwhile?

## Encouragement

There is a Norman Rockwell illustration which shows a young boy looking nervously over the edge of a high diving board. This child is on all-fours, gripping the end of the board, petrified it seems at the prospect of being in such a precarious position. Yet as we look at this picture something appears to have been left out. There is no one else in sight. No one stands on the diving platform behind the child, no one can be seen coming up the ladder. This child is alone on the end of the diving board, evidently experiencing great fear, although there is no one else present to account for his predicament. We wonder: how can it be that this child has ventured so far out on the diving board? How has this child found the courage not only to climb up to the diving board but also to go right to the edge of the board? Has the board itself become the challenge?

The diving board has indeed become the challenge for Marc. He sees his friends jump off the three-meter board with comparative ease, or so he thinks. They do not seem too worried by it. They try it many times while he stays below on the deck out of the way. "C'mon Marc," says Ben, "aren't you going to do it?" Eventually Marc climbs up the ladder to the board. He holds the railing at the top and looks anxiously over the edge of the board to the pool below. Some children climb behind Marc. He lets them past to have their turn before him. "C'mon Marc!" yells Ben from somewhere down below. Marc peers over the edge. He turns around and heads back down the ladder.

Is this the end of the matter for Marc? Not likely. The diving board has become the topic of his talk at home over the next few days. He mentions it so often that eventually his parents agree to take him and his younger brother, Matthew, to the pool so that he might try the three-meter board once again. But when they arrive at the pool, even the presence of the parents is not enough to allay Marc's apprehensiveness about going off this diving board. And to make matters worse, Matthew confidently mounts the ladder and runs straight off the end of the board. Matthew shows very little fear at all of this diving board.

"How deep is the water?" asks Marc. He sees the depth of the pool. He sees straight to the bottom of the pool. The water is so clear, what will stop him from plunging straight to the bottom? What will give him confidence to jump off this board? Marc backs down once again and looks wistfully at the board as Matthew and the children bounce off it.

"Can you show me how to do it?" Marc asks his father. It seems the challenge of the board weighs heavily upon him. But how can Marc be helped to respond to this challenge in the way that he wants? How can his confidence be built up? After all, it is not just a matter of showing him how to do it. He has watched the other children long enough already. No, the help given to Marc needs to be based on a knowledge of the board, in particular, Marc's knowledge of the board. Just as the dare is based upon some commonsense understanding of the riskiness of an activity, so too must the help that Marc wants stem from a shared sense of the riskiness of his activity. Marc wants to know how to jump off the board, starting from where he stands at the moment. He wants the sort of encouragement which allows him to find his own way of responding to the challenge of the diving board.

Tyler and Dorian are not on a diving board. Instead, they can be seen peering over the rim of a plastic casing which forms a partial roof to one of the platforms at Malmo Playground. A few of the older children have been half sliding, half jumping off this casing onto the sand some distance below. Tyler and Dorian have a bird's eye view of this activity from where they lie on a slanted wooden structure that buttresses the plastic casing. They lie in such a way that they can see what is going on, using the wooden beam that attaches the plastic casing to the wooden buttress in order to pull themselves up to gain an even better view of the action and then to slide back down the wooden structure and partly disappear from the view of those who are making ready to jump. At the moment they have pulled themselves up towards the plastic rim and are waiting to see Jonathan jump off. "Do it, kid! Do it!" says Tyler to this older boy. "You do it!" Jonathan snaps back. Dorian pipes in: "He doesn't want to. We did it before." Jonathan jumps. He picks himself up, brushes the sand off and turns to look up at the two younger boys who are now craning their necks to see where he has landed. "That's a cinch, kid!" says Jonathan. But before he can suggest they follow him, Tyler and Dorian have withdrawn from view. After a while Jonathan and his friends tire of this activity. They start chasing each other over the other pieces of equipment on the playground. Now it is safe for Tyler and Dorian to try out this plastic casing themselves. So they climb tentatively over the beam anchoring the wooden platform to the casing, and taking a firm grip on the beam, they try to find a way of sitting securely on the plastic rim. Now it seems they can really appreciate how far Jonathan had to jump to the ground below.

As they sit there leaning back with their arms draped over the supporting beam, becoming accustomed to the height, some of the older children return. Tyler and Dorian find they must shuffle along in order to make room for two of Jonathan's friends who have now climbed up beside them. But these children are not there for long. They jump off as soon as they see Jonathan coming their way across the bars that adjoin the platform upon which the two younger children lay only a short while ago. Tyler and Dorian watch closely as Jonathan approaches. As he comes near they retreat to the wooden platform, remembering, it seems, Jonathan's challenge for them to jump after him. They do not want Jonathan to know that they have been considering doing it. Much better to be out of Jonathan's way, to retreat to the platform so that Jonathan does not have his way with them. Discretion is, for the moment, the better part of valor.

A little while later I notice Dorian sitting again on the casing. Tyler is off to another part of the playground to watch Andrew play in the sand with the things he has brought from home. Jonathan and his friends sit talking under one of the slides. But Dorain stays on the plastic casing, unable to ignore the challenge of jumping off. He sits for a long time, saying things to himself and looking around for the others who are now below him on different parts of the playground. He sits alone above the chatter of the children. There is something grand about the position he is now in—to be in the midst of activity and yet to sit above it. It is a moment to be savoured. Still, the challenge is there to jump down. He jumps! Not once, but a second time, and then again. Even so, he has still not done what Jonathan did. Dorian has still to let himself slide off rather than merely lower himself down by hanging onto the supporting beam and then dropping the remaining distance to the ground when his arms can extend no further.

I climb up beside him. "You can go off here, can't you?" he asks me. "I'm not sure. I don't know if my knees can take it," I reply. Dorian comes back straight away: "It's easy. It's easy as one, two, three. See. I can sit here without holding on." Dorian holds his arms up and then, with a bit of a wriggle, he lets himself slide over the edge. Now he can at last do what Jonathan did. "It's cinchy!" Dorian calls to me as he picks himself up off the ground. "It's a cinch," he says again as he climbs up to sit beside me again. Dorian rests for a moment. "You gotta give your hands a rest," he tells me. "They go splat on the ground." He leans forward to see over the edge and then turns to face me once again. "Are you going to do it? It's easy as one, two, three. It's even easy as one." Having shown me how to do it, having shared this newly acquired knowledge with me, Dorian needs to ensure the value of this knowledge by daring someone else who hasn't the knowledge. So he surveys the playground and spies his former playmate. "Hey Tyler, come here and do this!"

No doubt there was a type of dare here, one envisioned in Jonathan's daring and articulated by Jonathan as a challenge to Dorian and Tyler. This dare was not so much a provocation as an enticement, a prompt to look more closely at the situation in order to find ways of doing what Jonathan appeared to do so easily. Whereas Tyler seemed happy enough to leave things as they stand, Dorian appeared from the outset to be caught up in the situation, intent on learning how to do it. Jonathan threw down the gauntlet to Dorian, but this has merely served to accentuate a possibility that was already implied in his being drawn to the plastic casing. The task for Dorian is not simply to respond to a dare; rather, it is to find out ways of jumping to the ground.

Whence arises the pedagogical moment: deciding if Dorian does in fact need encouragement or if he needs to work it out for himself. So I climb up beside him to take the place of Jonathan, thereby ameliorating the tone of his challenge and thus helping Dorian to find his own way of responding to a challenge that goes even beyond Jonathan's terms of reference. Sitting beside Dorian, I have found a place within his terms of reference that allows me to encourage his daring. Here I am no longer a passive observer but now someone who can act in concert with Dorian. Now I have a stake in the activity at hand. Now I feel moved enough to give Dorian a hand. There is in the first instance a pathic response to what Dorian is trying to do. Linschoten (1968) writes: "When one has urged someone to jump over a ditch and he hesitates it is almost impossible for us to encourage him and *not* at the same time make an initial movement for jumping with him" (p. 274). When we see Dorian attempting something risky and seek to encourage his efforts we have already begun "with bodily reactions that follow upon these things" (p. 278). On the basis of this empathy, we feel sympathy for what Dorian is trying to do, and we feel moved to encourage him.

Let us consider more closely the nature of this encouragement. Consider the case of Gerrard who can be seen reaching up to grasp the top-most bar of a series of parallel bars which slope towards the ground. He has already tried a few times to make it all the way to the ground by monkey-swinging from one bar to the next. His last attempt resulted in getting halfway across before losing his grip and falling to the sand below. Now, as Gerrard makes ready to try again, he calls to his mother. "Mom, look here! Watch me do this! Mom, are you watching? Mom! W-a-t-c-h!" She continues to talk with a parent of one of the other children on the playground. For the moment she is oblivious to her son's calls. Meanwhile a couple of the other children, close in age to Gerrard, push him to the side of the platform so they can swing on these very same bars. Gerrard appears frustrated and calls again for his mother's attention. "All right, Gerrard, I'm watching you now!" she says in an exasperated voice. Her tone mellows. "What is it you want to show me?" Gerrard reaches out for the first bar, and with legs kicking wildly, struggles to grasp the second, then the third. At about the same point as before he tires; he does not have the energy to reach the next bar, and just misses it. Gerrard falls heavily to the ground. But he does not hurt himself. He stays on all fours for a brief moment before brushing the sand off and climbing up the linked tires that lead to the platform from which the bars can be reached. "That was a good try," says his mother. "But I can't do it!" yells Gerrard. "It's too hot! The bars are too hot!" "Well, go and play on something else," his mother chides him. Gerrard suddenly becomes angrier. "Don't say that! You're not to say that!" he screams at her. "Look, Gerrard, if the bars are too hot then go and play on something else. The people here don't want to hear you yelling out all afternoon. Be a good boy and play on something else." Gerrard is in tears. "I told you not to say that!" he cries out for all the neighborhood to hear.

Gerrard has watched the other children on this set of bars and is anxious to do as they have shown him. He calls upon his mother to watch him, and he becomes distressed, not just because the bars are hot and he cannot yet do as the other children have done, but more because her words draw attention to the possibility of his being a failure.[2] Gerrard is clearly not ready to move on to some other piece of equipment; in fact, at this point in time no other piece of equipment matters to him. He wants to be encouraged to do as the other children have done on the bars. When he says "Don't say that" he means "Don't say that I can't do it. I want to do it and I am not prepared to admit defeat." In point of fact, his mother's words discourage him and, all power to Gerrard, he will not accept defeat so readily. Gerrard needs words of support to literally hold him up so he can find a way of swinging to the ground. There are, of course, limits to this support, yet Gerrard's growing frustration seems to indicate that he has been left neither a way of doing the activity nor a reasonable way out of doing it. His daring has not been sufficiently encouraged to have an appropriate outlet.

The encouragement given to children like Gerrard is often more than words can say. To encourage means to give heart to the child, to inspirit and animate him or her, to be with the child in spirit and flesh as activity is being attempted. Words are not enough. Too often they are only a means of praising the child, of feigning interest and of thus giving the semblance of our involvement while remaining at a distance. Praise without deed defeats the point of encouragement. We need to feel sufficiently moved to countenance the child's activity and to support the child's way of responding to playground challenges.

## Ways Out

But what if the child chooses not to respond to a challenge? Or what if the child seeks to avoid challenge altogether? For instance, on the way to Alice's Playground we pass one of the high apartment towers.

Rodrigo has been this way before. He knows about the service ramp at the side of this building. On previous occasions he has ridden down this narrow ramp and shot up it to the road on the far side. Now, with Paco in tow, he heads toward the ramp entrance. "Wait up!" I call out to the two of them. They have left me behind on their bikes and I need to check the ramp for obstacles before they disappear down it. The two boys wait impatiently for me to catch up. "We can go down," says Rodrigo, "there's nobody using it." I look to make sure, but before Rodrigo can turn his bike around he sees that Paco has beaten him to the ramp. Paco pushes his bike. He holds onto the handlebars and runs alongside his bike down the ramp and part-way up the other side before having to push it again. Once he reaches the other side he sits on the bike and waits for Rodrigo to join him. "You're supposed to ride down it," Rodrigo calls to him. Next moment Paco sees Rodrigo tear up the ramp past him. "Oh, I should've went down like that," he tells Rodrigo as if to acknowledge his mistake. It is significant, however, that Paco is quite anxious for us to be on our way to Alice's Playground.

On our return from the playground Paco stays with me. "Can we go this way?" he asks, pointing to a different way past the apartment building that had the service ramp. Too late. Rodrigo is already peddling his bike to the side of the building from which going down the ramp is a possibility to be reckoned with. So we follow Rodrigo. But Paco does not follow him down the ramp. He is content to ride around the pathway skirting the apartment block and joins Rodrigo on the other side. Later, out of curiosity, I ask Rodrigo: "Why do you think Paco didn't want to ride down the ramp?" "I don't know," he says matter-of-factly. For him, Paco's avoidance of the ramp does not matter. Other than indicating some seeming violation of a rule for riding down the ramp, Rodrigo has given no further thought to Paco's reluctance to ride down it. But what of Paco? Doesn't it matter to him? There is a distinct possibility that he has felt himself compromised by not responding to the challenge that Rodrigo articulated in word and action. Even my presence there prevented his finding a let-out, a way of saving face, although he obviously tried to create one for himself by suggesting we take a different route home.

The sequel to this situation comes the following day when Paco and Rodrigo are together at Malmo Playground. The two boys are chasing each other over the playground. During the course of this activity Paco climbs up to the highest platform. He sees Rodrigo coming up behind him, so he reaches out to grab one of the poles anchored off to the side in preparation for sliding down to escape Rodrigo's clutches. "Hey, this is real high. It's real scary," he says under his breath as he leans out to grasp the pole. He looks around and sees Rodrigo coming up closer behind him, turns back, hesitates momentarily, and disappears down the pole. Once on the ground, however, the chase seems less important than it did a moment ago. Instead of fleeing to another part of the playground, Paco takes a few steps back to watch Rodrigo prepare to follow him down the same pole. And he notices that Rodrigo, even though he has done this activity before, still approaches it with some hesitation.

"Rodrigo's a chicken! Rodrigo's a big fat chicken!" calls Paco. He laughs and says to me, "Rodrigo's too scared to do it, isn't he?" But Rodrigo does slide down the pole. "You bumped coming down," Paco tells him, apparently referring to the jerkiness of Rodrigo's descent caused by his gripping the pole too tightly. "I went down really fast," he adds with a bit of a sneer. They both do it again. "I didn't bump that time," Rodrigo says. To which Paco replies: "You did too. I heard you. You went bp . . . bp . . . bp . . . bp . . . bp." "Let's do it again, then. Let's see if *you* bump," says Rodrigo indignantly. "No," replies Paco, "how about we play TV tag? You're it!"

As Paco and Rodrigo engage in this banter I cannot help thinking of the incident of the previous day and wondering to what extent Paco is now playing out the inadequacy I assume he felt at the hands of Rodrigo. To what extent are his present actions related to being denied a let-out when faced with the daunting prospect of coming down the ramp? Is his taunting of Rodrigo some sort of retribution for his own humiliation the day before? And what of my contribution to this situation? To what extent did my presence determine the nature of Paco's responses? After all, Rodrigo thought little of Paco's reluctance to ride down the ramp. Perhaps it was more because of my presence there that Paco became disheartened at the suggestion of his failing to take a risk.

When left to themselves children find their own ways of doing things and their own ways out of doing things that appear too risky. Jesse and Matthew, for instance, are drawn to a hill where they see children rolling down the grassed slopes. Some of these children have found cardboard boxes to pull apart in order to make sleds. Others seem happy enough to run down at full speed. We watch as Matthew crouches down, buries his head in the grass, flops over onto his back, and then, having gained sufficient momentum, continues on with a few more forward rolls. "Can you do that?" he asks Jesse as he contemplates doing another series. "Can you do this?" Jesse asks Matthew by way of response. He rolls sideways down the hill. In doing so, Jesse has found an appropriate response to the challenge that Matthew creates. He has avoided a situation where he might not measure up. And in finding his own way of responding to Matthew's challenge, he is well satisfied.

Matthew's father, Tony, watches as the two boys roll down the grassy slope. He wanders over and tells them, "When I was a kid we used to somersault all the way to the bottom. We'd do twenty or thirty in a row. I think I could probably still do that now." He takes off his coat and prepares to give it a try. Matthew and Jesse stand off to the side. Then away he goes, not quite to the bottom of the hill, but certainly a good part of the way down. Matthew tries to follow suit. But Jesse wanders off to see if perchance there are any pieces of cardboard lying around that he can use to slide on. It seems that, for him, Tony has narrowed the choices he has for rolling down the hill. Whereas when it was just Matthew with him, it was easy to ignore the terms of Matthew's challenge and to find his own way of going down the hill, now that Tony takes Matthew's side, the possibility of failure looms larger. The adult's presence gives a stamp of approval to doing "this" rather than doing "that." So Jesse wanders off to find something else to do.

Such an option is often unavailable to children in more formal playground contexts. Chris tells his parents that today is the day they are going to be doing diving in their physical education lesson. That evening, as they are seated around the dinner table, his father asks: "Did you go diving today?" Chris stays quiet. "Did you hear me, Chris? I asked you if you went diving." Chris bites his lips and tears well up in his eyes. "I'm a coward," he blurts out. "All the other kids could do it. And I didn't. I had to sit on the side and watch them." In this situation the child has no way out at all. He is let off the activity only to face the accusing stares of his classmates and the censure of his teacher, and possibly the disappointment of his parents.

How much different it is for the children we see climb up the high diving platform at the aquatic center? Holding on to the railing, they peer over the edge of the highest platform and decide that they are definitely up too high. They descend to the next level and again peer over the railing that borders the rear of this platform. It is still too high, although not so high that they can't step out onto the platform. One of them even lies on the platform, his head over the end, to see where they might end up in the pool. It is tempting. They descend the stairs once again to the second lowest platform. Suddenly the one who was lying down a moment ago runs off the end of the platform and plunges feet first into the pool. The other one goes to the lower platform and does the same. For both children it seems that what they did was quite enough. Each found a way out of doing what appeared too risky, and yet both responded to the challenge of going off the diving tower.

Clearly children need options when challenges appear too great. And if left to themselves they tend to find their own ways out. This does not mean that children should necessarily be left to themselves, that "you should interfere as little as possible when the child is with other children," and that the child "must find out for himself how to get along with them and how to accommodate his interests to theirs" (Dreikurs, 1972, p. 56). Having already shown how dares can be mischievous when children are left to their own devices, and having indicated how the child looks to the adult to temper his or her daring, our task is to consider how we can in our dealings with children be especially sensitive to the nature of their "ways out" of playground activity. And we must be especially careful that we do not force responses that offer no way out at all—responses that risk a sense of failure or, at best, mute resignation.[3]

A poignant example is given by Crowe (1983) of a little girl who, for her own sense of security, carried around a "snake" made up of some cotton reels strung together.

> She didn't need it often, but sometimes we would see her hand slip into her pocket for a reassuring touch—or even hover near her pocket at the ready, in case. But one day she really needed it. We had created three solid steps up to the top of an inverted tea-chest, and the children were queueing up on the grass to climb the steps and jump off the top. Elizabeth was among them and when her turn came she confidently mounted the steps, moved over to the far side of the top—and froze. Suddenly the ground looked a long way down, and we watched her coming to the moment of decision. Risk it or jump? No. Accept the outstretched hand offering help? She hovered then averted her eyes. Turn around and go back? Suddenly she remembered, put her hand in her pocket to retrieve Snake, and with complete composure said "Snake doesn't want to jump today."
>
> I opened my mouth to say "Snakes don't like jumping, do they?" but suddenly saw two things simultaneously: she didn't need me to make it easier for her to climb down those stairs, she had managed it alone; and I would have blocked any renewed attempt to find the courage to jump later. If snakes "don't like jumping" then next time she climbed those steps it would be assumed that *she* wanted to jump— and what if her courage failed again? (pp. 124, 125)

We need to respect the options children create, and perhaps even view them as possibilities in themselves. To find out the way to ride down a steep ramp, slide down a pole, roll down a hill or dive into a pool, it is sometimes necessary to find ways out of doing it initially. This does not mean avoiding challenge; rather, it means seeking ways of meeting challenge. The child looks for the possible. And it is here, when we look with the child and recognize his or her response as an orientation to the riskiness of the playground, that our encouragement can be most helpful.

Here we can become attuned to the ways a child learns to take risks. Here we can see a pedagogy beyond daring the child.

## Limits of Challenge

I push a group of small children on a tire swing. As the pitch intensifies they start to chant: "We want a high push, we want a high push, we want a high push. . . ." They chant in unison: "Higher! Higher!" But how can I know how high to push them? How far can these children be challenged? Here we have a situation where there are seemingly no ways out of the activity, no ways the children may prudently let themselves off the swing if the challenge suddenly becomes too much; yet still the principle of letting children find out for themselves applies to the extent that it is their daring to which we respond. Here, where we are required to stand close to the children and contribute to their activity, we must be especially mindful of the limits of challenge.

Let me indicate the direction of this thoughtfulness. Picture a little girl of about four years of age. And picture her in a make-shift playground, a vacant lot which the neighborhood children have converted into a play area. I am walking through this lot and approach Sophie. As I come close I see Sophie reaching for the knot on a long rope attached to a tree that the older children have been using as a swing. I pick Sophie up and sit her on the knot. That's all I do. Then she says, "Push me." I haven't seen her on the swing before, so I cautiously push her just out of hand's reach. She had been quite calmly sitting on the knot, but now she is screwed into a tight ball, her face set rigid in terror. I am a little terrified as well, because I don't really want to frighten the little girl and she is obviously not enjoying herself, so I stop her. Relaxing slightly, she says again, "Push me." I wonder what is going on because I cannot match her words with her terror. This time as the swing slows, the terror abates and she looks a little happier, her lips turned up in a slight smile. The third time as the swing slows, Sophie relaxes and even eases back on the rope before again saying, "Push me." Before too long I cannot push her high enough (adapted from Jago, 1970).

Sophie sees a challenge and looks for encouragement. She wants to be lifted onto the rope and pushed, not simply because it is impossible for her to do it alone but because the challenge requires our complicity. She needs us there to give her the courage to extend herself until she can find her own way. Then, when she knows her way, there is indeed no way we can push her high enough. Hence our task is not just to push Sophie but rather to become attuned to the way in which she wants us to push her, which is to say, to the way in which our pushing may eventually become unnecessary. We look to a time when Sophie can do better by herself.

This means taking special care in the way we encourage children like Sophie and being sensitive to the manner in which we implicate ourselves in their risk-taking. Consider the case of four-year-old Tyler. The setting is now a fairly new designer-type playground full of ladders and platforms, bright yellow slides, geometrical climbing frames, assorted tunnels, and archways. Tyler and I are standing near the swings—the tires that are suspended by chains from a large beam, and that have a universal joint at the top so they can swing in all directions. But we are not the only ones on this part of the playground. Tyler watches a group of girls not much older than he enjoying themselves on one of the swings. After a while he moves onto the vacant tire swing. He lies across it with his feet scuffing the dirt. Next he runs in a circle still clinging to the tire. Then he pulls himself up, drops his legs through the tire, and stares down as the swing turns slowly round and round. "Can you push me?" asks Tyler.

I take hold of the chains, shuffle backwards, and release the swing. Then, as the swing returns I grasp the chains again, pull back a little further, and give the swing a little jerk as I launch it into a higher arc. This seems awkward, so I decide to push lower down on the swing, on the tire itself. Now the swing goes even higher, and as it does so, it starts to rotate such that the next time it can be pushed Tyler finds himself looking sideways at me. The swing continues to rotate, and with each push Tyler must alter slightly his position on the tire in order to keep from falling off. "Don't push me anymore," says Tyler. But I don't hear him since I am too caught up in the job of pushing him into the air. "Don't push me anymore!" Tyler says again, now with a sense of real urgency. This time I hear him. And I see the terror written all over his face. So I step back and watch as the slowing of the swing brings a look of relaxation to Tyler's face. The swing comes to a stop. Tyler sits with his legs dangling down, the swing moving ever so slightly. After a while he looks over at the girls on the swing beside him. He watches as they are pushed higher and higher into the air. Then he turns to me and asks: "Can you push me? But don't push me too hard!"

Tyler wants to do as the girls on the other swing have shown him. He is challenged by what he sees them doing, however he needs a push in order to respond to their challenge. Tyler wants to be pushed like Sophie. He wants to be pushed to the point of not wanting to be pushed anymore, not in the sense of being intimidated but rather in the knowledge that he can now push himself. For the sake of this knowledge, he needs to be encouraged. So he continues to ask me to push him as long as I remain in touch with him by not pushing him too hard.

It would seem there are not so much limits to challenge as there is a need to feel moved by children's desires to be challenged, and moved enough even to be able to follow the direction that the challenge takes. There is a need to stand in a physically construed relation to children whereby they can be encouraged to find their own way of exploring the playground risks which entice them and which we think are worth taking. A child's future is literally in the hands of the adult standing by. He or she can be dared, provoked, maybe even led by the words of the adult, but the best way of helping the child respond to challenge is if the adult's encouragement has the appearance of reaching out to the child, of making contact with the child, of making support palpable. How can this physical contact be achieved? Or better still, how can we remain "tactful" (literally, in delicate touch) in our dealings with children on the playground? Perhaps by looking more self-reflectively at what is happening when children respond to playground challenges, and especially, by considering situations in which the nature of their response is tantamount to a testing of our ability to stay in touch with them.

# 6

# The
# Encounter with
# Risk

Günther Anders tells the fable of a young prince who was forever stepping off the beaten track to explore the fields,
woods, and out of the way places where no path exists.

But since it displeased the king that his son, leaving the clearly marked
avenues, made his way across meadows and fields in order to get to
understand the world on his own terms, he gave his son cart and horse.
"Now you no longer need to walk on foot" were his words. "Now you
may no longer do it" was their intent. "Now you no longer can" was
their effect.  (Anders, 1902)

This parental consideration serves, in the first instance, mainly to bring
the child back to the straight and narrow pathway. The child loses the

freedom to ply his own way, for now he can only re-ply to the challenges before him in an adulterated sort of way. Likewise in the discussion of playground challenges we have seen how the adult can constrain the child from finding his or her own way.[1] But the lesson to be drawn from this is not that the child should be left completely to his or her own devices; rather that we must examine more carefully our motives for helping the child face challenges so that we can be better placed to eventually let the child go his or her own way along a path of risk-taking.

In this section of the study we seek a greater measure of self-reflection in our dealings with children. We seek to overcome that indifference borne of long-time experience which keeps us apart from the child's experience of risk and which lets us constrain the child's activity within an artificial safety. Our strategy will be to consider, first of all, situations unfamiliar to both adult and child and to contrast them with the supposed familiarity of the playground. Such a strategy will hopefully enable us to encounter the child's experience of the playground and to deepen the pedagogy of risk outlined so far.

## Apprehension

We follow the path along the top of the ravine, all the while looking for a way down to the river. But each clearing presents a major challenge, with thick vegetation barring the way and steep sides dropping to the water's edge. We must walk a little further before finding an easier access. Before long we come to where an earth slide has covered the vegetation and created a more moderate slope to the river, although we wonder if it is still too steep for the children who are with us. I take a few steps down to test the firmness of the ground, then call for Tyler to take hold of my hand. He says he does not want to come, yet his voice betrays a desire not to be left behind. "Here, take my hand," I tell him more insistently. A few steps more and I become concerned that perhaps this is not such a good idea. The earth is softer than I had thought and it is much more difficult to stay upright. Tyler becomes apprehensive as we continue to stumble and slide down the embankment. So I ask him to hold on to a protruding branch while I move sideways into a better alignment for the rest of the descent. But Tyler does not want to let go of my hand. He is visibly upset at this turn of events. At this moment Tyler is afraid; futhermore, it seems that we are in a position where, because of the difficulty of the activity for us both, I cannot be totally mindful of his fearfulness. Or so it probably seems to Tyler.

Just at this moment we hear Matthew laughing above us. Turning around, I see Matthew tumbling toward us, earth and stones scattering in his wake. Matthew has decided to throw caution to the wind. If there were any fears in his mind they were put aside when he left his father behind on the slope above us. The sight of Matthew changes things for Tyler. He laughs with Matthew as his friend comes crashing into us. Suddenly the hill does not appear so steep, so hard, so dangerous. In fact Tyler now wants to careen down the slope as well. He wants to do as Matthew has shown him. Matthew's father and I stand and watch as Matthew first and then Tyler scamper down the rest of the slope, giggling all the way to the bottom. Later on when it comes time to leave, we are not so concerned to find an easy way out of this river valley. The first open area we come to seems accessible enough. We watch as Matthew heads off with Tyler close behind. We follow directly after them, since there are places where they need some help to climb up the steep and slippery sections. Yet such difficulties do not worry the boys. Soon we reach the path at the top and stop to catch our breath. Tyler says: "I climbed up all by myself, didn't I Daddy?" I nod in agreement. "Can we do it again?" he asks.

How can it be that a child can be so fearful initially going down the slope and yet show such bravado coming up? And in what way are we implicated in this child's coming to terms with this challenging place? Perhaps it is significant that Tyler was being led when his fearfulness became apparent, and that he became most anxious when he was left momentarily by himself on the hill. This was also the moment when the accompanying adult felt most concerned about the difficulty of the climb down to the river. This was when I felt least connected to Tyler. Then, just as the situation became charged with apprehension, a child the same age as Tyler shows us how things might be grasped, how Tyler might have been led down the embankment, and how the encounter with risk might have been a fortifying experience for us both. Consider, in this regard, a more dramatic situation, that of leading a large group of children down the slopes of a mountain. On the way down, which is difficult at the best of times, we are surprised by a thunderstorm. We take shelter while it passes, but now the descent is made especially difficult. Previously firm attachments have become slippery while once safe ledges and overhangs must be negotiated with care. In a very short space of time the storm has changed the face of this mountain. Mount Danger has become a threatening place for us all. As we continue our descent some of the adult leaders seem as frightened as many of the children. One of them, Therese, hangs back at the end of the group. She is literally in tears at the prospect of going any further, and has to be coaxed down by one of her friends. Meanwhile the children are finding themselves increasingly on their own. They are still being led by the adults who stay in front of the group; yet it is the anxiety of those closest to them that makes the way seem so very dangerous.

In many ways the situation of the children on this mountain parallels that of Matthew and Tyler on the slopes of the riverbank. Children become fearful in both situations, however their fearfulness is much more than a psychological state; it is an expression of our own implication in the situation. The children's fears, while having some objective meaning, are more an expression of how we as adults maintain a relation to them in situations that hold risk for us both, albeit in different ways. Children sense adult anxiety and nervousness and they feel their own grip on a situation loosening as adults become increasingly apprehensive about what might befall them.

By way of contrast with these landscapes of risk, consider a much more familiar site, one so familiar that we can easily lose sight of our stake in the child's fearfulness. Serafino (1986) provides the example of a young child who, at the age of three, develops an aversion to bathtime. As an infant Rachel was happy to be bathed and would delight in having water poured upon her. Then, when she grew too big for the bathinette, she was no less happy to be bathed in a tub. Even before she could sit up, she would lie on her back, her head supported, and kick and splash water over the edge of the bathinette with mirthful abandon. And by the age of eighteen months the suggestion of bathtime was enough for her to saunter off to the bathroom and begin prying off her clothes while trying to climb into a partially filled tub. Having her hair washed, with shampoo inevitably getting in her eyes, was not much fun, but aside from this unpleasantness, Rachel could have stayed in the tub forever playing with the collection of toys ring-a-rosyed around her. She would often pull on the faucets, draw herself upright, and on occasion, slip and fall awkwardly, and sometimes, mistaking water for air, emerge from her activity spluttering and coughing. But there was never an accident that would explain why, at three years of age, she should suddenly become so averse to taking a bath.

According to Serafino, her "fear arose from incorrect ideas she thought up all by herself that involved extensions of things she had seen" (p. 59). It appears that during one of her bathtimes, Rachel was playing with the drainage plug and began letting water out of the tub. Since she had already been there for some time already, her father did not close off the drain; instead, he had Rachel stand up and dried her down as the water level dropped lower and lower. Rachel stood still as the frothy bath water that blanketed her a moment ago seeped around her legs, her feet, her toes, until the last of it swirled and gurgled down the plughole. "Suddenly Rachel grabbed onto her father, saying 'Take me out, Daddy.' He hadn't realized what she was thinking, and, since she was dry, he picked her up and carried her off to bed" (p. 59).

In questioning the nature of Rachel's thinking, Serafino suggests that she probably thought that she would disappear down the drain with the last of the water. She did not see herself as impossibly large for that drainage hole nor did she yet understand the essential differences between solid and liquid matter. In fact, it was the loss of a substantial body of water that threatened her own embodiment. "So, as she watched the water drain, she noticed that the original amount of bath water was 'bigger than me,' and *it* went down the drain" (p. 60). Serafino speculates that there may even have been an association in her mind with a genie figure from, say, a Walt Disney *Aladdin* movie, who can be sucked into a spout. He concludes that "Rachel's thinking may have been faulty, but it seemed logical to *her*—and that's what counts. Her *thinking* provided the source of her fear" (p. 60, original emphasis).

It follows from this analysis that we could help children like Rachel "work through their fears by recognizing the causes, building up their . . . self-confidence, and helping them attain mastery over what they dread" (Graeber, 1996, pp. 49, 50). We could help Rachel by pushing her through Piagetian-type stages of rationality, by giving her a watered down scientific explanation such as "using different-size toys to show her that she's too big to go down" (p. 50), and she would, no doubt, become less fearful. The trouble is we may overlook the fun of taking a bath, though I guess this happened when the father thought Rachel was just messing around in the bath water and that its disappearance would not matter. Furthermore, this procedure of explaining things to Rachel strikes me as a diminution of the child's natural intelligence. Even I as an adult feel some despair at the sight of an empty swimming pool, a pool that has had all its life sucked out of it, a pool in name only. Also, the beach where I swim is a different place when the tide is out. The outgoing tide creates dumping waves that ruin the experience I was having in the water. I feel robbed of the experience of being present to the world, of being caught up totally within this water. Similarly, when the water drains out of Rachel's tub it takes away that in which she was immersed. And it threatens to suck her away in the process. Experientially, though not according to rational thinking, Rachel is in very real danger of disappearing down the plughole.

Seemingly remote situations on mountains and alongside rivers, coupled with the very familiar situation of giving a child a bath, cast light on the encounters that occur more frequently on playgrounds. In the normal course of playground activity children are challenged, they become fearful, anxious, and find themselves in situations which are fraught with danger. The thing about the playground is that these trepidations often appear to be too much the concerns of children. The familiarity of the playground, like that of the bathtub, disguises the ways we could entertain the child's perspective; and yet, like the unfamiliarity of the mountain or river embankment, we might also see the playground anew as offering the possibility of a shared encounter.

Van den Berg (1961/1975, p. 81) says that when we are in the company of children, especially in places that are familiar to us, we assume an experiential commonality, although on our own terms. The child is encapsulated in our sense of the orderliness of the world—in our sense of time and space. If we should take the child for a walk to, say, the corner store we simply assume that this little journey is the same for both of us. The cul-de-sac we leave hardly bears thinking about and the lane that bypasses busy Jolimont Street is a route taken daily, whether on an errand, taking the dog for a walk, or going for a jog. The familiarity of going this way to the store, the same cars parked in driveways, the same houses, the same manicured and overgrown lawns, makes it difficult to appreciate what the child might be seeing.

We do not realize there is a distance separating us from the child, an indifference coming from habitual actions, that prevents us from remembering how we might have experienced our home and the surrounding neighborhood when we were children. When the child stops and gazes we regard this as an inconvenience, simply a waste of time. "Come on, stop dawdling," we admonish the child. A little further on she says: "Step on a crack and you'll break your mother's back!" The child plays a game we vaguely remember. She hops over the lines in the pavement, stopping constantly to assess her direction of movement. We watch for a moment and then hurry on our way. The memory of this game offers only a temporary respite from the pressing goal of getting to the corner store with as little bother as possible.

Such "memories are vague; and besides, they are so intertwined with mature interpretations that they have lost almost all of their childhood qualities" (p. 81). Even the amusement of watching the child bound over the cracks is but a concession to the "playfulness" of children.

> The adult is inclined to think that his own childhood gradually merged into maturity (although the smell of an old book immediately proves how different things really were then, in that vague past which looms up so suddenly), and he presupposes the same gradual transition for his child. If he digs in a sandbox, he assumes that it has a more childlike quality, but apart from that, an entirely identical meaning for the child. (p. 81)

The same assumption of common meaning occurs when we take children to playgrounds. We see recognizable games, equipment that has not changed at all since we were children, and actions that have identifiable meaning in terms of children's physical growth and development. What we fail to recognize is the relative newness of these things to children and that "a swing or a slide might have a different meaning for the child, that it might be an entirely different thing" (p. 81). Should we be surprised if the child cannot get enough time on the swing, if again and again he wants an "under-duck" that launches him high in the air, yet he will not go anywhere near the carousel slide? Should we be surprised if another child refuses the offer of a swing and avoids all the playthings in the park, but is happy to dig in a rotted tree stump, scratching for ages in its crumbling bark? Maybe we will recall that not all things appeal to all children in the same way. Maybe we attribute certain activity preferences to children. But will it occur to us that these things appear quite different to children and that "besides being a place of bliss, [the playground] can be no less a place of fears. And these playthings are *meant* for children" (p. 81, original emphasis).

Van den Berg draws our attention to the yawning gulf between the experiences of adults and children, and the gulf which the familiarity of the playground tends to obscure. Familiarity gives adults a sense of the continuity of experiences such that children's playground activity appears to be totally explicable in its rudimentary, developmental form. Thus, when playground activity becomes especially troublesome to children we become surprised, quite unaware of the lopsidedness of our interpretation, and most unprepared to reckon with children's fears. For adults, the playground is a domain encapsulated by a notion of maturity; for children, the playground is an arbitrary collection of things that call to them in differing ways. "The swimmer enters the water because the water is proving to him in a thousand ways that it is prepared to receive his body. The child digs in the sand because the sand cries out to it: dig!" (Van den Berg, 1972, p. 76). The bars ask to be scrambled over; the swings ask to be driven higher and higher; and the slides ask to be mounted, even to be climbed up their slippery and shiny face. These same things speak of difficult things to do and things that often seem to the child to be out of his or her reach. They dare the child. They challenge the child. They make the child anxious, fearful, afraid. And this is how unfamiliar the playground may appear to the child.

The fearful child brings us back in touch with the playground as a place of lived experience. Our efforts to encounter the playground with him or her require facing up to the possibility that the playground can be no less a fearful place for us as well. We empathize with the child's fearfulness, not only by remembering the fears that were once instilled in us, but also by understanding how unfamiliar the world can be outside a comfortable maturity. After all, maturity is not so much some knowledge we possess of the world's familiarity as it is a feature of our engagement with children such that we forsake the familiarity of their activity in the interests of bringing them up out of their fearfulness and into a confident relation to the world around them.

Encountering the fearfulness of children, we seriously question the way the playground's familiarity masks our potential involvement in their activity. Fearfulness is what we see and feel as we countenance playground activity. It is not just a state of mind we impute to the child; rather, it is a mood of understanding the clinging, grasping, tentative, cautious movements we observe, and the words and sounds of alarm, nervousness, fright, and false bravado that we hear coming from the child. The child's emotional state (even the supposedly objective conditions of the child's experience) has its corollary in the adult's empathic responsiveness to the tone of his or her playground activity. The perspectives of adult and child might even be considered two aspects of the same affective medium (cf. Bollnow, 1970/1989) by which the playground can be encountered. Fearfulness is fundamentally a "state-of-mind" implying "a disclosive submission to the world, out of which we can encounter" that which is of particular concern to the child (Heidegger, 1962, p. 177).

So when we look at children on the playground and see them become fearful, perhaps even afraid, and it is tempting to pass off this fear as if it indicates a phase through which all children pass, we might also reflect upon how children's presumed fearfulness is related to our efforts to become mindful of them. In other words, it is not sufficient to say that children become fearful if our observation explains away their actions and avoids the question of our responsibility for their fears; on the contrary, we might well imagine ourselves taking risks when we look at fearful children. We can watch as they navigate between the familiar and the unknown, we can share in their discoveries, and we can share in their failures. Their apprehension strikes at the heart of our concern for them, our fearing for them, and also, our becoming aware of how the world appears to them.

## Becoming Mindful

In the previous chapter we considered situations where children are fearful and where they can be encouraged to overcome their fears. But what if we take to heart the unfamiliarity of the playground—the fact that it is a domain over which we have no certain, fixed knowledge of what might happen there? How might apprehensiveness, which is not necessarily confined to the child, bring us in touch with the child? How might our fearfulness make us more mindful of the child? How might even a remembered apprehension allow us to lay hold of a familiar situation and recognize in it the merits of the child's activity?

"What's this for?" asks Paco, pointing to the knotted rope hanging down from the large willow tree in Andrew's backyard. Although Paco and Tyler have only just arrived, the first thing they see is this suspended rope. "Can you swing on it?" Paco asks Andrew. The presence of these two smaller boys allows Andrew to show something of what he has been up to these past few days of the school vacation. He has strung a rope over one of the lower branches of the willow tree, threaded it up towards the top of the tree, and then tied it off on one of the outer limbs so that it then trails almost to the ground and forms the rope swing that Paco and Tyler first saw when they entered the yard.

Andrew takes hold of the end of the rope. He mounts the high wooden fence that stands a few paces away from the tree. He then launches himself on this rope, swinging out over the lawn, and with a degree of practiced agility, returns to his precarious footing on the top of the fence. "How did the rope get up there?" asks Paco. "Did you put it there all by yourself?" Andrew jumps down from the fence. He moves to the base of the tree, clasps the part of the rope that is draped against it and starts pulling himself up while walking his feet up the tree trunk. Before too long he reaches the first place the rope is secured, and then, entering the thick cluster of branches, he moves steadily towards the second rope attachment higher up. Andrew moves above the level of the garage, above the surrounding houses, until he reaches a spot where the branches are becoming much thinner and no longer press firmly against his movements. He nestles into a vee created in the top-most stem of the tree, and with his back against the more solid branch of the tree stem, settles back to survey the scene spread out beneath him.

"What can you see from up there?" calls Andrew's father who has been sitting all the while with a group of adults only a short distance away from this tree. "Can you see the school?" "Yes," answers Andrew. "And I can see the river, and I can see the tennis courts." He continues to rattle off a long list of things that can be seen from this perch at the top of the willow tree. As Andrew continues this listing of things within his purview, his mother confides in us that she cannot bear to look at Andrew when he is up in the tree. She says: "It gives me a shiver whenever I see him going up there." And as if to prove her point, she remains seated with her back to the tree, never once turning in Andrew's direction. She is not the only one to be put off by Andrew's antics. Andrew's father is also ill at ease. He speaks haltingly. He is distracted as other adults talk. Every so often he glances up at Andrew who seems happy enough just to sit looking out from his roost up in the tree. "Ah Andrew, I think it's time to come down now," he says at last. But Andrew does not move. "Why don't you come down and show the boys the tadpoles you brought home from school." The ploy works. Andrew starts making his way down through the branches. He reaches the ground and, a few moments later, he and the two younger boys disappear around the corner of the house in search of the bucket that contains the tadpoles. Andrew's parents are noticeably relieved, which is understandable, although it is also clear to those who have watched him that Andrew is a very good climber of this tree. After all, this is his tree, the tree that he has made safe.

In the situation described above we are aware of a certain fearfulness on the part of Andrew's parents, a fearfulness motivated by a sense of danger, yet a fearfulness that does not necessarily resonate with the child's sense of his own explorations. This fearfulness reflects a mindfulness of the child that seems to fall short or an understanding of what the child is actually doing. Even Paco and Tyler are far more understanding of Andrew's achievement, although it could be argued that they are too young, too inexperienced, too immature, to fully appreciate the risks involved. On the other hand, just as children can watch a circus performance which puts fear in the hearts of adults and makes them avert their gaze at critical moments, perhaps Tyler and Paco are in closer touch with what Andrew is up to. They are not scared, although they are certainly in awe of what Andrew is able to do.

The adult's apprehensiveness is a way of denying Andrew's place of maturity. The younger children recognize his accomplishment, however the adults are afraid to look. Their fearfulness places them at a distance from the things that matter to the child. In truth, they cannot bear to see him up there. It would be best if Andrew came down out of the tree to a place that is safer and more familiar.

Some weeks later, while Andrew is away visiting relatives, a fierce storm hits the area. It splits the willow tree in half. Andrew's father is concerned when he sees the damage, and saddened at the thought of having Andrew return to find his tree no longer there. His concern might easily be dismissed as simply regret for a lost plaything, or maybe it is disguised concern for the damage to the landscaping of the backyard, however something more is involved in this fretting over a damaged tree. This damaged tree stands out in his thinking about Andrew. It brings to mind the experience of seeing Andrew perched up at the top of the tree, although not so much the apprehension that was felt at the time, as now a feeling of having been involved in Andrew's explorations. What was not recognized in the apprehension of the moment is now the basis of nostalgic regret.

What was the nature of adult involvement in Andrew's climbing activity? Better still, how had Andrew been helped to become so adventurous and independent? Clues to the implication of adult sensibility in Andrew's activity can be found in tracing his movements back to more familiar playground activities where we are less apprehensive.

Consider a young child pulling herself up the bars of a climbing frame. Her mother stands behind and holds onto this little girl's waist as she moves ever so cautiously upwards. Upon reaching the top rung, the little girl becomes afraid. She begins to cry. She twists around to partially face her mother, and still being held at the waist, lets go of the climbing frame. Her mother places her down on the ground and smiles as she watches her daughter begin once again to climb the frame. For this mother, there is little to fear in watching her child climbing. After all, the frame is not very high and she is standing right there beside it. But how different it is for the child! The climbing frame even brings her to tears. Although the little girl is not discouraged from climbing up the rungs, her tears create a striking contrast with her mother's smile.

Consider, now, an older child. We watch as Kyler climbs the large frame at Lansdowne Playground. Then, not being content with this achievement, she tries walking across a beam that connects this frame to an adjoining platform. We become a little anxious as we see Kyler so far off the ground, although she moves so sure-footedly that very soon she has safely reached the platform. She comes back along the beam and, like a seasoned tight-rope walker, swivels around, balances on one leg, before regaining her place on the platform. She moves so easily, we wonder about the basis for our concerns. Could it be that she scares us by doing things that we are no longer capable of performing? Could it be that our first impulse, which is to stop her from venturing out onto the beam, is a fearfulness we would have for our own safety?

We may extend this concern even further to the situation of watching Andrew up in the tree. The parents' fearfulness, which is so easily explained away as a concern for the danger of the situation, discloses a direction of Andrew's activity which extends beyond the competence of the adult. Andrew might easily have said: "To me it was so high up I felt I could look out upon my whole world. With my friends and family below, it left me alone up there to ponder my thoughts and feelings and wonder what lay before me" (Marcus, 1978, p. 38). Whereas the balance of fear in the example of the little girl on the climbing frame was all on her side, in watching Andrew it appears to be on the side of the adults. Such apprehensiveness, which might so easily prompt us to curtail Andrew's explorations, is the register of Andrew's growing independence. It is, positively speaking, a mindfulness of where the child's grasp of the world exceeds our own.

But then the question arises: Is there no real danger in such situations? Should we not warn children of the potential hazards and dangers to which they are exposed? Before we ask such questions, we should first consider how a sense of danger arises and what it does to the child. Then we can be more mindful of the inappropriateness of imposing a sense of danger on children's activity and seek better ways of involving ourselves in the risks they choose and those we encourage them to take.

## Sensing Danger

All children are from time to time fearful, timid, and afraid. But how is it that these fears turn into a threatening sense of danger that limits a child's capacity for being at home in the world? Bledsoe (1977, 1978) provides a telling example. His fear from childhood arose from the challenge of exploring a tunnel system near his home.

"One day," he says, "I decided to crawl inside it and explore it to its source" (p. 121). Bledsoe gives us a sense of what this experience was like as he describes the cold water seeping through his pants, the cobwebs brushing his face, and the sounds of little creatures scurrying off into the darkness ahead. "Sound amplifies in such places and the imagination is influenced. I remember listening to the dripping water and looking ahead into the tunnel's darkness—populating it with imaginary creatures" (p. 121). He writes of the hesitation he felt in responding to the lure of the tunnel: "Some thought that I could not fully comprehend was telling me to turn around and go back" (p. 121).

Bledsoe turns around and heads back into the light, but not without feeling some regret for what he now regards as a "a risk I had once refused to take" (p. 120).

> The places above and the sound of water running from some mysterious source were not to be my destination that day. The silence and darkness were more than I was prepared to handle. I wanted to make my way further into the tunnel but I was beginning to lose my nerve. I was chicken! I couldn't have crawled up inside that tunnel more than 60 feet at most. Once more I looked ahead up the passageway. Water trickled from the walls. Slowly, I drew backward and began to crawl back down the way I had come.  (p. 121)

A risk was not taken and Blesdsoe, the child, faced the indignity of having to back down the way he had come since there was no other way out. He ran up hard against his fears, lost his nerve, then turned about face from an uncertainty that was all too alluring.

For the young Bledsoe there was a way out of taking a risk, but it was at the cost of a lingering sense of danger and a fearful relation to the world. As Heidegger said, "what is detrimental as coming-close close by carries with it the latent possibility that it may stay away and pass us by; but instead of lessening or extinguishing our fearing, this enhances it" (Heidegger, 1962, p. 180). When Bledsoe remembers the tunnel he senses an impending danger, something monstrous standing before him. He withdraws to a dubious safety, ever more fearful of the dangers that have now tunneled into his life.

His sense of danger reminds us of a similar experience another child had of turning back. Instead of a tunnel, though, this child's adventure takes place in a stolen rowing boat.

> I dipped my oars into the silent lake,
> And, as I rose upon the stroke, my boat
> Went heaving through the water like a swan;
> When, from behind that craggy steep till then
> The horizon's bound, a huge peak, black and huge,
> As if with voluntary power instinct
> Upreared its head. I struck and struck again,
> And growing still in stature the grim shape
> Towered up between me and the stars, and still,
> For so it seemed, with purpose of its own
> And measured motion like a living thing,
> Strode after me. With trembling oars I turned,
> And through the silent water stole my way
> Back to the covert of the willow tree;
> There in her mooring-place I left my bark,—
> And through the meadows homeward went, in grave
> And serious mood; but after I had seen
> That spectacle, for many days, my brain
> Worked with a dim and undetermined sense
> Of unknown modes of being; o'er my thoughts
> There hung a darkness, call it solitude
> Or blank desertion. No familiar shapes
> Remained, no pleasant images of trees,
> Of sea or sky, no colors or green fields;
> But huge and mighty forms, that do not live
> Like living men, moved slowly through my mind
> By day, and were a trouble to my dreams.
>
> (Wordsworth, 1850/1959, Book 1,
> lines 374–400, pp. 25, 26)

Withdrawing from the forbidding form, it looms larger still. An imaginative presence darkens the child's mood, instilling a fearfulness of once-familiar sights. A sense of danger now prevails because a risk was not taken.

Similarly with Bledsoe, we can almost sense how he must have been on the very brink of a great childhood discovery. Now, as an adult, he says not only he has often thought of that tunnel, trying to picture what might have been beyond the point at which he turned back, but the experience itself stays with him as "an inescapable fact from my own biography" (p. 122). As well as being a trouble to his dreams, Bledsoe says:

> What stands out in my mind is the vividness of my original experience—the encountering of the first crude sense of fear, but a sense of fear that was also tantalizing. For tied up in the memory as well is the not entirely unpleasant sense of latent danger, dark discovery, and uncertainty. (p. 122)

This is not to say that there was no danger in Bledsoe's explorations and that he was not wise to go no further. But such assessment of potential hazard should not be confused with the inevitable sense of danger that comes with turning back. The tunnel now stands out as a place of danger. What originally led somewhere, perhaps to an opening not far beyond where Bledsoe turned back, is remembered as the closing in of fear, as "the coming on of the night fear" (p. 122). Bledsoe says:

> I carried something back down that sloping tunnel with me. It has existed there in my mind unnoticed, but now and then, over the years, it comes back to me. A shadow crosses my mind sometimes when I lie awake at night and I remember with bitterness that I hadn't gone in that tunnel all the way. I hadn't found out what had been around the first bend. Instead, I had been careful. (p. 122)

Compare the bitter aftertaste of this experience with the recollection of one who dared to go beyond the first bend.

> It was dark in the tunnel—darker the further you dared go in. I knew the Giant Spiders lived there. I just didn't know how far in. About ten feet in there was a second culvert branching off. It was smaller and had metal reinforcing bars covering the opening. These had been pulled back (by the spiders?) and were twisted and rusted. . . . I conquered the spiders eventually and travelled great distances through the tunnels. I conquered countless foes there. I was alone there, but secure, knowing

the tunnels connected me with hundreds of others. I was nearly always silent there, but was surrounded by gurgling, trickling water, deep resonant earth sounds, and rustling leaves. (Marcus, 1978, p. 38).

This child's daring led not to danger but to a familiarity with the tunnel system. Although there were surely dangers there, this child's fearfulness was subdued by the sense of security that came with his explorations.

One child fails to take the risk of going any further inside the tunnel. But what did he in fact lose? It would seem that his failure to take a risk has significance for the rest of his life (as is evident from his later recollections of this experience). For him, the failure to take a risk has been a very valuable experience since he now knows something that will help him conquer the tunnel many times over in adult life. He now has a sense of limit: that he could and perhaps should have gone further inside the tunnel. The other child's experience is valuable also in terms of the confidence his explorations have given him; but his success did not provide him with a sense of limit. For him, the tunnel does not stand our so clearly as a motive for his subsequent actions.

One morning, some twenty-five years later, Bledsoe hears a radio news report about a nine-year-old child who has disappeared from his home and who now eight days later is the object of an extensive community search. The plight of this boy has received wide media coverage, and there is speculation that the boy may actually be in hiding in the tunnel system under the city. "People started talking about mysterious clues, missing suitcases, boys taking food down to Simon and warning him when adults got too close. It was reported with all the intrigue and fascination of prowling through unknown and secret places under cover of darkness" (p. 123). What gains Bledsoe's attention, however, is hearing a radio interview with a child called Billy Sandborn who not only lived in the same apartment block as the missing boy, but who was also something of an expert on the tunnels where the boy was supposed to be hiding. Bledsoe listens as Billy answers the interviewer's questions about the risks of being down in the tunnels. His ears prick up as he hears Billy speak of how he and his friends navigate their way through the tunnel system, learning how to run through the pipes without getting wet, creating maps and identifying the routes they have taken, learning the geography of these underground spaces and becoming at home there.

Bledsoe catches "a glimpse of an earlier tunnel and a figure of a small boy" (p. 124). So he makes contact with Billy Sandborn and convinces him and his friends to take him down into the tunnel system and teach him what they know. In so doing, he recovers the inchoate knowledge of a child who ventured only so far up a tunnel near his home. He draws upon "a ghost knowledge" that has "always existed there ... waiting to be spelled out—to offer its solutions, to help me form intelligent and informed ways of seeing the larger world without ever losing sense of local vitality" (p. 126).

A lesson to be drawn from Bledsoe's preoccupation with "a risk I had once refused to take" (p. 120) is that in failing one can win, which is to say, in backing down from a challenge, in refusing to respond to a dare, the child can be inspired to grasp things more thoughtfully. Real risk-taking takes more than just the bravado of the moment. To take a risk means to push a limit, and in order to push a limit it is necessary to already have a sense of what that limit is and of what it ought to be. Without a sense of limit it is doubtful if risk-taking, in a personally meaningful sense, can be said to have occurred. With a sense of limit we can say that the child stands a greater chance of taking risks head on, by which it is meant that risks can be taken with a sensible, thoughtful disposition to the activity at hand. It may take twenty-five years to fully take that risk. It may even take a lifetime. A thoughtful, memorable, responsible sense of risk extends far beyond the sense of danger felt in the initial decision to turn back.

Through these examples of presumably dangerous and forbidden places we can now appreciate the way a sense of danger arises in the normal course of playground activity and how it is understood by an adult in attendance. Children do sometimes find themselves in situations where they must back down; but as we have seen already, there is more than likely a way out which does not necessarily carry the threat of danger. Where it seems more likely that a sense of danger will be experienced is in situations where the adult undermines, even inadvertently, the child's resoluteness by making a "way out" seem a "way of backing down." Recall the situation of the mother and her three very frightened children on the slippery slide. Until they felt the degree of her concern they were happy enough to be on the slide. Her pointing out a danger changed the face of this activity. It then became necessary for the children to back down from this dangerous place.

Consider a similar situation involving a woman following close behind her child up the ladder of a different slippery slide. She holds on tightly to the supporting rails at the side, and with each step we see that she would rather be someplace else. "I think Mommy's too big to sit on the slide," she says partly to the young child who leads her up the last rungs to the top of the slide and partly to herself as if thinking about how to avoid getting any further involved in this activity. She sits on the landing with Matthew in her lap. But as she waits there Matthew utters a faint whimper. "Are you scared?" she asks him. "Do you want Nicholas to go down with you?" Matthew begins to cry. "All right, let's go back down then. Nicholas, will you let your brother past?" she says to her older son as she helps Matthew get around her so that he can go back down the ladder.

Here, in this seemingly well-intentioned effort to have the child go down the slide, the result has been the cultivation in the mind of the child of an unfounded sense of danger. The child was afraid sitting up there on the slide, so was his mother, and this confirmation of his fear undermined his resolve to go down the slide.

Russell (1926) once said, while it is necessary for the child to be aware of real danger, which involves some degree of fear, "this element is very much diminished when it is not present in the instructor" (p. 86). He advised that "A grown-up person in charge of a child should never feel fear" (p. 86). But he was only partially correct. What he might have said is that the adult should not always reveal his or her fears to the child since it is this disclosure which often magnifies the child's fears and contributes to an irrational sense of danger. The child needs not so much to experience the dangers which our fears magnify, as to be in a relation of care with one who is mindful of the consequences of the child's activity and is fearful for that child's well-being. To be on a slide with a child requires our being careful, not our sharing fears with the child. If our fears must be made evident, and especially if our fears are well-founded, then neither the child nor us should be where we are. The situation is, in actual fact, far too dangerous and the child has been put at risk.

Children know implicitly that a careful relation can mollify an impending sense of danger. For instance, Kyler comes running over from the large slide. "Did you see me? Come and watch me." She grabs my arm and starts hauling me towards the slide, not desisting until I am standing almost underneath it. "Stand right there," she tells me. "This is a very dangerous slide, she cautions me." "Why is it so dangerous?" I ask. "It just is!" She goes down the slide many times, so many that soon we must head off in search of drinking water to slake her thirst. "Is it still dangerous?" I ask Kyler, thinking she may now be better disposed to reflect on the activity. But her answer strikes me as somewhat obtuse. "I like that slide," she says. "It's much better than the little one." It seems my question about danger is now irrelevant. For Kyler the danger has past. The dangerous slide is a thing of the past.

The element of danger becomes a significant feature of playground activity not only because we have an implicit sense of it but also because it defines the sensible limits of activity and of our involvement in the activity of others. For instance, an after-school playground supervisor walks hand in hand with one of the children in her charge. She stops to say something to a group of young girls, and then she and Eduardo continue on a little farther. Eduardo points to the roof of one of the little huts upon which he has seen some children perched not so long ago. "Can you lift me up?" he asks. His words are ignored, so he breaks free and then tries to pull himself up. But the gap between the ground and the first of the logs that make up this roof is too much for him. He struggles in vain, for he cannot quite lift his foot up onto the purchase afforded by the spaces between the logs. Eduardo looks around at the playground supervisor; and anticipating his request she says: "If you can't get up there on your own, then I think it's too high for you. It's too dangerous."

Eduardo has no sense of danger here, especially after having seen children on this roof only a short while ago; however he is told by the adult standing by him that there is indeed danger here. "If you can't do it by yourself, then it's too dangerous." Because Eduardo cannot climb up onto the roof by himself, then it must be too dangerous. Is this not the same lesson that Bledsoe learned as a child? In a sense the lesson is correct, provided we downplay the significance of having an adult standing by. But if we acknowledge the adult's involvement in the child's playground activity, even the tacit approval of standing close by, then we might contemplate the extent to which a sense of danger reflects the feasible limits of our involvement in the child's explorations. Thus, Eduardo can be helped up and he can be supported while sitting on the roof, in which case there is no real danger for him. But this will not satisfy him for long. Soon he will want to try it for himself. He will want to risk the security he has when being helped, to relinquish his ties to the adult for the sake of finding his own way of climbing onto the roof. And it would be difficult for this to happen if Eduardo is told from the start that "if you can't do it by yourself, then it's too dangerous." This lesson only reinforces a premature independence.

Our sensing danger in children's playground activity is, therefore, as much a precaution for the sake of ensuring the child's physical safety as it is a measure of our sensible involvement in the child's activity. We sense danger, not only when the child is at risk, but also when his or her risk-taking exceeds our grasp. He is too high up in the tree; she balances on a beam beyond our reach. From where we stand we cannot encounter the same things as these children. They have moved beyond us. So we try to understand their movements by questioning their distance from us, and by seeing what they do as taking them even further from us. The trouble is that in making such a summary judgement of danger we fail to see the nature of our dislocation. Danger represents the risk that should not be taken, yet so often it represents the risk we do not wish to see the child take, and thus, the risk we do not wish to take of trusting the child. So before we conclude there is danger we might consider the predicament of the child more carefully. We might consider our physical relation to the child upon which our sense of the child's risk-taking is predicated.

A child climbs up the chain holding one of the tire swings to a beam radiating from a central pylon. Upon reaching the beam she manages to pull herself on top of it. Then she sits for a while, her legs dangling down either side, delighted it seems to see people watching her from down below. Next she starts walking along the beam towards the center, being very careful not to overbalance and fall that great distance to the ground. Upon reaching the center she stands tall, towering over the playground. Then a thought crosses her mind. Her mother should soon be here to pick her up. She hopes she has arrived, in which case "she wouldn't be half-frightened" (cf. Lowenfeld, 1969, p. 223).

Is this a terror of a child, a daredevil, an audacious show-off, or is it more that this child realizes intuitively that her actions test the limits of her relation to her mother? She wants to frighten her mother not so much to cause her any real concern, but in order to support the sense she has of a conquest being made and her growing sense of independence. There is risk, to be sure, but it is risk that ought to be taken and will be taken, if not here, then in some other place beyond the playground where real dangers lurk. As the Opies remind us, when children play on streets, "it is not they who are afraid of traffic, it is traffic that is afraid of them; and the children are aware of this, and willing to take advantage of it" (Opie and Opie, 1969, p. 269). The playground also offers such encounters only now the potential for harm has been greatly diminished. Now, as part of the normal course of activity, the child can risk his or her attachment to the adult. In a far less threatening way, in a far less dangerous way, the child can counter the adult's hold on him or her.

## Letting Go

As a very small child Shayle liked to be held in my lap as we sat on a gently swaying swing. As if being rocked in a cradle, on a number of occasions she would fall asleep while being held in my grasp. Now she seems big enough to be put on a playground swing, the type that has a metal bar in front to hold her in place. At first she appears somewhat apprehensive, however she grasps the bar in front of her and seems composed enough for me to begin to move the swing, not a great deal, but just enough to let her feel the to and fro motion. I hold onto her while easing the swing forward and back. Then, after she becomes used to this motion, I release my grasp on the swing. I don't dare push it yet, but merely release this young child and then catch her on the return. Shayle continues to enjoy this activity, even laughing now as I let go of the swing and then catch it again. I wonder if she may now want a little push to make the swing go higher. Perhaps she might like some freer motion.

But how much freer? Certainly this intentional letting go of the child on a swing contrasts with the mere recognition from a distance of a child swinging freely. A mother says:

> I remember on a lovely golden September day, looking out of the window and seeing my three year old daughter swinging back and forth by herself under the huge window at the bottom of the garden. Her hair streamed out behind her catching the sunlight and she was swinging alternatively into dappled shadow and bright light. She was singing gustily but tunelessly to herself, happily lost in her own world. Looking at her at that moment the shadow crossed my mind that she soon must leave this charmed world of childhood. (Smith, 1987, p. 136)

Could it be that the shadow into which the child swings, the shadow that crosses this mother's mind, is similar to the shadow that crosses Bledsoe's mind late at night as he recalls with bitterness the risk he did not take? Could this shadow be the "darkness" of "solitude" or "blank desertion" that hung over Wordsworth? There would seem to be too much regret and nostalgia, too much of a backward glance, and too little bodily remembrance evoked in watching the child on the swing. The example is less of "letting go" and more of "hanging on." It does not exemplify a situation of deciding to be there for the child such that she can be encouraged in her movements. It does not encounter the risks of swinging into shadows.

These thoughts about so simple an activity as pushing a small child on a swing disclose something of what is at stake in "letting go," especially in more risky situations. Shayle trusts me. She is happy enough for me to hold on to the swing. And she is confident enough to permit me to let her go momentarily. Her confiding in me brings a confidence in the activity itself. The same holds true for the older child, except that now we realize it is not just the swing we release, but the child as well. Now, partly because the activities are less familiar to us, and carry a greater degree of risk, we along with the child must gain confidence. The older child is being challenged, just as Shayle was; the difference is that now we must sort through our own apprehensions, our own fears, even our sense of danger, in order to catch hold of the child again.

To countenance letting go of a small child on a swing suggests a particular kind of experience, and one that is accentuated with bigger children on much larger swings, climbing frames, slides, etc. Here we experience the "to and fro" movement of inclining ourselves towards children, apprehending their situations, while finding that contact with them discloses a necessary separation. We encounter, in this "to and fro" motion, "the experience of an actuality appearing opposite to the person that questions him in his innermost being and before which he must affirm himself" (Bollnow, 1972, p. 311). The bigger child's actions are not as easy to grasp; indeed, these actions may express a personality much different than our own. We encounter not merely a child but another human being by virtue of no longer being able to guide completely the child's actions. Here we must confront the possibility of not being needed anymore, or at least not in the obviously helpful way that a young child requires assistance, since we meet the child at the point at which the child is inclined to be on his or her own way.[2]

Children should not gain independence through the failure of adults to understand the nature of their activity. This would be a pedagogy of neglect, denying the depth of experience that makes an encounter with another human being possible. Actions that surprise us and that reduce us to silence are understood quite differently than those that scare us or bring on vertiginous feelings and make us concerned about dangerous activity and the child's safety. Surprising actions are those of a child we encounter rather than merely look after, supervise, or otherwise relegate to a place in our adult scheme of things. They are actions we can recognize as testing out our ability to stay in touch with the child and our capactity to understand the meaning and significance of the child's movement preferences.

The encounter is essentially a differentiation of experience. It is coming face to face with that which must surely diverge. Letting go of the swing helps us let go of the child. It engenders the confidence to follow the course of activity even to the point of encountering a child who is confident enough to be let go completely. We stand and watch such a child's accomplishments, maybe even get involved, however the child now has something to show us. Like Billy Sandborn knowing more than Bledsoe about being in tunnels, like Andrew who is so at home climbing up a backyard tree, and like younger children who become so proficient on playground equipment, we can be most helpful if we know when our help is needed and when it is not. Letting go of our apprehensions, our fears, and our unfounded sense of danger, we become more appreciative of what children know and more admiring of their accomplishments. Relinquishing our fearful, safety-consciousness hold on them, we grant them an independence. Letting go, we catch hold of the child as someone who is already well advanced on the path of maturity.

# IV

## The Educational Significance of Risk

# 7

# The
# Practice of
# Risk

We have heard through the silences of risk how our questioning of what is the best thing to do with a child leads to the encouragement of risk and to the encounter with risk. We have heard and felt that the way we understand risk is bound up with the way we are present to the activity of children. Such actions in turn rest upon a certain visibility of risk, upon a perception and reflection of action which shows risk to be involved in a testing of the adult-child relation and eventually its dissolution. The direction of risk-taking discloses our letting-go of the child, our realizing his or her growing independence. We recognize, through an awareness of risk, that the child needs to find his or her own way. Accordingly the discussion so far is an educative description of how we might prepare the child to be on his or her own, that is, of how we can contribute to the child's ability to be on his or her own in the most helpful way possible. But the account falls short of being an educational theory of risk.

Langeveld's (1966) initial requirement of "the theory of education" has been taken to heart: that what is needed is "a serious analysis and interpretation of what the child is, what the relations to the child are, what the child's own relation is to himself, what his world is, and what the relationship of the child to self-reliance, to responsibility, and adulthood *means*" (p. 97, original emphasis). An awareness of risk, as a term of our pedagogical relation to children, did indeed require questioning the status afforded childhood and lead to a reflexive analysis of how we customarily understand children. A responsiveness to risk, as a term of our pedagogical relation to children, required an analysis of the way we are present to children in risky situations, along with an interpretation of how children can experience the world in challenging ways such that they can define for themselves a sense of identity. Furthermore, an interrogation of our responsiveness to risk allowed us to disclose the conditions that enable children to become self-reliant and responsible for their own actions. But, for an educational theory of risk, there is a further requirement.

We need "to undertake a serious analysis and interpretation of what the child means to the adult, to the adult as parent, as an educator, as a person living in a given community, in a given society, in a *given world of meanings*" (p. 97, my emphasis). There is, in other words, the requirement of showing what it means to be aware of risk and responsive to it in the context of being one who already values certain kinds of activities, performances, and proficiencies. An educational theory of risk ought to resonate with the conditions of current educational practice. It should show the significance of risk for those curriculum practices that constitute the contemporary educational scene. The terms of an educational theory of risk could even establish a sense of order, perhaps a standard, against which such practices can be analysed and interpreted.

So let us review the description given so far and seek some educational orderliness to the notion of risk. Let us be careful not to impose a "given world of meanings" upon the sense of risk we have been working out, although this sense of risk is only understandable in light of such meanings; but rather, let us look again at the visibility of risk-taking situations for some principle, some value, some intrinsic sense of order which lends itself to a deeper understanding of current educational practices. We shall see if the pedagogy that is disclosed in our dealings with young children on playgrounds provides a basis for thinking about how to teach children in more formal educational contexts.[1]

## Tricks

In order to grasp the meaning of children's experiences of risk we have realized it is necessary to observe children closely, and that means putting aside "the myopic lenses of our adult-centered theories" (Beekman, 1986, p. 41). Just as we have been careful to use a method of inquiry that places us in the midst of children's activity, so we need an educational way of thinking about the meaning of risk in children's lives that retains a focus on concrete events and their experiential meanings.

We observe the child first-hand, up-close, and interactively. Invariably this boy or girl before us wants to show us what he or she can do. "Did you see me?" the child asks. "Look here. I'll show you again." The child wants to be seen. Yet with our knowledge of developmental patterns, our planned curricula, our premeditated learning experiences, our lessons for children, we tend to lose sight of this initial inclination on the child's part to show us something. I am not suggesting we proceed without any expectation of what children should be able to do; in fact, anticipating situations through planning and environmental design is essential in order to avoid sensing danger in children's activity and thus cutting ourselves off from the child's experience. But once we know the domain of potential activity is secure, once children know the basic safety expectations, once we have set an appropriate tone for children's interactions, it is then up to the children themselves to show what they are inclined to do before we can position ourselves to influence the course of their activity.

"Can you come and watch?" asks Tyler as he pulls me in the direction of a horizontal bar at Lansdowne Playground. Holding onto the bar, he walks up the side support until he is able to hook one leg over the bar. Then he swings his other leg up and over. He brings both legs together, first by releasing one hand, the hand between his legs, and then grasping the bar again on the outside. "Are you watching?" he calls out from this upside-down position. Next moment he lets both hands go of the bar, flopping back like an upside-down rag doll, and with the the the bar held firmly in the crooks of his knees, he swings and swivels freely. He stays in this position for only a moment or two before reaching up to take hold of the bar once again. "Did you see that?" he asks. "It was a pretty good trick, wasn't it?" Tyler feels a sense of accomplishment in showing what he is able to do. He has done this "trick" a number of times before, even though this is the first time we have seen him hang by his knees from the horizontal bar. We have seen him before on the climbing frame, his knees wrapped around one of the rungs while he reaches down to touch a rung lower down; and we have helped him back up when first he got stuck in such a position. So when he says "watch what I can do," already he is confident in his ability. He shows us a movement that, while seemingly novel, is rooted in a bodily history.

Children who want to be seen by an adult standing close by want very much to be successful. This fact is not immediately obvious, especially when we watch a child having difficulty where only a moment ago the action could be executed perfectly well on his or her own. Perhaps we watch too much as a spectator would, hoping to be entertained. When children want us near to observe them they desire an empathic response, a morale boost one might say, that tells them, "Yes! You can do it!" In the former case, hanging by the knees would be something done primarily for the adult. It would indeed be a trick, a stunt, a feat designed to impress an audience. At worst it would be a deceitful practice, a concealment or a subterfuge, or simply a hare-brained action which overlooks the element of risk involved. This "pretty good trick," as Tyler calls it, is something he has worked out for himself, but it is not yet a contained action over which he has a sense of control whereby a performance can be given. He still wants us there to observe his movements and to give him a hand if need be. It is not simply our approval he desires nor our admiration. He needs encouragement for the risk he is taking.

The child's words mislead us, because what he shows us is not really a trick at all. A trick can go wrong, or as we say, "it just doesn't work." One can be unsuccessful at a trick, but as we have seen from risk-taking situations, there is really only a failure to take a risk, and even this is not simply a mistake, an error, but something very personal with which the child must learn to live. It is a lingering doubt that is worked out in future explorations. A trick is merely some action done for show. It is intended to show off ability by concealing know-how.[2]

When children like Tyler have something to show us, there is the danger of losing sight of how we should be present for them. Tyler flops backwards from his inverted hanging position. We gasp, not yet noticing the sturdy crook of his legs over the bar. We overlook the physical thoughtfulness about what he is doing. He sees a risk which brings a measure of reflectivity to his actions and discloses a tangible end-in-view.[3] By acknowledging the riskiness of what the child does, we bring attention to this direction that is implied in what he is able to show us. The child's words "it was a pretty good trick, wasn't it?" are a request to see with him that which is being worked out even in this seeming display of ability. He asks for some acknowledgement of that which has been worked out so far, and only so far.

I feel inclined to show him a better way of hanging by his knees. Instead of struggling to get his legs up and over the bar, I think it would be easier if he learned how to tuck up and bring them through between his hands. So I stand alongside him and cradle him, one arm against his back while lifting under his knees to bring his feet up to the bar. I push underneath him, forcing his feet through and hold him around the waist while he gains his composure upside down. I take hold of his hands and begin to swing him back and forth. "Now, on the count of three I want you to let go of the bar. Ready—One—Two—Three—Away you go!" With a look of apprehension he lands safely on his feet. Do it again!" he says as he stands underneath the bar waiting for me to lift him up once again.

The child's initiative is taken from him. I take full responsibility for setting him in a position he already knows, for holding him in a familiar upside-down position, and for showing him a way to dismount the bar that takes him by surprise. He now looks to me to support, guide and instruct him and even to evaluate the degree of his achievement. But is the child any the wiser for this? Like balancing a toddler on one's feet, or having a five-year-old put his hands between his legs and, reaching from behind, flipping over in an aerial sommersault, there seems to be a far greater reliance on the ability of the adult to give children a thrill by doing a movement to them than there is on children's ability to take up the movement as their own. The trust that children show holds as long as they do not become tired or anxious and as long as the adult is prepared to keep the child amused. Such trust in the adult and the physical excitement that this trust allows contrasts with the earlier, more determined and serious action which Tyler wanted to show us.

It is the potential for autonomous movement which we are questioning in this adult intervention. We see potential in the child's activity and try to draw it out by getting the child to do something that we think fulfills it. But in so doing should we not also encourage a thoughtfulness about what he can do and what he might hope to accomplish? Adult intervention is most meaningful when it occurs within a "zone of proximal development" which Vygotsky defines as the discrepant space between what children are capable of doing alone through independent problem-solving and what they can perform when given assistance by those more competent than they (Berk and Winsler, 1995, pp. 5, 18–20, 26). Although a cognitivist construct, the notion of a "zone of proximal development" helps us appreciate the significance of those interventions that guide, support, and challenge children in what they can already demonstrably and bodily do.

Better still, children's receptivity to being shown new tricks tends to mask a deeper motivation, namely the desire to stay in a relational zone of risk. They look to adult participation to make their activities sensible and, if not to adults, then to one another. This relationality of risk is evident, as we saw earlier on, when one child responds to the dare of another, however it is even more pedagogically meaningful in that far more practical articulation of the challenge of an activity where one child watches closely the tricks another child can do. Maybe if Tyler had seen Dorian swinging by his knees from a bar, and if he had had the time to try it for himself, then quite possibly he might have been inclined to ask for my help. The trick of landing on his feet might then have made sense to him. He might have eventually realized how to do the trick all by himself by better grasping the steps leading up to it.

Simply telling children what to do and putting them thorough the motions, we deny our own part in working through their "e-motions" (cf. Cataldi, 1993, pp. 44, 184). Recall the child on the slide at Lansdowne Playground. Remember how hesitant Christine was to try the larger spiralling slide, even after I had agreed to come down it with her. This encased, spiralling slide, which presented itself to me as a way of showing Christine a "new trick," was for her something quite foreign to her earlier experiences. Her backing down the slide illustrates in a dramatic way the consequences of not being attuned to the child's sense of movement. The lesson from this encounter for the present situation with Tyler is that, rather than showing the child some "really good trick," we might better assist the child by encouraging his activity in a way that is mindful of how he encounters the bar from which he hangs.

What should be the degree of our assistance? The child gives us a lead. After trying the inverted swing and dismount a few more times under my guidance, Tyler has had enough. He does not gain any intrinsic sense of how he might swing upside down on his own, only a sense that swinging upside down is what is being done to him. The dismount from the bar is even further from his physical comprehension, his grasp. So having seen all he can of the trick I have shown him he wants to try something else, something by himself. He leaves the horizontal bar and wanders over to the mushroom-shaped climbing frame. A little later Tyler calls to me. He has lowered himself through one of the spaces in the frame and is now hanging by his knees, just like before. "Watch what I can do!" he calls out.

If Tyler could have actually seen the movement, if another child had shown him the "really good trick" by doing it in front of him (even by turning it into a dare), maybe it would have attained more relevance. Yet even with such visualization, the relevance of the trick, the dare, or the challenge would be due to its impinging upon the child's sense of what he is already trying to do by himself. The child wants to be helped, to be encouraged, and for us to encounter the playground with him. He wants "participatory guidance" (cf. Rogoff, 1990) that does not lead him too far from the activity at hand and the challenge that it poses.

Using a term drawn from the teaching of tricks and stunts, we could say that the child wants to be "spotted" (eg. Boone, 1985). He expects us to look at his activity in a way that is mindful of the direction of his achievement, and that is respectful of the extent of his present achievement. He wants us to watch him up close, to spot him by, say, standing underneath, securing his grip on the bar as his fingers begin to slip, and even by helping him down if he becomes stuck. The "scaffolding" metaphor captures even better the kind of teaching that is required. "Scaffolding" learning means giving feedback and direction in accordance with the competence children demonstrate, encouraging them to take responsibility for their activity (Berk and Winsler, 1995, p. 20). "The adult remains closely in tune with the child's actions, carefully anticipating the child's next moves and remaining engaged in the activity just enough to provide support as it is needed" (p. 29).

But the "scaffolding" metaphor does not capture our complicity in children's activity, the value we ascribe to their actions, nor the meaning we lend to the situation by the way we encounter risky activity with children. In showing us a trick, the child invites us to look beyond the activity per se to recognize what is at stake for him when he wants to show us what he can do. We begin to discern an inner logic to this tricky, risky movement.

## Repetition

Children pursue those activities that have an experiential register of familiarity. Tyler likes hanging by his knees, and notwithstanding the enjoyment the subsequent rush of blood to his head must bring, he likes to hang upside down for the increasing familiarity it brings to a topsy-turvy world. He is content to hang there, and when it becomes almost too much for him, he pulls himself up towards the bar into an almost upright position whereby he can again view things around him in a more or less normal way. He is happy enough doing this over and over again. Such repetitive activity seems characteristic of the playground. While it may appear that children run from one piece of equipment to another in what seems to be a constant seeking of novelty, closer observation shows them to be often caught in the spell of certain equipment. Here on a swing or a slide they will want to be pushed again and again, or to have "just one more turn." Is such repetitive activity an avoidance of the risks of playground activity, or might we see in repetitive playground activity a certain orderliness to the practice of taking risks?

"When a situation has been experienced repeatedly without harm, familiarity kills fear," says Russell (1926, p. 88) in what almost amounts to a truism. But what is really meant by this idea of killing fear through repetition and the subsequent sense of familiarity? If we recall the various encounters we have with children on playgrounds we will remember that it is the suggestion of a child's apprehensiveness that raises fears in us for his or her security! We fear for the child. We wish to avoid a fearful state-of-mind where "what one 'is apprehensive about' is one's Being-with the other, who might be torn away from one" (Heidegger, 1962, p. 181). This requires being with the child such that we might come to see ourselves on, say, the horizontal bar. It requires becoming child-like, reawakening to the landscape of the child. So when we talk about killing fear we must be careful that our preoccupation is not merely with our own peace of mind. In other words, we need to distinguish between the ways children familiarize themselves with playground things and the way we, on the other hand, become accustomed to seeing what they are doing. A sense of familiarity might even be the correlate of an increasing insensitivity to what children are doing. Earlier on it was said, following Van den Berg (1961/1975), that the playground, while seeming very familiar to us, can be no less a fearful place for the child. Likewise, the activities which we have become accustomed to seeing over a lifetime can be a source of much anxiety on the child's part. That which seems so unexceptional to us, that which the child tries over and over again, this seemingly repetitive activity can engender an indifference on our part to what is before us and what lies before the child.

Seen in terms of an adult familiarity which kills fear, the repetitiveness of children's playground activity is but a step away from being considered a type of self-imposed drill. Is this how we wish to view what the child does? Is it the rigor and exactness of movement that we want to stress as opposed to its risk and uncertainty? When Tyler tries hanging upside down from different pieces of equipment, we might conclude that he is looking for the invariant features of his activity, that he is mastering a technique of hanging upside down which can be applied farther afield. Doing the activity over and over again may be thought of as the development of a technique whereby he might do away with risk altogether.

Viewing the repetitiveness of a child's activity in terms of developing techniques of controlling, managing, and manipulating the body diminishes our own sense of the activity's riskiness. Instead of being mindful of the child's experience, we simply see movements that conform to empirically generalizable patterns of physical development. We see hanging upside down as preparation for greater feats of strength and agility. Consequently we try to show the child some new trick, some more difficult way of hanging from the horizontal bar. We lead him through it and in the process we leave his activity behind.

The fact that a child returns to hanging from the bar by his knees when we leave him alone shows us that he does not see any real connection between that activity and the trick we have shown him. He shows us, by repeating his earlier activity, that he has a different sense of technique, a different sense of progression and order. So perhaps we ought to reconsider what it means when an activity is done repeatedly without harm. Does it simply mean that the child is attempting to overcome a sense of the riskiness of the activity so that he or she can attain some higher level of difficulty and hence some greater level of skill? Or is there some more intrinsically grounded principle of movement at issue here? Perhaps it is not so much the logic of physical skill development with which we should be concerned as it is the manner in which a familiar sense of risk-taking evolves. Seemingly repetitive playground activity provides a place of comfort for accepting a dare or a challenge. In its fluctuations this activity provides an experiential measure of the risks that can be taken. Were it simply repetitive, the child would soon lose interest.

Van den Berg reminds us that our adult sense of an activity's repetitiveness is not necessarily the same as the child's, "for repetition is not repetition to the mind of the child."

> The tot who skips up and down the stairs ten or twenty times, does not repeat: it perseveres in the present. If we grownups ascend the stairway it is because we have something to do upstairs. It would be altogether senseless to run up and down repeatedly. Once we are upstairs we no longer need the stairway. But if we should send a child upstairs, to fetch some object or other, it could still be tarrying on the stairs after a quarter of an hour, all taken up with the wonders of the stairway, a stairway such as hardly exists for us adults. The child is altogether taken up, for example, in the experience of going up and down and in the actual experience the object it was sent for is readily forgotten. (Van den Berg, 1959, pp. 28–34).

Children may readily forget some instrumental purpose for their activity, some end beyond it, however they do not necessarily have no sense of purpose such that their activity is endless. We would do better in understanding the repetitiveness of children's playground activity if we discerned a motive to their motions—how the purpose of the activity is somehow contained within, how each descent of the playground slide brings new confidence, how each time the swing is pushed higher and higher brings that time nearer when children will want to try swinging by themselves. What seems repetitive at first glance attests to a series of movements towards increasing autonomy as we look at children's activity more closely.

"Although children often seem to realize both when repetition is needed and when they are ready to explore, they do not always know, and an adult may help by gently urging the over-repetitive child out of his routine, or by drawing the over-exploratory [child] back to necessary repetition" (Ministry of Education, 1952, p. 65). Such is the purposeful intervention that is at times warranted. But what of the far more subtle influence that comes from a manner of watching what a child is up to?

Each time on Malmo Playground Matthew invariably finds his way to one swing in particular. On this occasion the other children are on the far side of the playground, which allows me to take a closer look at the fascination of this particular tire swing. Up to this point in time it has seemed as if Matthew finds this swing when he is tired of playing with the other children. And as I have glanced at him every so often, he has not appeared to be doing much of anything on the swing. "You must like that swing, Matthew," I say to him. "It's the best swing," he replies. But what is so special about this swing, this tire swing that looks the same as the other three beside it? I watch as he pushes the swing back and forth, pushing it as high as he can before letting it drop. Then he tries to jump onto it as it swings back to him. But the swing moves too quickly. Besides, it has too much force and ends up dragging him forward with his legs trailing on the ground. A little later I see Matthew pushing the swing in a circle, his legs spinning out on the soft sand below, only this time he manages to lift himself onto the swing. He sits down on the tire and holds onto the suspended chains until the revolutions finally end. He does this again, and again, and again, almost tirelessly. Matthew glances over and sees me looking in his direction. "Look! No hands!" he exclaims while balancing on the edge of the revolving tire.

For Matthew and for those of us who care to watch his activity closely, there are subtleties in what he does on the swing. He is not bored; he is not prevented from doing other things on the playground; it is just that the tire swing discloses possibilities of the present that are far from being exhausted. Our interest in Matthew's being on the tire swing draws out the possibilities of movement which the swing allows.

## Practice

Can we discover a principle which embraces the seeming novelty of the "tricks" the child wants to show us, the "new tricks" we want to teach him or her, and the repetitiveness of activity which is the basis for the child being able to show us anything at all? Here we might appeal to Dewey's analysis of the relation between interest and effort, particularly what he regarded as the unfortunate juxtaposition of these terms as a direct consequence of assuming that the action to be done exists as an entity separate from the person who is to take it up.

> Because the object or end is assumed to be outside self it has to be *made* interesting; to be surrounded with artificial stimuli and with fictitious inducements to attention. Or, because the object lies outside the sphere of self, the sheer power of "will," the putting forth of effort without interest is the principle of the recognized identity of the fact to be learned or the action proposed with the growing self; that it lies in the direction of the agent's own growth, and is, therefore, imperiously demanded, if the agent is to be himself. Let this condition of identification once be secured, and we have neither to appeal to sheer strength of will, not to occupy ourselves with making things interesting. (Dewey, 1913/1975, p. 7)

Dewey referred to an "*intrinsic* connection as the motive for action" (p. 25), or rather, to the fact that any momentary activity is interesting to the extent that it has "its place in an enduring activity" (p. 42). Thus a trick is amusing only because it is perceived as having some bearing on the activity at hand, or better still, because it extends the present activity in the direction of its own perfection.

The trouble with this formulation of interest and effort is that it reduces the motivation behind children's playground activity, the motivation behind the "tricks" which children want to show us, to "a consideration of their *powers*, their tendencies in action, and the ways in which these can be carried forward by a given subject-matter" (p. 62). To be sure, Dewey did acknowledge the social dimension to a child's interests, saying:

> This social interest not only, then, interfuses and permeates his interest in his own actions and sufferings, but it also suffuses his interest in *things*. Adults are so accustomed to making a sharp distinction between their relations to things and to other persons, their pursuits in life are so largely specialized along the line of having to do with things just as things, that it is difficult for them, practically impossible, to realize the extent to which children are concerned only as they enter into and affect the concerns of persons, and the extent to which a personal-social interest radiates upon objects and gives them meaning and worth. (pp. 85, 86)

However this social interest still falls short of a pedagogical interest (cf. Vandenberg, 1980, esp. pp. 245; 248–49). Dewey's analysis of interest fails to acknowledge the significance of the relation between adult and child for keeping interest alive and moving in the direction of physical accomplishments—the pedagogical relation which holds interest in the riskiness of the playground. His analysis leaves us groping for a principle that embraces not only interest and effort as aspects of a child's disposition towards the playground, but also the pedagogical motivation suggested in the distinction between novelty and familiarity, between the tricks we want to show the child and the repetition we see in what the child shows us, between the challenges we articulate and the child's present accomplishments. Instead of appealing to a psychology of interest, we need to draw from the present analysis of risk a pedagogical principle that shows the "intrinsic connection" between these seemingly juxtaposed terms.

Bollnow (1974) provides just such a principle in his treatment of the notion of "practice." He says that practice is necessarily repetitive, however it differs from being simply repetitive in that it is motivated by "a special ability" which is acquired in the course of repetitive movements and which seeks its own perfection (p. 65). Practice means trying to do better than the last attempt, desiring improvement, striving for a level of ability, a standard, which is intimated in each repetitive attempt. The child tries to reach higher than before, swing upside down a little longer, or jump farther, each time "wishing for ability to do ever better. . . . [Practice is] essentially an experiment and *risk*, [that] seeks to approach the latent precision and limits of its own nature" (p. 65, my emphasis).

Consider the situation of Dorian and Matthew playing on a tire suspended from a large cross-beam by means of three lengthy chains. There is a game of sorts developing here. At first the boys are content to push the tire to and fro, for both of them to stand on it as it spins around, or for one of them to pull himself up to touch the beam. As they play, Dorian sees that when Matthew sits with his legs inside the tire, and when he clings to the chains with one leg looped over the tire, they can swing far enough to almost brush against a set of wooden stumps imbedded in the ground. These stumps can also be a platform from which Dorian can leap onto the tire as Matthew maintains its momentum. I watch as Dorian performs this trick. He stands poised on the blocks, waiting for the right moment to jump. Unfortunately he misjudges the swing, and with a futile attempt to grasp the chain, he falls heavily to the ground. Undeterred, he tries again, and again. Dorian performs a number of successful and not-so-successful jumps until Matthew protests that it is time for his turn. As I watch this activity I see that, to a certain extent, these boys seek to be in control, and yet the risks of the activity mean that more is involved than the simple pursuit of mastery. Referring back to Bollnow, their desire to perform this trick may involve technical skill development, however the risk factor means that the practice itself is what truly matters.

> Every individual attempt holds directly a claim to the greatest possible achievement. Along with this the attitude of the person necessarily changes: in the place of interest in the subject-matter or the object to be gained comes pure satisfaction in achieving complete ability in the task. And when this is not achieved, the earlier experience of attainable progress offers a spur to ever renewed effort. (p. 68)

After resting and watching Matthew have his turn, Dorian wants to try again. He is spurred on by the bodily echo of Matthew's attempts to do better himself.

Bollow warns of a consequence of this type of practice, that it can result in "soulless virtuosity (technical skill) as a refined form of self-indulgence" (p. 69). Such practice can turn into the mere display of physical powers, although this consequence is more likely when the child's attention is diverted by the look of another person away from the possibilities of perfection which the movement itself contains. The child who cries out "Look at me! See what I can do!" is not displaying virtuosity, but is bringing our attention to the risk which makes ability something to strive for through practice. The actions performed are ones she lives through. They express who and what she might become.

"See that one," exclaims Christine, after bouncing over a speed bump on her bicycle on our way to Malmo Playground. "That's the first big jump I ever did!" "That's not a jump," Kyler snaps back at her, "not a real one." Kyler circles round on her bike behind us and, peddling furiously, she hits the same bump and bounces up into the air. Christine follows suit, although not quite as fast as Kyler, but certainly much faster than she went before. She stops peddling just before she reaches the speed bump and braces herself. She hits the bump, keeps control of the bike, and then comes to a stop a little farther along the road. "Did you see?" she asks. "I did a real one!" Kyler looks on in silence, satisfied that Christine has now done a "real jump." Later on these same children can be seen jumping over the edge of the pedestrian path onto the road. They even find a couple of steps to take their bicycles down.

"Watch me," Christine says one day. "I can do three steps now!" For Christine and Kyler there is a certain possibility of risk-taking suggested in the way they first encounter the speed bump. A challenge is found in jumping over the bump, and this initial challenge opens up a host of related challenges. Likewise on the playground, there are ladders which the young child sees other children climbing, there are slides she sees children coming down, and there are swings on which her parents put her. The child is introduced to the playground in particular sorts of ways—ways to which the playground things lend themselves (ways for which they are for the most part designed) and ways which point to future playground encounters. Playground objects, like bicycles and speed bumps, set the child on particular courses of risk-taking. Yet without a comfort in taking risks, reflected in large measure by the kind of encouragements given, such possibilities may very well remain hidden.

There are certainly progressions to the child's risk-taking practices. But the practice of taking risks cannot be explained away by appealing to the "skill talk" that has become so rife in education circles (Barrow, 1987, 1990).[4] For the most part, the motivation behind "skill talk" is a fear of taking risks (Hart, 1978); moreover, the very notion of skills draws from an instrumental reason which is not the practical reason exemplified in risk-taking situations (see Carr, 1981, p. 93). The practice of risk-taking discloses a different sense of progression to the playground activities of children we have been observing than a skill development hierarchy and "the individual practice acquires a significance going far beyond the individual skill it seeks to reproduce" (Bollnow, 1987, p. 108).

We have seen Gerrard before on the sloping parallel bars. He returns to them again; besides, he has still to make it all the way from the top to the bottom rung. On this occasion we see him as he reaches out, takes hold of the first bar, and letting himself swing forward, hangs for a moment in mid-air. He kicks his legs, and jerks back and forth, until the next bar comes within reach. And so on for the next few rungs. Then he misses. It is the second to last rung. His fingers graze the metal pipe at the very second he relinquishes his grip on the preceding rung. Gerrard crashes to the ground, his energy spent for the moment. But Gerrard is not discouraged this time because now he has almost done what he intended to do. Perhaps he thinks to himself, "if only I can hang on a little bit longer I can surely make it all the way." Just a little more effort, a little more application, and Gerrard will have made it.

Some months later Gerrard is again on this playground. "How are you doing on those bars?" I ask him. Gerrard doesn't answer, although a few minutes later I see him swinging across a different set of bars that is much higher than the inclined rack he had been on before, and much more difficult because all the bars are set at the same height. Gerrard cannot let himself drop down from one rung to the next on this playground equipment; he must use his body to swing forward to grasp the bar in front of him. And Gerrard seems to be doing extremely well at precisely this movement. "How far can you go, Gerrard? Can you turn around and come back again?" With this challenge he is off again.

What is happening with this child who sees so much in sets of parallel bars? For him the challenge is ongoing. On another part of the playground stand the horizontal bars of differing heights. Gerrard has not gone near these bars yet. Will they be the next things to draw his attention? Our thinking about challenges for Gerrard derives from a perception of a progression to his penchant for bars you can swing on. We envisage a direction for his actions which has an effect on his present activity. Our challenge to him is evidence enough of this.

## Being in Practice

For the child to accept a challenge to his ability and one that is well within his capabilities requires that we encounter the risk with him. Simply daring him or challenging him requires too little of us. We need to enter the spirit of the child's practice.

Too often playground activity is seen as distinct from us, which at times it is; and all too often we stand outside children's activity through an inability to practice what we teach. But being mindful of children's experiences, especially sensing the riskiness of their activities, admits our complicity in the practice that unfolds. Having children extend themselves thus requires showing something of ourselves. After all, we take children to adult-designed playgrounds, so from the outset we carry responsibility for the possibilities they offer; and once there our presence influences the way these possibilities unfold by the manner in which we either guide, support, instruct, or evaluate children's movements from a position of detachment or alternatively, challenge them and encounter the risks of their activity from a position of close reflective engagement which lends credence and direction to what they practice. It is not a matter of showing children new tricks—that would constitute mere amusement; nor is it a matter of developing skills—that could constitute mere training. The risks that play at our relation to the child and give this relation tangible form exercise a "practical wisdom" (Aristotle, 1925, 1140–42) whereby the child is guided to new plateaus of achievement. They require us to stay in practice with those activities we see children doing.

Does this mean we should be able to do those same activities? Yes and no. We should be able to imagine the space and time of children's movements; bring back the past in anticipation of what might unfold in the present situation. We should also be able to reimagine our past practices by experiencing the fullness of the present practical moment. Then again, to be immersed in our own physical capabilities risks running rough-shod over the child's practice. The notion of being in practice stresses not so much the exemplary character of teaching as it does the "mimetic" dimension to pedagogy. "Mimesis is the ensnaring of me by the other, the invasion of me by the other; it is that attitude whereby I assume the gestures, the conducts, the favorite words, the ways of doing things of those I confront" (Merleau-Ponty, 1964, p. 145). Mimesis is the bodily imitation of what one sees whereby the child takes on the actions of another, more confident and competent, performer. Not only do the children imitate each other, performing movements which they feel the urge to attempt, they do so in contexts where adults feel for them and can provide imitative possibilities (see Gardner, 1983, pp. 228, 229, 234). Risk is the sense we share of the purpose of the child's activity, and it is our awareness of, and responsiveness to, its riskiness that defines the mimetic character of how we can best teach the child to become confident and competent in doing the activity. Being in practice with the child is the physical capability of showing the child some new movement, tempered by the emotional register of that movement's riskiness for the child.

Recall the situations where children back down. They would suggest a lack of support and a presence of risk that is not ameliorated by the presence of the adult. And how much more serious are those situations where it is the adult whose fearfulness makes the child back down from a seemingly risky situation? Such situations, except those in which danger is the reality, show an adult who is out of practice in responding to the riskiness of the children's activity. Of course, one can have ability yet still be out of practice. From the child's side, he or she may be physically capable of some activity, yet be in need of encouragement in order to try it. From the adult's side, we may have done the playground activities we see taking place before us at some earlier time in our lives, but we may be quite reluctant to try them now. Even worse, we may disregard the initial trepidation we experienced when trying the activity as a child and hence overlook the risk the activity now holds for the child before us. Here, again, we are out of practice.

This notion of being in practice avoids the separation of teaching and learning, adults and children, purposes and activities. It avoids the reduction of pedagogy to teacher skill, strategy, and technique that affect the development of children's physical or motor skills. According to one recent formulation: "Pedagogy has to do with the design and management of the teaching and learning transactions involving subject matter (i.e. content knowledge) and a variety of academic appreciation, skills, and understanding" (Gordon, 1995, p. 33). Formulations such as this one deny the relationality of risk. Our "teachings" ultimately make sense when they are couched within a situational understanding of what the child is attempting to do. The value of what we teach the child on the playground depends, first of all, upon our acknowledging the primacy of a relation of practice, of our being in practice with what the child wants to do. Teacher skill, strategy, and technique are either self-conscious constructions of experience or categorical interpretations made by other adults. Like the skill taxonomies with which we define children's activities, movements, and experiences, they are second-order, adult constructions of a first-order, practical relation premised upon the encounter with children whom we perceive to be taking risks.

The same logic holds more generally for the constructions of "child development" that have become commonly accepted in our educational talk.[5] The prevalence and acceptance of such constructions is evidenced in the manifesto of the National Association for the Education of Young Children, called *Developmentally Appropriate Practice in Early Childhood Programs Serving Children from Birth Through Age 8*, which defines appropriate practice as that which is not only geared to the characteristics of the individual children but also guided by an understanding of the "universal, predictable sequences of growth and change that occur in children during the first 9 years of life . . . in all domains of development—physical, emotional, social, and cognitive" (Bredekamp, 1987, p. 2).[6]

According to Spodek (1988), there needs to be a synthesis of teacher knowledge "growing out of experience and one's interpretation of those experiences" and developmental theories of childhood (p. 170). Unfortunately the commitment to a particular theory of development suggests that teachers may "not even be aware of a particular child's development or behavior because their adopted way of knowing precludes them from receiving that form of input" (Haberman, 1988, p. 37). Silin (1988) argues that child development discourse is in fact "a potent form of technocratic mindedness" that removes decision making with respect to children from "the realm of moral and political consideration to which it more properly belongs" (p. 125). Polakow (1989) extends that line of thinking, railing against the "hegemony of development discourse" that surveys, regulates, and controls the lives of children according to a managerial adult gaze (p. 78). These constructions potentially define in advance what is to be observed irrespective of how one might encounter particular children. They reinforce a view from above, a supervisory gaze, that sets adults and children apart.

The notion of being in practice provides a deepened understanding of "developmentally appropriate practice" as well as a critique of those ways of talking about "developmentally appropiate practice" which undermine its relational significance. Though we can sit on a park bench and survey the developmental levels of the children before us, we can also commit ourselves to observe more closely the activity of any particular child. We can approach children, observing their activities up close, and question the categories of experience normally assigned. We can observe children at close range and attempt to support them, guide their actions, instruct them, even evaluate what they are attempting to do; and we can dare to encourage children to extend the range of their movements as far as possible, while remaining conscious of the level to which certain children can, for the moment, be challenged. It is through our reflective engagement in the playground activities of children that the supervisory gaze is softened. We avoid a hardening of the categories of childhood experience by encountering the riskiness of the playground with children, becoming more fully aware of our practical responsiblity for what they do. This reflective engagement is what the experience of risk calls for. This is what is meant by being in practice. And this reflective, relational quality of risk is what makes "developmentally appropriate" physical practices, such as those exemplified on the playground, educationally worthwhile.

# 8

# The
# Possibility of
# Risk

Although risk is a term of our pedagogical relation to children
on the playground, we have seen certain possibilities of this
relation in activities beyond the playground. A pedagogical
awareness and responsiveness to risk occurs in bathrooms, on mountains, in swimming pools, by rivers, on the streets, and in the neighbor-
hoods of children. Playground situations stand out because playgrounds
are places reserved for children and places where we are prompted to
thematize our interactions with children in terms of risk, even if only to
ensure the safety of children. They are places of risk-taking where a certain manner of challenging children and encountering the world with
them is practiced.

The temptation now is to apply the results of our analysis of the
riskiness of the playground to domains of activity that bear a strong

resemblance to the playground. Hence we might show the applicability of the practice of risk to, say, gymnastics and outdoor pursuits which resemble the playground activities we have observed. After all, a child hanging upside down from a horizontal bar is learning the rudiments of an olympic gymnastic event, while the child climbing a cargo net or walking up the vertical side of a playground structure aided by a fireman's pole is becoming aware of what it takes to climb rock faces. The danger of such an extension of the analysis of risky playground situations is that it may lose hold of the relational quality of risk for the sake of taking a conceptual grasp on its visibility. Just as the didactics of skill development can obscure what is at stake in the practice of risk, so the premature design of an activity sequence may hide the possibilities intrinsic to the pedagogical relation of risk. At the very least, we should first consider the possibilities of risk as they are suggested in the activity preferences of the children themselves before prescribing any apparently logical activity sequences.

## The Playing Field

"Do you want to go to Malmo Playground?" I ask my child. "No, I'm busy," he replies. He and his friends have just started a backyard game of ball hockey. The gloves are on, the goalie has padded up with the leggings he made earlier in the day, and the rest of the children are sorting out who is playing where and which team they are facing. Tyler is too caught up in this activity to be much interested in going to the playground.

This game is not a particularly special event, although increasingly it seems there are more reasons for not going to the playground than there are reasons for going. Only when there are no other children around to play with does this child feel inclined to go to the playground. He will change into his soccer outfit well ahead of time, and then practice kicking the ball around the backyard until it is time to head off to the game. Has this child outgrown the playground? Certainly he is not alone in his current preference for more organized games. Most of his friends, including those who have gone with us to the playground on previous occasions, play in the soccer league. So is there a point at which the playground no longer holds such a strong appeal for children? There is still the school playground to be considered, although even here the children's activities extend beyond the climbing frames, slides, and swings to the surrounding spaces and playing fields.

It would be too easy to conclude that the child has outgrown the playground, or that the pressures of little league sports intrude upon the child's liking of the playground. A stronger conclusion is that the qualities of the playground become manifest in activities that draw the child beyond the playground. "Tell me, Tyler, what would you rather do, go to the playground or go to soccer?" "I like both," he replies. "But if you had a choice, what would you rather do?" He is confused by the question. He says: "You mean I can't play soccer anymore? Why can't I play?" He becomes increasingly upset at such a thought. For this child, it is not a matter of alternatives. It seems there is something to playground activity that can be preserved not only in "pick-up" games, but also in little league activities where the overriding considerations often seem to have more to do with uniforms, coaches, inviolable rules, and tournament schedules than with the quality of children's experiences (Orlick and Botterill, 1975). The fact that Tyler still comes back to the things of the playground from time to time shows that there is a certain connection between the playground and the playing field. Tyler can still enjoy the playground in much the same way as before. It is just that he enjoys other things as well.

Soccer does not appear to be an inherently risky pastime, compared to the other formal and informal activities that children may take up. It is a preferred activity for both boys and girls because it does not have the intimidatory physical contact of the other forms of football and ice hockey; it contains fewer occasions for embarrassment and even humiliation than, say, continually striking out or dropping the ball in baseball; and it requires less attention to drills and choreographed routines than is required in swimming, gymnastics, and dance. If our task is to see how the sense of risk-taking that is first acquired on the playground can be transferred to new and potentially challenging contexts, then the soccer field would not be the most obvious place to look. But since the child shows such an inclination to move from the playground to the playing field, maybe we need to look more closely at the nature of this activity preference to see how the principles that are at work in our coming to terms with playground activity apply here as well. Consider how the playing field discloses the possibility of "risk as a term of our pedagogical relation to children" for some of the other children of this study.

## Christine

This child whom we have seen before on the playground slide is the only girl on the Malmo soccer team. She is also one of the quieter children on the team and is often overshadowed by the more boisterous ones, some of whom come with ready-made friendships. As if this is not cause enough for her to be a little timid, during the first game Christine is hit in the face with the soccer ball. She holds up well as the coach tries to confort her; but when as she is led away by her father we wonder if she will want to remain with the other children on the team. Our fears prove unwarranted. Christine turns up in fine spirits the next game, and although somewhat reluctant to get involved, she seems content enough to be on the field with the other children.

Both parents come to watch Christine play in the last game of the short soccer season. On previous occasions only one parent has come for any particular game. This time, with both of them on the sidelines, Christine is noticeably more confident than we have seen her before. She sits chattering to her mom and dad when the coach sends her off for a spell, and she is anxious to enter the fray again when it is her turn to replace one of the other children. Her parents look on approvingly as Christine kicks the ball. And though she has still to learn how to take possession of the ball by, for instance, dribbling it upfield, Christine now seems prepared to take the risk of getting involved in the play. "Kick the ball!" her mother challenges her. "Oh, good one. Well done, Christine!" Being on the sideline, Christine's parents are limited in the encouragement they can give, yet on this occasion their presence is enough to help Christine play better than she has played before. Their presence creates an atmosphere of security for their child's endeavors on the soccer field.

### Gerrard

"Go hard, Gerrard!" "Run hard! All the way!" Gerrard runs hard. He is the most involved player on the team. Perhaps he is the best player on the team, although this is difficult to judge because whenever Gerrard is on the field the other children tend to move aside to let him have the ball.

Gerrard is a little hard on his team mates. "Heads up," he chides them. After all, this is what the coach keeps telling them. Gerrard has simply taken it upon himself to remind the others of this rule. By contrast, Stephen, the coach's son, is not too much bothered by this rule. "Heads up," Gerrard tells him, and Stephen wanders around staring at the clouds. Later on, Stephen lies down on the field while the game goes on around him. "Get up, Stephen!" Gerrard screams at him. Substitutions are made and Gerrard comes off the field. He is in tears and weeps in his mother's arms. "He won't play properly," he tells her. "Stephen won't get up and play properly."

Gerrard is not afraid to get involved, in fact he is probably afraid not to be involved. "It's all yours!" he hears as he takes control of the ball once again. It seems that Gerrard knows only one way to play soccer and that is, as his mother tells him, to play it hard. "Way to go, Gerrard!" And with these words, we wonder to what extent such glib responses to this child's activity may actually gloss over the nature of his experience. What risk is Gerrard taking when being told to play so hard?

## Paco

Paco is the leading goal scorer on the team. Although he does not have the same determination as Gerrard, he knows how to get into a position to score goals. For instance, as the opposing goalkeeper makes ready to kick the ball into play, Paco is hovering directly in front of him, ready to pounce on it when it comes his way. And a number of times it will come to him, whereupon he will surprise the goalkeeper by kicking the ball past him ever so quickly. It is not too many games, however, before goalkeepers learn to kick the ball away to the side of the net instead of directly in front of it. This puts an end to Paco's scoring from directly in front.

Paco learns a new way of scoring. The children cluster around the ball until some child manages to kick it free for a brief time; yet increasingly Paco stands apart from this melee. He waits for the ball to come his way so he can take it upfield with the other children following in his wake. He stands farther and farther apart from the other children until eventually he is so far off-side that it becomes necessary to teach the children the rule.

"How many goals did you score today?" his father asks him. "I only got two," he tells him. But Eduardo insists that Paco did not get any goals at all. An argument develops between the two boys and is settled only when Paco's mother arrives and confirms the fact that Paco went scoreless today. Why does Paco lie about the goals he scored? Hasn't he scored enough goals already? Perhaps Paco thinks that scoring goals is all there is to playing soccer. At first it comes so easy to him, but then, as the other children begin to understand the facets of the game, the opportunities which brought Paco early success begin to disappear. Eventually he thinks he must lie to win his parents' approval.

## Matthew

Children like Christine, Gerrard, and Paco are not concerned solely with the responses of their parents. Their own standing in the eyes of their friends is also important. One notable illustration of this is the constant squabble over who should go in goal. So much fuss does this position create that before too long an order of turn-taking is devised to give each child a chance to stand out in goal. "When is it my turn?" Matthew asks the coach. His team has already scored four goals, and with none scored against them, perhaps it is a little odd that Matthew is so anxious to be in goal when all the action so far has been at the opposite end of the field. "Is it my turn yet?" he asks the coach for either the fifth or sixth time.

Matthew eventually has his turn. The coaches of both teams have by this time worked out ways of balancing out the field of play, and as a result, Matthew finds himself busier than he would otherwise have been. Eventually the other team scores, not just once, but twice. Matthew looks dejected. He asks the coach if he can come off. To be held responsible for letting the other team win, that would be humiliating. All the good saves he has made so far could not compensate for this possibility of failing in front of his friends. The risk is not worth it.

Matthew has become very aware of the presence of his friends. We recall how on an earlier occasion he did not want to be on the Royal Gardens Playground opposite his school because a group of smaller children were there at the time with their supervisor and Matthew did not want any of his friends from school to see him for fear of being ridiculed. Certainly his concerns in this regard are understandable, but it is unfortunate that his concern for how he looks in the eyes of his friends should become a hindrance to his activity. Like children on the playground who are too influenced by the approbation of their friends and for whom it helps to have a more benign presence, perhaps the coach or some other adult should be there for Matthew so that the risk of going in goal is a risk worth taking.

## Dorian

Dorian is one of the biggest children on this soccer team, and at first sight, he looks like he should be one of the best players. It is therefore surprising to see him overshadowed by Gerrard and Paco for most of the games. Although Dorian can easily chase the ball down, often being the first one to reach it, he seems unsure of what to do next. Dorian lacks confidence in his ability to play this game. He sees the ease with which Paco scores and wonders why he cannot do the same. Paco scores once again and Dorian lifts him off his feet as if in celebration, then drops him heavily on the seat of his pants. Dorian's frustration is turning to malice. He longs to score a goal himself.

As the end of the soccer season draws near, Dorian learns an important lesson: he can outrun the other children. If he can break free with the ball then there is no one fast enough to catch him. Five times during the second to last game he breaks away with the ball. And five times he either kicks the ball wide of the net or else straight into the arms of the goalkeeper. Before he can try a sixth time, he is called to the sidelines to make way for one of the other children to come back onto the field. "Did you see me? I nearly scored," he tells his father. "How much time have we got left to play?" Eventually Dorian goes back onto the field. Again he manages to break away with the ball. He kicks it upfield and follows in hot pursuit with most of the adults on the sideline cheering him on, anxious for him to get that elusive goal. Determination is written all over Dorian's face. Now it is his turn to get a goal. Sure enough, he does. This time he kicks the ball firmly past the goalkeeper. Dorian is elated. So are his parents. He finally got one!

Dorian scores two goals in the first half of the last game. As the children come off the field for oranges, Dorain says: "I think I'll get two more." He doesn't, although it is evident in the confidence of his announcement that he has discovered how to score them.

A sense of risk, first evident on the playground, underlines Christine's, Gerrard's, Paco's, Matthew's, and Dorian's experience of the playing field. Although not so obviously a place of risk, there is indeed a texture of risk which is apparent in the way these children respond to their parents who sit on the sideline. And because the adults do sit on the sideline (somewhat like the adults who sit on park benches), there are the silences of risk that this distance creates and that give the children the freedom to find out how to take risks for themselves. Children can be challenged—we can encounter this attenuated form of risk with them. In turn, they can become practiced at the cultural form of physical risk-taking called soccer.

How similar, then, are the risks of the playing field to those of the playground? A clarification would seem to be indicated at this point, since the risk-taking described above would not appear to be of exactly the same kind as the physical risk-taking we see on the playground. In fact, the fear of failing, of looking inept, of not living up to parental expectations, and so on, would seem to lie well beyond the more physically-rooted fears of, say, falling off the slide. And yet, are there really different kinds of risk involved? Does physical risk simply include those different kinds of risk which have in common the fact that they pertain to certain physical activities, or should we consider that which is physical in a far less restrictive manner?

Such questions disclose my intention not to lose sight of real physical existence, of the Aristotelian notion of *physis*, the internal principle of movement which is the essence of human nature (cf. Peters, 1967, pp. 158–60). The physicality of risk-taking lies in the realm of growth and maturity and that which fosters such growth. The root *physis* "means the power that emerges and the enduring realm under its sway" (Heidegger, 1959, p. 14).

We oppose the psychic, the animated, the living, to the "physical." But for the Greeks all this belonged to *physis* and continued to do so even after Aristotle. They contrasted it with what they called *thesis*, ordinance, or *nomos*, law, rule in the sense of *ethos*. This, however, denotes not mere norms but mores, based on freely accepted obligations and traditions; it is that which concerns free behavior and attitudes, the shaping of man's historical being, the *ethos* which under the influence of morality was later degraded to the ethical. (p. 16)

Accordingly, by talking about physical risk-taking in the context of those physical activities undertaken by young children on playgrounds and playing fields, it is intended that our discussion will indicate the more comprehensive nature of physical risk-taking: that although evidentially physical, risk is primarily social and ethical, and essentially pedagogical.[1]

The question we now take up is that of the broadly physical and essentially pedagogical nature of risk in activities beyond the playground. It is a question of how the pedagogical nature of risk might unfold as we follow the child beyond the playground.

## Beyond the Playground

We stop at Malmo Playground on our way home from the soccer game since Tyler wants to play for awhile. "You're it," he says as he climbs up the ladder to one of the platforms. With these words I am drawn into the game. His call does not allow me to stay on the sidelines. I must enter into the spirit of the game.

It would be tempting to contrast my engagement with Tyler on the playground with being a spectator to his actions on the playing field. One might even appeal to the critics of organized children's sport to show the impoverishment of our relation (eg. Orlick and Botterill, 1975) in the latter situation and to explain the problem of the zealous parent. But just as we had to see beyond a sociology of knowledge of the playground in order to appreciate a pedagogy of risk, so too must we see past a sociology of knowledge of the playing field in order to realize the possibility of risk that exists there. In other words, were we to speak of the playing field only as a socially constructed space, as if none of us had ever enjoyed playing there, then we would deny the place where, like the playground, we were sometimes thrilled and scared, sometimes intimidated and dismayed, yet many times challenged and encouraged to find our own limits. We would lose our grasp on the lived experience of the risks of the playing field and the connections between the sense of these risks and our prior experiences of the riskiness of the playground. We would also fail to see that our adult presence is felt on the playing field through the actions of coaches and referees, and that the playing field brings the child closer to the adult world by being a place where adults can still be seen to play. The child moves onto the playing field because it seems to him or her a more grown up place to be.

So what can we say of the possibility of risk? How should the pedagogy of the riskiness of the playground apply specifically to situations beyond the playground? The present study leaves the question partly unanswered. After all, this pedagogical question must be taken up anew in each situation in which we find ourselves with children, whether it be on the playground, on the playing field, or farther afield. And yet, to simply leave the matter here would allow us to overlook the responsibility we have for directing children's activity. We are the ones to challenge the child, to encounter the playground with the child, and to stay in practice with what the child is attempting to do; and our responses are only possible because of a maturity that anticipates the risks a child might take, and in that anticipation, provides a direction for the child's activity. Thus we could say that the possibility of risk is more a measure of the maturity we have acquired along the lines we presently help the child.

It is not simply how much more experience we have than the child, but what that experience holds for the child. Our greater experience means that we are better placed than children to assess their efforts and provide the necessary support, guidance, and instruction. This experience allows us to discern the direction in which their activity is headed and to challenge them to greater physical accomplishments.

> Failure to take the moving force of an experience into account so as to judge and direct it on the ground of what it is moving into means disloyalty to the principle of experience itself. The disloyalty operates in two directions. The educator is false to the understanding that he should have obtained from his own past experience. He is also unfaithful to the fact that all experience is ultimately social: that it involves contact and communication. The mature person, to put it in moral terms, has no right to withhold from the young on given occasions whatever capacity for sympathetic understanding his own experience has given him. (Dewey, 1938/1963, p. 38)

We stand in relation to the child not only as an adult, but also as a parent, teacher, or a coach, with a sense of the continuity of the child's experience and of the particular forms this experience might take. As we look, for instance, at Marc on the high diving board we see a child known to be overly aware of the possible consequences of his activity. We see as well a child who, from his first inclination to step out onto the board, has embarked upon a particular course of activity. Our responsibility is to help Marc along this way and to confront the risks that we know to be along the way. The possibility of risk is in this regard an expansion and extension of our motives for first helping the child take risks in his or her present activity on the playground. It is premised by "a reflective sense of the Good, a sense of the meaning of being human, a sense of hope for the personal becoming of the child" (Bollnow, 1970/1989, p. 11) which we obtain from these relatively immature risk-taking activities.

The possibility of risk puts greater stress than before on our responsibility for the riskiness of the playground. Even when the child prefers at some point in time to play soccer rather than go to the playground, it must be kept in mind that both the playground and the playing field already bear an adult stamp of approval. This fact should put to rest any thought of us simply following the child from one activity to another. Such indulgence of the child's whims would deny our educative responsibility for the unfolding possibility of risk. As Dewey (1902/1956) put it: "The systematized and defined experience of the adult mind, in other words, is of value to us in intepreting the child's life as it immediately shows itself, and in passing to guidance and direction" (p. 13). The possibility of risk pertains to such "interpretation and guidance." As a term of our pedagogical relation to children, it provides a peda-logic for an expanded, physical domain of childhood experience.

Children must find their own way, yet ways that always and already conform to what has been laid down for them in general terms. The dimensions of risk are, on the one hand, ways of interpreting what children do, and on the other hand, ways of directing the course of children's explorations and disclosing ways of acting which they would not necessarily follow by themselves. The possibility of risk is thus a reflective sense of the connections between the playground and the playing field. But it is first and foremost a measure of the degree to which we can actually challenge, encounter, and be in practice with children, even as they now take up activities leading beyond the playground.

## Towards a Curriculum

Risk marks out a humanly significant domain of physical activity. There is, first of all, the physical space of the playground, that place of risk where a fundamentally human relation can be defined. This place provides us with a conceptual space for reflecting upon the significance of our relation to children. The domain represented by the playground becomes even more significant when we see it in light of the world the child must come to know. For instance, we consider those things in the region of the world to which playground activity lends itself. We consider games, sports, and physical recreations which take the child beyond the playground and connect his or her actions to the wider world. But the question to be drawn from the present study has to do with how we can best help the child enlarge the space of the playground. How can the child gain self-confidence, self-knowledge, movement proficiency, and feelings of self-worth in activities such as games, sports, and physical recreations which lie beyond the playground? That is the paramount curriculum question for this pedagogy of the playground.

And what shall we call this wider domain of the possibilities of the playground? A "periculum"? from the Latin "to risk," but absolved of the negative connotations of being endangered, at-risk, or in peril (Simpson, 1959, p. 437). Or shall we look to current practices and call it Movement Education, Physical Education, Adventure Education, or maybe even Outdoor Education? Such labels as these may make the child's experiences of risk the subject of deliberate, formal learning, however in thematizing content, subject matter, these labels risk denying the subjectivity and intersubjectivity of the experiential engagments of adults and children that create a course of risk-taking. While it is important to plan and organize such learning experiences for children and to provide a rubric for acknowledging their place, especially when one is a teacher of many children and not just an adult who has the reflective luxury of accompanying a few children to playgrounds, our efforts are for naught if in the process we lose sight of the relationship which makes these experiences meaningful. Risk is fundamentally a term of our relation to children. It carries certain possibilities of physical experience, so long as these possibilities play out the relation which we observe on the playground.[2]

A problem arises at this point, for we want to reconcile our analysis with current conceptualizations of the domain of physical activity where risk is prominent, and yet we note a disparity between the pedagogics of the playground and our curriculum formulations of that type of physical activity which lends itself to risk-taking. Do we then agree with Macdonald (1986) that "the domain of curriculum is grounded fundamentally in the boundaries of the activity of schooling, and influences outside the action context are only relevant as they can be observed and/or inferred from this context" (p. 212)? Do we see the playground in the shadows of the school curriculum? Or should we see the school curriculum as more the "presence of an absence?" "Present is the curriculum. . . . Present is the window. Absent is the ground" (Grumet, 1988, p. xiii). Absent is the playground. Should we not bring to our thinking about curriculum an understanding of the critical ground for what we do with children, even in more formal situations of physical activity? Shouldn't what we do with children on the playground for the sake of their maturity, how we treat the riskiness of the playground, be seen as the "lived curriculum" (Aoki, 1986; Aoki and Shamsher, 1991) as well as the critical ground for understanding the more formal and systematic designs, plans or curricula which one might wish to develop for the benefit of children?

The task that remains is, I suggest, to extend our analysis of the domain of the playground much further into the conceptual reaches of the school curriculum. Further reflection needs to apply itself to an understanding of how we might practice this pedagogy that arises on the playground. We might look favorably, for instance, at how the curriculum of Movement Education challenges the child, at how the equipment we use in following this approach resembles the equipment found on the playground, and at how the "limitation" and "indirect" teaching methods of Movement Education (cf. Kirchner, 1988, pp. 116–20) allow children to discover the nature of an activity for themselves. But here again, the most significant curriculum questions we can ask stem, first of all, from attending to the experiences of children. What is the child's experience of the riskiness of physical activity? What can we do to improve the quality of these experiences? Can we structure them in such a way that all children might experience what only a few experience when left to their own devices? Then we ask: what language, what terminology, will allow us to extend a child's range of experience in ways that lead to a maturing of movement? What language justifies the improvements we seek to make? Can our designed lessons, our formal curricula, allow for this pedagogical direction? Can we structure the child's experiences of the riskiness of the playground in pedagogically significant ways?

We structure children's physical experiences by the type of space that we make available. The playground, the playing field, the gymnasium, and the swimming pool—such spaces bring an adult frame of reference to bear upon children's experiences. They put a general curriculum border around them. Within this framework, we further structure children's physical experiences by the way we interact with them. Consequently, our task is to keep returning to the landscape of the child so that we can continue to see things with the child in mind and so that our designs for the child's learning can be in tune with the nature of the child's experience. This, after all, is the message for playground designers, although the message runs deeper than this application. My contention is that the playground provides critical ground for understanding the curriculum designs we have for children and for making these designs pedagogically, as well as developmentally, and culturally, appropriate.

An ongoing task is to realize how risk, as a term of our pedagogical relation to children in physical activity contexts, can be used to make sense of the teaching that occurs in the more formalized physical activity programs which we design for children.[3] For this we need to look anew at the experiences of children, especially as they disclose this possibility of a pedagogy of risk in activities which extend beyond the playground. What has been sketched out as the educational significance of risk needs to be explored in much greater detail as we continue to talk about a curriculum that extends the riskiness of the playground.

# 9

# Practical
# Insights

Spiecker (1984) defines the pedagogical relation as both a conceptual framework and a relation *sui generis*. "This relation
which makes human development possible, and which makes
it possible to become a person . . . is highly practical in nature: parents
are guided by it in their relationships with their young" (p. 208). Risk
stands out in this regard as a practical term of our pedagogical relation
to children. We see that the playground is not only a place of risk, but
that it is also the place where we see evidence of the modulation of the
atmosphere of risk to which children are exposed. The silences of risk,
in particular, disclose a way of being with children whereby we can
challenge them to take risks with confidence. We can see our interventions stemming from things held in common with the child, from an
attempt to relate to the child's experience of things, from a shared

encounter with risk. And through this practical engagement, which brings the maturity of our experiences to bear upon those of the child, we can help to define what risks are worth taking and why.

Risk, as a very practical term of our pedagogical relation to children, has a "contrafactual character," since what are presupposed in our relation to children are precisely those notions and principles that need to be realized (p. 208). Ultimately we cannot value the child's experience in itself because the very sense of a pedagogy of risk (and pedagogy in general) is to lead the child out of childhood. Our pedagogy is, therefore, intrinsically paradoxical, for it must respect the child in his or her childness and personhood only for the sake of being lead out of childhood. One is faithful to a pedagogy of risk in not taking the child solely on his or her own terms.[1]

This tension, between respecting children's experiences and knowing what is good for them, characterizes our encounters with children on playgrounds. In our practical engagements with children the course of their activity becomes apparent to us, and through our reflection upon these situations the question of what we should do can be answered with some degree of confidence. Risk serves to bring us in touch with the child at the same time as it obliges us to act in certain practical ways on the basis of what we think the child could become. To be sure, the child must inevitably go on his or her own way, but only after the direction has been vouchsafed by the actions we take with the child and on the child's behalf.

These reflections on risk thus serve a very practical purpose, namely that of holding up a notion which lends significance to children's growth and development. But these reflections are not practical in any technical or managerial sense. They serve to outline a "communicative understanding" (van Manen, 1977), a knowledge that is practical not so much because "it provides for the justification and legitimation of common practices" (p. 219), but more because it establishes a normative sense of how we might approach "common practices" such as those represented on the playground. So, from this study of risk in the lives of children, what can we now say about the practical requirements of a pedagogical relation which is sensitive to risk?

## Practical Ways of Acting

*The relation requires close and careful observation of children.* The playground stands out as an important place where an interest can be taken in the actions of children. We can see, first of all, that the playground is designed with children in mind. It is designed for their safety.

Second, the playground allows for the supervision of children. It allows for more than a passing interest in their activity. Third, and most importantly, the playground allows for children to be observed at close quarters. It is a place where adults can participate in the activities of children and a place where children can take risks in the relative safety provided by having an adult close by.

By observing children closely and carefully in places like playgrounds, we allow them to show something of themselves. Our teaching is bound by the situation in which we find ourselves with children. Effective teaching requires that we first observe the child's sense of an activity, and that we observe the child as he or she shows something of what is possible. In other words, our interventions are meaningful when they reflect what it is that the child wishes to show us. This is the difference between "educare" and "educere." According to educare, the educator brings up the child into the world of responsible adulthood according to a maturity presented to the child. But educere carries the sense of bringing or drawing out the child's latent talents and capabilities (Onions, 1966).

*The relation requires us to question our approach to each and every child.* A pedagogy of risk becomes possible when we see that the playground is not only a place of risk, but that it is also the place where we see how we are implicated in the risky situations to which children are exposed. The silences of risk, in particular, disclose a way of being with children whereby we can see how our help can be given. In fact, the knowledge of how to be most helpful to children comes as a questioning silence. There are the silences that accompany our approach, the silences that are necessary so as not to disturb the activity that takes place before us. Then there are the silences that result from not knowing what to do, the silences that disclose the tension between our understanding of the activity and the child's understanding. To these silences we feel the need to speak. We want to see the difference between our respective views of the activity as the basis for coming to terms with the nature of the child's experience. We want to speak of this difference in a way that acknowledges the integrity of the child's experience while pointing the way to more mature forms. So we trust the child, we place our trust in what the child can do, and within these silences of our approach, we see how each child can be best helped.

The consequence of questioning our approach to each and every child who needs our assistance is that we remember what it means to follow children. We follow children who already know how to follow other children. We see children dare each other, imitate each other, and at times give assistance to one another. And we see within these interactions a form of peer teaching from which we can develop a pedagogy.

Especially when we observe older children helping younger ones, we find a direction for how we might follow children and how we may, on occasion, lead them.

*The relation requires a thoughtfulness of how maturity comes to the child.* To the extent that the playground is a refuge for children, we need to consider our actions with children on playgrounds against an understanding of a more general and prevailing atmosphere of risk. This atmosphere is affected by the sense of security that the adult brings to the events of everyday life as they concern the child. The playground, in particular, can be made a secure place between the safety of the home and the riskiness of the outer world. On the playground we can be mindful of the atmosphere of risk by supporting, guiding, instructing the child, and evaluating his or her efforts. But we can be tuly mindful in bringing a sense of security to the child's explorations when we challenge the child to take risks and when we find within the terms of such challenges an opportunity to experience the riskiness of the playground alongside the child.

By thinking about how maturity comes to the child, our interventions carry significance beyond the immediate situation in which we find ourselves with children. What we do with children, how we challenge them and encounter the playground with them, has an effect on their sense of security not just when they are on the playground but also when they move into the world beyond the playground. In fact, the relation we establish on the playground brings a certain clarity to our understanding of how we might generally help children become independent in a world which extends far beyond the security of the playground.

*The relation requires us to see and articulate challenges for the child.* We consider the terms of the dare and the level of common sense which a dare contains. Surely, we say, there can be more positive encouragement than this. The hard edge of the dare can be softened. Instead of being pressured into trying some risky activity, the present activity can be made inviting. Words can be offered which give the child courage. However the child will often attempt an activity without realizing what it holds. The child may then find some way out of going through with the action. Our words of encouragement should therefore acknowledge the somewhat varied paths that children take in coming to terms with a risky activity. And we should be cognizant of the limits to which a child can be challenged.

By seeing and articulating the challenges of the playground, we instill a measure of self-confidence in the child. The child learns to be responsible for his or her actions, and with this independence comes a knowledge of what he or she can and cannot do. Indeed, the child's increasing sense of maturity is contingent upon sensing the limits of challenge—the limits to which challenge can be responded to, the limits to which one can be challenged by another person, and thus the extent to which an action is something done through one's own initiative.

*The relation requires that we know when to leave the child alone.* We become fearful for the child, apprehensive about what is being attempted, yet our fearfulness is, more positively, a way of becoming mindful of what the child can do. Similarly, we sense danger, and yet other than the hazards of being on faulty equipment, danger signifies the point at which we do not wish to be concerned any more about the child's explorations. More important than a sense of danger is the grasp we have of children's activity and the confidence we have in letting them do something for themselves.

By knowing when to leave the child alone, we give the child a sense of self-direction. Although the direction of the child's activity has already been outlined in terms of our earlier responses to what we see happening, there comes a time for the child to feel in charge of the direction of his or her activity. The child needs to move beyond the sphere of direct adult influence and to feel increasingly responsible for his or her own actions.

*The relation requires us to be in practice with the child.* We look at the tricks which the child shows us. We also see the repetitive nature of much of the child's playground activity. Out of this interplay of novelty and repetition we can formulate a notion of practice which shows the stake we have in the child's playground activity. Practice, we say, makes perfect. Practice defines those actions which disclose the direction of their own perfection. This notion of practice brings us in touch with the course of a child's activity, because it implies our being or staying in practice, enjoying a spirit of practice with the child, and acting on the child's behalf with a wisdom borne of our experiences of those activities which the child presently undertakes.

By being in practice with the child, we lead the child to movement competence. We bring the child to attend to the demands of playground activity and to the specific action requirements which extend this activity in what are normally called directions of skill development. There are, for example, the actions of hanging, swinging, jumping, diving, sliding, climbing, and balancing which can be perfected, although such actions are, as we have seen, already imbedded in the riskiness of the playground. By being in practice with the child and thus attending to the riskiness of the playground, we do better in inculcating such movement competencies than were we to see them as discrete actions that can simply be extracted from the playground context. We take "great care [that] the process of developing confidence and competence [does not become] secondary to the production of certain outcomes, largely assessed in terms of skilled performance" (Boorman, 1987, p. 237). The movement competence we want for the child is, after all, a physical confidence in the world rather than a technical confidence in what the body can do.[2]

*The relation requires us to follow the child in risk-taking activities beyond the playground.* The extension of the child's activities from the playground to the playing field and then farther afield carries with it a consideration of the more physical dimensions of childhood experience. In fact, the riskiness of the playground serves as a point of reference for those physical practices that go far beyond the playground. The situations of risk-taking which we have observed and described in this study provide "paradigmatic examples" (Bollnow, 1987, p. 144, 145) for the much broader domain of physical risk-taking. They can even be regarded as situations of "exemplary learning" (Flitner, 1972) for those cultural forms, namely games, sports, and physical recreations, which extend this physicality in particular sorts of ways.

## Practical Ways of Being

We started this study with a formulation of risk as a term of our pedagogical relation to children and left open the decision as to whether risk was the relation itself. By following children on playgrounds we see the extent to which risk characterizes our relation to children and that it is more than just a single term of our pedagogical relation to them. Being fully aware of, and responsive to, risk in children's lives suggests requirements and preconditions of the relation which have to do with "trust," "patience," "hope," "care," "love," "serenity," "humor" and "goodness" (cf. Bollnow, 1961, 1970/1989, 1979; Noddings, 1984, 1992; Spranger, 1971; Vandenberg, 1975). A comprehensive analysis of the pedagogical relation would require paying further attention to these "affective presuppositions of education" (Vandenberg, 1975, p. 36), including their corollaries of "gratitude," "adoration," "obedience," "expectation," "morningness" and "cheerfulness" which apply particularly to the child's situation. In this undertaking we could go back to Pestalozzi who was the first educator to trace out "how the seeds of love, confidence, gratitude, brotherly feeling, patience, obedience, and sense of duty develop in the child's mind and heart through the tender care of his mother and by family intercourse" (Downs, 1975, p. 82).

The present study is certainly not the final pedagogical statement on the affectivity of educating children. But, defining risk as the term of our pedagogical relation to children, showing how an atmosphere of risk is mediated by the ministrations of an observant and responsive adult, and describing how such ministrations enhance a child's confidence and competence, makes a bolder statement about pedagogical relationality than much theory that affectively characterizes the education of children.

*Risk is essential to being with children.* Risk is the essence of the pedagogical relation because it is in the first instance the distinctive feature of children's experiences. And children's experiences are inherently risky, not because they are anxiety provoking for us, but because it is of the very nature of experience to become apprehensive, uncertain, fearful, afraid, or alternatively, confident, controlled, adventurous, strong, and daring. We could say that "every experience has something about it of an adventure," something that "lets life become felt as a whole, in its breadth and in its strength" by venturing beyond the familiar margins of existence (Gadamer, 1975, p. 62).[3] Rather than seeing risk merely in terms of the fears, doubts, and threats that lie on "dark side of the child's world" and about which an adult knows enough to comfort or, at the very least, warn the child, our analysis shows risky experience to be the summons to pedagogical relatedness (*contra* Bollnow, 1989, p. 10).

The existential reality of risk for children is understood pedagogically as a "solicitude" (Heidegger, 1962) characterized by becoming apprehensive about children's activity and trying to encounter its riskiness with them. Being indifferent to the predicaments of children, simply passing them by, is the deficient form of "solicitude" that potentially puts children at-risk. The positive response, on the other hand, is initially, an anxious concern where one is inclined to take away the concerns of children by ensuring their safety. But this "solicitude" gives way to a more authentic response where one is with children, leaping ahead of them to where their movements might take them, in order to leave them be for the moment. Being in practice with children, one does not take away the cares of children, but is kind, loving, considerate, patient, forbearing, trusting and hopeful in letting children take prudent risks (cf. pp. 157–59).

*Risk is essential to growing up.* Risk as a defining feature of children's experience is not to be explained away in terms of prior causes (although there are a variety of scientific explanations that can be made of risky behavior). Risk is better understood teleologically as an intention that prefigures activity and the course it takes. Taking risks and being challenged to take risks lead, as we have seen, to ends such as self-direction, self-confidence, movement competence, and proficiency. These outcomes, these bodily learnings, accrue demonstrably from games, sports, and physical recreations that extend the domain of the playground. They serve to "enlarge one's lived space, thus increasing its mobility and one's willingness to undertake new activities with positive feelings regarding the probability of success" (Vandenberg, 1988, p. 70).

What defines these ends as educational goals and purposes is our adult validation of them as necessary for children's maturation. We cast them in terms of established attributes of maturity like "expertise, efficiency, autonomy, and so on, which allow us then to categorize children's risk-taking experiences more generally in terms of developmental stages of cognitive, psycho-social and motor-skill maturation.[4] But these categorical ends and means refer, in the first instance, to the experiential meaning of coming to terms with living in a risky world.

*Risk is essential to becoming at home in the world.* Egan (1988) points out that the hoped-for ideal for children is that they have "a sense of being at home in the world, experiencing a oneness, an immersion and participation that absolutely takes the world for granted, about which there may be endless questions but no doubts" (p. 87). This is a wonderful ideal, except for the fact that taking the world for granted can only be a transitory experience. There is a fundamental anxiety, giving rise on occasion to fearfulness, that characterizes living in a world that can all of a sudden become unfamiliar. Being "not-at-home" is indeed the "more primordial phenomenon" (Heidegger, 1962, p. 234). What distinguishes childhood is not that children should have a sense of being at home in the world but that this is a time when they first become aware of the ongoing project of "becoming at home in the world" (cf. Vandenberg, 1971, p. 21). They learn that becoming physically at home in the world is a temporary achievement reached through being curious, inquisitive, adventurous, and exploration-minded, by continually risking, in other words, the security of that which is physically familiar and comfortable.

Vandenberg (1990) writes of the ever-expanding sense of the world that comes through the exploration of things that lie at hand.

> To become at home in an advanced industrial society [a risk society],
> children and youth ought to explore fabricated things, playthings, nat-
> ural things, human things, and societal things. The exploration should
> be both perceptual and conceptual to include both the things and the
> previous disclosures of their characteristics to older people. To make
> these previous disclosures available requires the exploration of writ-
> ten things and quantified things. The regions that should be explored to
> become at home in the world therefore include the tactile, manipulable
> world; the play world; nature; society; the lived world; and the world of
> books and numbers. Their curriculum corollaries are the arts, crafts,
> and trades; sports and the dance; the natural sciences; the social sci-
> ences; the humanities; reading; and mathematics. (pp. 200, 201)

Vandenberg insists that it is the "exploration of the things in the manipulable and play worlds [that] is chronologically and phenomenologically prior to any conceptualized exploration of things in the natural and social worlds" (p. 201). This is because the feeling of becoming at home on the playground, by learning new tricks through repetition and practice, is a bodily register of the world's riskiness. Becoming physically at home in the risky domain of the playground is the formative and decisive step towards becoming at home in risky places beyond the playground, even in those places which Barell (1980) has termed the "playgrounds of our minds."

## Conclusion

Redefining risk as a term of our pedagogical relation to children has moved us beyond explanatory theories of risk into the experiential realm of risk-taking. And here, with reference to the playground, matters of meaning and significance have been foregrounded.

Maturity has been the term used to organize these matters—a maturity that prefigures our pedagogical relation to children, that constitutes the difference between our experiences and children's experiences of risk, that comes to bear upon children's activities and makes sense of them, that allows us to follow children's activities and influence them in ways children are only beginning to understand, and that highlights the meaning of children's activity for their growth and development. This sense of maturity has provided practical insight into a deliberate manner of bringing up children. It has provided an answer to the instructional question of how we should teach children to become responsible adults as well as an answer to the curriculum questions of why such an education is important and what it might comprise.

But for sheer practicality of insight we need to question the presuppositions of maturity that establish in advance the course of children's activities and the thoughtfulness of the responses we choose to make. Risk and our pedagogical relation to children is primarily a study of the shifting and sometimes ambiguous meaning of a maturity that can never be the sole property of an adult who remains interested in the things of childhood. Children risk the security of the playground in order to explore more mature activities, however adults never really leave this place of risk. We return there in silence, unsure at times what to do, but knowing that our presence makes a difference to children's explorations. We are conscious of the atmosphere of risk and how certain responses can make children feel secure in their activity. Daring, encouraging, and challenging children, we encounter risky situations with them. Why? So we can be most helpful by remaining in practice with what they are attempting to do and, in so doing, open up possibilities for a sustained practice of living with children. Risk is essential to being with children, to growing up with them, and to becoming at home in a world where their presence helps us appreciate those risks worth taking. Risk is essential to a maturity that unfolds in the course of living with children.

Froebel's motto was "Come let us live with our children" (Downs, 1975, p. 113). I suggest that we take up this motto, reminded of a risky world where many children are at-risk, or unnecessarily exposed to danger, and where all children need to learn how to take risks that enrich their lives. I suggest we take up this motto conscious of how risk is the term of our relation to children and the very idea of living meaningfully with them. So come, let us take risks, with our children.

# Notes

## 1. Introduction

1. We cannot actually understand children "on their own terms." We can only do so in a manner of speaking, since children are *essentially* in need of adult assistance and indeed are children only if they stand in a some dependent relation to responsible adulthood. All of which ought not to diminish the significance of the playground, but rather, to show that the playground, if we consider it as a place where the effort can be made to understand children "on their own terms," is a very important pedagogical place.

2. It is the decision to take a risk that brings the magnitude of that risk into relief and that, in fact, constitutes the risk itself. Merleau-Ponty (1962) used the example of the "unclimable rock face" which means nothing to someone who does not intend to climb it and who thereby fails to see it as inherently risky (p. 436). Through this example he showed that attributing "unclimability" to the rock face which, were one to try climbing it would present very real danger, is only possible by approaching the rock face with the intention of climbing it. "It is, therefore, freedom, which brings into being the obstacles to freedom, so that the latter can be set over against it as its bounds" (p. 439). By the same token, freedom of choice, which includes taking a risk, remains conditional upon the capacity of certain things and events to solicit choice. I do not absolutely choose to take a risk because I am already caught in a risky world that makes certain things and events more challenging than others. "We choose our world and the world chooses us" (p. 454).

3. See Trimpop (1994) for an extended review of the diverse theoretical explanations of risk-taking behavior.

4. It is not my intention to blur necessary distinctions between teaching and parenting since the demands made on a teacher of twenty to thirty young children are quite different than the demands made by one or more children on a parent. But these respective demands, insofar as they arise from interacting directly with children, are not sufficient to distinguish pedagogically between teaching and parenting. What primarily makes the difference comes from another quarter altogether—from the political, institutional, and administrative

framing of teaching, and from the culturally-framed actions of women and men, adopting the roles of fathers and mothers, that preclude the kind of awareness and responsiveness to risk that is described in this study. Teaching is then geared to a "rationalized sphere of pedagogy" which relegates the informal life of pedagogical relationality to the margins of curriculum life (van Manen, 1992, pp. 181–83). (Hence the informality of the playground qualifies it as being an extracurricular rather than a primary curriculum site.) This technological framing of teaching is modified somewhat by the call for "individualized instruction," "integration," and "mainstreaming" of special needs children, more "open" education, "developmentally appropriate practice," and so on, where the focus shifts back to the child. But it is challenged mostly behind closed classroom doors by teachers who get to know the children with whom they work and who make their pedagogy co-extensive with being a "significant other" in these children's lives (e.g. Paley, 1981 and subsequent books; Sinclaire, 1994). It is the latter view of teaching which has much in common with the sensitivities of women and men who are in their best parenting moments animated by a sense of the well-being of their children. Here we could look back to Pestalozzi, Froebel, and Herbart whose educational systems developed out of a sense of pedagogical relatedness in the home or as a result of teaching and tutoring students with whom they lived. But we could also look to those who have seen the dangers of pedagogical systematizing and who choose instead to draw out the lived meanings of pedagogy as they are to be understood in the particular encounters one might conceivably have with particular children (e.g. Adan, 1991). To the extent that pedagogy is a theory addressed to individual children, it is a refined way of seeing children that is confined neither to schooling and the institutionalized practices of teachers nor to the home and the nurturing actions of parents. I maintain and attempt to show in this study that the most practical pedagogical theory is that which we derive in becoming aware and responsive to risk in the lives of particular children who may be our own but could also be our children's friends, our friends' children, and the children other parents entrust to us for their extended upbringing.

5. The playground observations that form the basis of this study were made over a three year period. During this time I had unlimited access to the internal playgrounds of a large university residential community in western Canada that was, even for young children, within easy walking distance of two community playgrounds attached to elementary schools. The children I observed hailed from places across North America as well as from Mexico, Columbia, Japan, Australia, Korea, Northern Ireland, Trinidad, South Africa, and Great Britain.

6. That boys are greater risk-takers than girls, being more inclined to embrace challenge, seek out risks, and respond more calmly to dangers, is a belief that continues to have "popular" support (e.g. Segell, 1996). There is also increasing "popular" support for encouraging girls to become equally-active risk-takers as boys (e.g., Ryan and Stock, 1996). Given such support, it would seem that much of the difference between the risk-taking behaviors of boys and girls is a consequence of the limited access to, and encouragement of, girls in

those activities which have traditionally highlighted the risk-taking propensities of boys.

7. There remains a potentially gendered aspect of playground interaction, a "rite of manhood," that bears upon the experiences of risk-taking addressed in this study. For example, Keen (1991) describes a situation involving two boys, four and six years of age, who are playing on a rope swing in their backyard. All is well until the older boy takes possession of the swing and refuses the younger one his turn. Undeterred, the little boy insists on his turn. He takes hold of the rope and is summarily told to "bug off!" He is knocked to the ground. Then, getting to his feet and trying his best not to cry, he tells the older boy: "That didn't hurt" (p. 41). Such bravado in the face of aggression is evident in those more subtle interactions where a child is dared with malicious intent to take a risk. It is also evident, to some degree, in the responses of many children to the hurts that occur in the course of engaging in risky activity. This bravado becomes a gendered construction of children's experiences when different expectations of resilience apply to boys and girls and when a risk-taking machismo on the part of boys is expressly commended through adult praise and encouragement, or when it is foisted on the sensitive, cautious child through adult reproof of the child's timidity. We shall have to exercise care in this study that we do not unwittingly support this gendered construction of children's risk taking experiences.

8. Collateral support for writing anecdotally about our relation to children, specifically in risky situations, comes from a suggestion made by Earle and Cvetkovick (1994) that "risk communication" be "shaken up. . . . The era of the domination of risk communication by techno-rationalism is over. Enter narrative. Enter literature. Enter poets and artists, talking about new, better worlds that we can't now imagine. We suggest they be welcomed" (p. 176).

9. The phenomenological notion of the lifeworld, referring to that which is prior to and constitutive of all our experiences of the world, is first articulated by Husserl (1970). But it was Schutz (Schutz and Luckmann, 1973) who developed what came to be known as lifeworld phenomenology. The turn towards existential phenomenology that we find in the work of Heidegger (1962) is also prompted by an acknowledgement of the primacy of the lifeworld, such that "being-in-the-world" is recognized as the facticity, certainty, and condition for one's experience of any particular things in the world. Worldliness and relationality are seen to be the ontological grounds against which things stand out. Merleau-Ponty, however, brought the body to the fore in lifeworld phenomenology in the process of articulating his thesis that "the perceived world is the always presupposed foundation of all rationality, all value and all existence" (Merleau-Ponty, 1964, p. 13). His phenomenology of perception is grounded in an interrogation of incarnate subjectivity—in the bodily-experienced relations that configue one's manner of being at home in the world.

10. This study has primarily to do with the experiential realm of risk-taking. In continually referring to children's and adult's experiences of risk, I draw upon a "phenomenological concept of experience [which] is expressly distinguished from the popular one" (Gadamer, 1975, p. 59). This concept of experi-

ence refers to that "unit of consciousness" which is not merely a duration in the passage of life, but rather, is essentially an "intentional relation" characterized, on the one hand, by "a definite immediacy which eludes every opinion about its meaning," and on the other hand, as "something unforgettable and irreplaceable that is inexhaustible in terms of the understanding and determination of its meaning" (pp. 59, 60). The ambiguity between immediate and inexhaustible meaning is resolvable in terms of the relationship of experience to life. Life is represented "in the experience of the moment" (p. 62). Its meaning is an experienced one. I quote Gadamer at length on this important point: "Every experience is taken out of the continuity of life and at the same time related to the whole of one's life. It is not simply that it remains a living experience only until it is fully integrated into the context of one's life-consciousness, but the very way in which it is 'preserved' through its being worked into the whole of life-consciousness, goes far beyond any 'significance' it might be thought to have. Because it is itself within the whole of life, in it too the whole of life is present" (p. 62). Lived experience, as intentional, finds a place within the "teleological structure of consciousness" (p. 60), for what is presupposed in that experience is that it will become meaningful and memorable.

## 2. An Awareness of Risk

1. Huizinga (1950) made a similar etymological claim regarding the common meaning of play and risk (p. 39).

2. It may even be argued that the history of play theorizing, as it is reflected for example in the works of Schiller, Groos, Huizinga, Caillois, even Nietzsche, Gadamer, Fink, and Derrida, bears out Heraclitus' famous fragment 52, that "Time (or lifetime: *aion*) is a child playing, playing at draughts. Kingship belongs to the child." See Hyland, 1984, p. 83.

3. See Sutton-Smith and Kelly-Byrne, 1984b, and Sutton-Smith, 1987, on the "idealization of play," the legitimation of a distinction between child play and adult play, and hence, the denial of adult-child interaction within play.

4. To be sure, we can follow his line of thinking and serve similar notice on other public attempts to ensure the safety of children. Bicycle helmet legislation, for instance, is based upon extensive research indicating the mitigating effects of this piece of safety equipment on the severity of head injuries (reducing serious head injuries by more than 70 percent, according to Laudan, 1994, p. 54). Yet, similar to Wood's indictment of playgrounds, it can reasonably be suggested that this concern for safety, particularly the bicycling safety of children, is a way of not being more practically concerned about the welfare of children on the road. Simply legislating mandatory helmet-wearing precludes thinking about how roads can be designed as far more inclusive and child-friendly, public spaces.

5. Unfortunately the expressed concern for safety does not result necessarily in structurally safe playgrounds. A major conclusion drawn from a survey

of playground equipment in 206 elementary schools throughout the United States of America was that, due to design problems and maintenance neglect, "the safety of our children is in jeopardy each time they play on the playgrounds of our schools" (Bruya and Langerdorfer, 1988, p. 196).

6. Friedan (1996) draws attention to a recent shift in public concern for children. Set against an "identity politics" which asserts rights on the basis of "narrowly defined grievance and goals," she discerns the emergence of a more inclusive, inter-generational, political paradigm. "In seminars and schools, in community centers and union halls, in churches and the offices of public-spirited businesses, a new paradigm has been quietly taking shape. Perhaps its strongest unifying theme is a concern for children, who represent not only the greatest vulnerabilities of our institutions but also the future of those institutions" (p. 6).

7. Grumet (1988) makes the very reasonable point that caring for other people's children is a matter of doing things with them rather than simply having some general sense of responsibility for them. "When I have typed the story that your child reads or have tied his shoe or found his scarf, when you have told my child a story of your own or have helped her catch the bus, other people's children become our children" (p. 179). Such contact with a child holds the promise of caring for that child in the manner of his or her parents. It enjoins our experience with theirs and enlarges the sphere of pedagogical influence.

8. See Smith, 1957, and Sutton-Smith, 1950, for equally nostalgic though more tellingly real accounts of "play" activity that occurred outside adult control and, we are led to believe, outside the realm of adult interest. See also the listings in the Edith McKeever Cobb collection (Cobb, 1977, pp. 119–36).

9. Metsuru (1992), a playground designer, refers to the "safety cage " that we have constructed for children. "Preschools, schools, and parks are all pervaded by this insistence on safety, and utmost care is taken to ensure that the children are not exposed to the slightest danger, but children must learn to avoid great danger by being exposed to small dangers" (p. 4).

10. To this initiative can be added the variety of violence-prevention programs being implemented in schools which give instruction in such matters as empathy skills, anger management, conflict resolution, peer mediation, and bullyproofing. Many of these programs arise from a concern for youth violence, however some programs like *Second Step* (which was developed by Seattle's non-profit Committee for Children and has been widely accepted in school districts with which I am acquainted) target elementary children. Here children learn to become attentive to the expressions of other children, to rehearse nonviolent responses to the actions of others, and to become increasingly aware of, and responsible for, the consequences of their own actions.

11. Empathic understanding from the vantage point of the park bench is wonderfully described in the Japanese children's story *The Park Bench* (Takeshita, 1988) where the bench itself seems responsive to the events that happen over the course of a day.

12. See Peter Petersen's definition of an "educational situation" and its moral prerequisites (Dietrich, 1987).

# 3. The Silence of Risk

1. This detachment contrasts with the more visible and at times active presence of Thorne (1993) and Opie (1994) in their observational studies of children's playground interactions. It contrasts even more dramatically with Diana Kelly-Bryne's (1989) year-long ethnographic study in which she interpreted the "play" of a seven-year-old child as the term of her relationship to that child. As a co-participant in the construction of Helen's play world, Kelly-Bryne acknowledged, methodologically and thematically, her part in making sense of, and giving sense to, the child's experience. Whether she, Opie or Thorne fully acknowledged their pedagogical responsibility, however, is a question that might be answered indirectly by the present analysis of risk and our pedagogical relation to children.

2. Cf. situation/site: from *situs*, derivative of Indo-European base se(i) meaning "to leave off," whence also the Latin *silere*, meaning "to be silent" (Klein, 1971, p. 687).

3. Although it has become popular to speak of the "inner child" (e.g., Bradshaw, 1992), Beekman's words are more akin to the "poetics of space" in which Bachelard (1960) wrote: "Our whole childhood remains to be imagined" (p. 100). Beekman's empathy for John is not as one child (albeit an "inner" one) to another; it is as an adult who feels the resonances of the child's activity and thereby imagines what it is like to be a child playing hide-and-seek. Beekman puts the events of his life to "creative use" (See Bettelheim, 1987, especially pp. 14, 25, 25, 44, 45).

4. I have taken pains to avoid casting the present study in more conventional methodological terminology which would distinguish the ways of the researcher from those of the parent, teacher, or child care-giver. At the same time, I still want to claim a "method" of inquiring into the conditions of children's lives to understand how their lives can be pedagogically construed. A phenomenology of childhood, our inquiry stands in opposition to psychologies of childhood "whose present images of childhood are so intertwined with adult visions of development and self-actualization needs that the landscape of childhood is left barren by excessive psychologizing" (Polakow, 1982, p. 15). It differs, as we have seen, from an anthropology of childhood which would epistemologically categorize the experiences of children in terms related more to the context of action than to its experienced structure. It even differs from a hermeneutics of childhood which would appropriate the experiences of children within an expanded adult self-understanding where "Childhood is in me a form of knowledge" (Kennedy, 1992, p. 48). We have seen there is a memorable reflexivity to addressing the experiences of children that recognizes "the mutual necessity of the terms 'adult' and 'child'" (p. 48), however there is an otherness,

an alterity (Levinas, 1969) to the child's experience, that maintains a difference (a silence) between adult and child that ultimately makes a difference. A phenomenology of childhood signals a move from epistemological to ontological research—from knowing about children through viewing their actions from above, to understanding one's relation to children, and its limits, by becoming mindfully engaged in their activities. What distinguishes the present study, as a phenomenology of childhood, is the attentiveness to a certain manner of being in the world, as a parent, teacher, or child care-giver, who is aware of and responsive to risk. Pedagogical "intentionality" is understood by means of a comprehending silence, a phenomenologically quiet "comprehension" (cf. Merleau-Ponty, 1962, p. xviii), of what it might mean to observe the riskiness of children's lives at close quarters.

## 4. The Atmosphere of Risk

1. Bowlby (1969; 1973; 1980) and subsequent researchers (e.g., Ainsworth, Mahler, and Winnicott) have shown how a sense of security can be cultivated. Two main sets of influences contribute to a child's sense of security, namely, the influence of a trustworthy person who can "provide the kind of secure base required at each phase of the life-cycle," and the capacity of another individual to respond in a trusting manner and "to collaborate with that person in such a way that a mutually rewarding relationship is initiated and maintained" (Bowlby, 1979, p. 104). But the pedagogical question of the security of the child's world takes us beyond attachment theory. First, although it requires us to consider the need for attachment to one or more specially loved adults, it stresses the responsibility adults share for ensuring the conditions of children's security. Second, it is a pedagogical question about how things ought to be for children, rather than a psychological question of why things are as they seem to be for many children. And third, the issue of the security of the child's world has not only to do with the trust, confidence, and self-reliance exhibited in adult-child interactions, but also with the grounds for being able to respond to children. In other words, it requires attentiveness to the conditions that give rise to a child's sense of security in particular risky situations. A fourth consideration, which is only touched upon in this study, is that the question of security requires attention to those "wild places" in the world where children can and should learn to be at home. The attachment that children need is not only for their own preservation but also for the preservation of the earth. See Nabhan and Trimble (1994) for an excellent account of how "a sense of wildness" can be encouraged in children.

2. I do not mean to trivialize the disturbing riskiness to the lives of many children. The daily reports of neglect and abuse compel us to seek public, legislative reponses to alleviate the tragic circumstances of at-risk, high-risk children and to ensure their right to protected and secure childhoods. (See Jensen and Goffin, 1993, for an extensive coverage of children's rights and entitlements.) My address is to those who work and live with children, who care on a

daily basis for them, and whose actions show me that a public responsiveness to the plight of children at large is best cultivated through the care shown for particular children in one's everyday dealings with them. Noddings (1984) writes of the "concentric circles of caring" (p. 46) that characterize being receptive to the plight of others. Through one's everyday dealings with children one can learn to see the children of others as much like one's own. The strange child, the abandoned, homeless, "latch-key," "home alone," child is someone we can care about and someone we can care for to the extent that there are means at our disposal to be practically responsive to that child's immediate situation. Too often the vulnerability, neglect, and abuse of children becomes an occasion for public hand-wringing and political expediency. I suggest that it become a challenge for us to look at our own dealings with each child we encounter to ensure that we, too, in some small measure, are not guilty of contributing to the riskiness of that child's world. In contrast to the callous insensitivity of certain teachers to at-risk children (Polakow, 1993), I suggest looking to the sensitive, kind, loving, caring, thoughtful actions of parents and other educators for whom the riskiness of children's lives is a statement of fact as well as a call to action.

3. Thinking about Marc's sense of responsibility involves a rather tenuous balance. "Responsibility," as the term implies, entails the "ability to respond," although mature responsibility is not just the recognition of risks and obligations that one takes upon oneself, but the ability to discriminate what risks and obligations are *appropriately* taken upon oneself. A pedagogy of responsibility and indeed of risk must have that "epistemic" component which would indicate what responsibilities are truly mine, what risks are genuinely worth taking.

4. See also van Manen's (1990) pedagogical analysis of various situations of children "being left" (pp. 79–90). The popularity amongst children of the recent *Home Alone* movies, where the child who is left behind plays havoc in an adult world, speaks directly to the riskiness that children experience when left to their own devices.

5. On this score it is worth remembering that the word "danger" actually derives from the late Latin "dominiarium" meaning dominion or rule (Shipley, 1959, p. 107), but with the sense of the power to dispose of, to hurt, and to harm. The earliest uses in English had the sense of "being in someone's danger," i.e., under their power or control, in their debt, etc. So what was "dangerous" in the danger was your being subject to the other's control. Not to perceive danger, or to be daring in the face of it, was to miss or confront this control.

## 5. The Challenge of Risk

1. One does not have to look too far to see the adolescent extensions of this approach to risk-taking. I read in the local newspaper of yet another car accident where the "Jaws of Life" are used to free the trapped and injured occupants. The incident occurs just after lunch outside a nearby high school where the teenagers were playing a game of "chicken" involving two cars being driven

at high speed head on. Then there is the fourteen-year-old girl whose joyride with a friend hanging on to a freight train turns sour as the train picks up speed and the pair begin to panick. She tries to jump free but is caught and dragged underneath the train. I think also of that "rite of passage" at a local tourist site where mostly teenagers, but sometimes young adults as well as some younger children, can be found diving from canyon cliffs into the rock pools below. The dangers of this activity are spelled out in the warning signs that surround the area and in the monuments placed on the trail in memory of those who have died. To these examples could be added many more that indicate what portends for those children who understand risk-taking along the narrow lines of physically daring and potentially dangerous activity.

2. Grumet (1988) indicates how the child's request to be watched is an effort to recapture "the look that has captured her . . . the look that constitutes her identity. . . . 'Look, look,' the child implores, begging the glance that will ratify her activity" (pp. 102, 103).

3. Keyes (1985) writes that: "No risk is avoided more often by taking even dangerous physical risks than that of looking foolish. In fact, much apparent 'risk taking' is little more than activity engaged in to head off the greater risk of losing face. In such case we're not *taking* the risk of physical injury so much as avoiding the risk of humiliation" (p. 168). The measure of one's responsivity may well be the child's willingness to try the action again rather than his or her one and only successful attempt.

# 6. The Encounter with Risk

1. The story of the child whose explorations are confined to the mobility of a horse and cart provides a more than passing analogy for how curriculum constructions rein in the experiences of children. Curriculum comes from the Latin "currere" meaning a course to be run with "curricle" designating a two-wheeled carriage (Onions, 1966). By turning our attention to the risky experiences of journeying alongside children we reconceive curriculum not so much as a course of learning defined in advance as it is an exploration of the essential meaning of tarrying in places like playgrounds. Following such a reconceptualization, the pedagogical method used in this study to make theoretical sense of our lived encounters with risk is akin to the curriculum reconceptualists' method of "currere" (cf. Pinar, 1975; Pinar et al., 1995, pp. 414–17, 518–25).

2. Bollnow (1972) has written of the "unpredictable," "fortuitous" nature of an encounter with another person, which he extended to the encounter with the work of another person and, by further extension, to the encounter with specific subject matter. But this fortuitousness and unpredictability is apparent "if," as he says, "we understand education in the usual sense as a matter of deliberate and planned influence" (p. 312). Alternatively, the encounter becomes "pedagogically important" and, let us say, anticipated, if we define the pedagogical relationship "in a much more complicated way" than the ways of being obviously helpful (cf.

p. 312). If, beyond the supportive, guiding, instructing, and evaluative responses we care to give, we try to understand the intention to challenge children by truly encountering risk with them, then pedagogical relationality will encompass matters of subjectivity that could be regarded as constitutive of subject matter. The practical terms of this "more complicated" definition of pedagogical relationality is the subject of the next section on the educational significance of risk where we will consider in particular those practices and possibilities of risk-taking that have instructional and curricular applicability.

# 7. The Practice of Risk

1. Elsewhere I have developed a phenomenological analysis of a more formally taught physical activity (Smith, 1997). This analysis, which focuses upon the olympic gymnastic movements a child is learning to perform on a balance beam, provides a more philosophical account of the embodiment of pedagogical relationality than the present study. Common terms of reference are the "tricks," "repetitions," and "practices" which can be discerned in both informal and formal movement settings. But, whereas these terms refer in the case of gymnastics to a particular curricular domain, the present consideration of less formal playground events allows us to define a practice of risk and suggest possibilities of risk-taking that are not confined to a realm of movement experience where physical risk-taking is so clearly circumscribed.

2. See Carr (1981) on the distinction between "ability" and "know-how" in physical performance.

3. Gardner (1983) would define this physical thoughtfulness as a "bodily-kinesthetic intelligence" characterized both by "the ability to use one's body in highly differentiated and skilled ways, for expressive as well as goal directed purposes" and "the capacity to work skillfully with objects, both those that involve the fine motor movements of one's fingers and hands and those that exploit gross motor movements of the body" (p. 206). But this definition rests too heavily on a perception of the "body as an object" (p. 235), which is the perception of the adult who stands at an emotional distance from the child and in so doing objectifies the child merely as some body.

4. More general support for the position I am taking against the exclusivity of "skill talk" comes from the work of Sutton-Smith (1995) who sees in the adaptive function of play a questionable emphasis on the discourse of "progress." He writes: "Maybe the function of play is quite different from the kinds of things we have been looking at, or perhaps we have been looking at the wrong kinds of function. Perhaps we need another kind of rhetoric for human beings and their play than the one that focuses always on some kind of skill—physical, cognitive, or emotional" (p. 282).

5. Although dating from the time of Pestalozzi, it was in the nineteen-forties and fifties when "the normative studies of children by Gesell at Yale took hold" that a developmentalist frame came strongly to the theoretical forefront

(Silin, 1988, p. 119). Because of the cognitivist emphasis in the sixties as a result of the popularity of Piaget's work on cognitive stage theory, a child development perspective became foundational to the education of young children (Goffin, 1994, p. 191). Erikson and Piaget both subscribed to the "epigenetic principle" laid down by Froebel, "which holds that just as certain organs of the body appear at specified times and allow the individual to perform life sustaining functions so, too, does the personality and intellect of an individual form through series of interrelated stages" (McNeill, 1995, p. 36).

6. A developmentalist perspective is not confined to the field of early childhood education. As a recent proponent of developmentalism points out: "A generation of research in genetic epistemology and developmental psychology by such people as Piaget, Kohlberg, Loevinger, and others now offers educators relatively clear blueprints of what people are like at various stages in their lives and what it is that stimulates their intellectual, moral, and personal-social growth" (Mosher, 1995, p. 4).

# 8. The Possibility of Risk

1. The difficulty in appreciating this expanded sense of the physicality of young children's experiences lies not only with the empirical distinctions drawn between individual and group activities and those that involve large movements versus those that are sedentary and involve, at most, only fine movements; it also has to do with the fact that "while early childhood educators have always paid attention to physical development and growth, [only] recent thinking has suggested the centrality of the body as a vehicle for learning" (Silin, 1988, p. 127). An expanded sense of physicality would acknowledge the bodily consciousness of children and the physically mimetic consciousness of adults interacting with children. Instead of restricting children's physicality to categorical observations of skills, techniques, and patterns of motor behavior, we should instead try to discern the expressive and communicative qualities of those bodily movements enacted before us.

2. Yerkes (1988) has called attention to the risk-taking qualities of children's playground activities and has argued that "the ever present playground of nursery schools and day care centers remains a potentially powerful but neglected educational tool" (p. 22). Her claim seems to be that those who advocate "experiential education" and emphasize its risk-taking dimension (e.g. King, 1988) might well look to the playground activities of young children as providing a sound basis for curriculum development.

3. In the case of physical education programs, we can well understand the desire to formulate a "developmentally appropriate" pedagogy based upon analysis of how physical educators effectively motivate children to become practiced performers (cf. Graham, 1992), and we can appreciate attempts to mediate the developmentalist logic of motor skill acquisition through teacher sensitivity to the particular explorations of an individual child (e.g., Gallahue,

1993). But a recognition of risk as a feature of children's physical education obliges us to forge even stronger programmatic connections between children's and adult's experiences of activities that extend beyond, but do not fully surpass, the domain of the playground. Program designs, such as those of Hoffman et al. (1981) and Hellison (1995), with their respective emphases on themes and goals of psycho-social development, provide useful guides for reconceptualizing the subject matter of physical education; although the relationality of risk requires that even greater emphasis be given to the intersubjective constitution of meaningful, physical education subject matter.

## 9. Practical Insights

1. A more positive term than "paradox" for such an apparent contradiction is that of "antinomy." The pedagogical antinomy to which I refer has been extensively considered by representatives of the *Geisteswissenschaftliche Pädagogik* tradition. Beginning with Schleiermacher and Dilthey, the notion of "antinomy" and the antinomy of the uniqueness of the child and our responsibility for ensuring that the child acquires values we hold in common, even at the expense of his or her individuality, have been at the center of pedagogical thought (van Manen, 1987).

2. It is interesting to note that even in the positivistic studies of movement confidence on the playground (e.g., Butcher, 1988; Crawford and Griffin, 1986; Griffin and Keogh, 1982) it is admitted that: "A particularly important indicator [of movement confidence] might be the amount and kind of support an individual needs and seeks during participation" (Griffin and Keogh, 1982, p. 234). In other words, it is conceded that a relation to the world, which is first of all a relation to a trusted adult, might be the most important consideration for instilling in the child that sense of movement confidence which we see expressed in particular movement competencies.

3. The word "experience" contains the Indo-European root "per" which means "to try, "to test, or "to risk." Hence in modern English we have the word "perilous." "Per" is found also in the Latin "experimentum" and in the more recent coinage, "experiment," which refer to a "trial" or a "test." Related meanings of "per" refer to motion: "to cross space," "to reach a goal," or "to go out." Experience thus takes on the features of an ordeal and refers to a duration of activity that provides a measure of one's character (Onions, 1966).

4. I have been especially critical of the "skill talk" in education and of that "developmentalist" thinking that keeps children at a distance and prevents us from seeing how their risky, "physical" activities are meaningfully lived. My point is that these categorizations of children's experiences preclude a mode of physical presence wherein, say, Erikson's (1968) stages of "trust," "autonomy," "initiative," and "industry," would make pedagogical sense. Learning and development are not separable entities, and one does not necessarily follow the other. They are degrees of abstraction of an embodied sense of behaving well in

response to activities where we sense a degree of risk. Lived pedagogical relationality precedes talk of learning or development since what the child comes to
know and do is first of all determined by how we stand in relation to him or her.

# Bibliography

Aaron, David, and Bonnie P. Winawer. *Child's Play: A Creative Approach to Playspaces for Today's Children.* New York: Harper and Row, 1965.

Adams, John. *Risk.* London: University College of London Press, 1995.

Adan, Jane. *The Children in Our Lives: Knowing and Teaching Them.* Albany: State University of New York Press, 1991.

Anders, Günther. *Kindergeschichten,* 1902. Unpublished book, text taken from handwritten copy made by Eva Michaelis-Stern in Jerusalem and translated by Wilfred H. O. Schmidt.

Anderson, Walter. *The Greatest Risk of All.* Boston: Houghton Mifflin, 1988.

Aoki, Ted T. Address to members of the Canadian Association for Curriculum Studies. CACS/CSSE Conference, Montreal, May 28, 1985. Printed in *CSSE News* 13, no. 1 (January 1986): 3–5.

Aoki, Ted T., and Mohammed Shamsher. *Voices of Teaching.* Vancouver: British Columbia Teachers' Federation, 1991.

Appelbaum, Barbara. "Creating a Trusting Atmosphere in the Classroom." *Educational Theory* 45, no. 4 (1995): 443–52.

Aptekar, Lewis. *Street Children of Cali.* Durham, N.C.: Duke University Press, 1988.

Apter, Michael J. *The Dangerous Edge: The Psychology of Excitement.* New York: Free Press, 1992.

Aries, Philippe. *Centuries of Childhood.* New York: Vintage Books, 1962.

Aristotle. *Nicomachean Ethics.* Translated and edited by W. D. Ross. Oxford: Clarendon Press, 1925.

Azarov, Yuri. *A Book About Bringing Up Children.* Moscow: Progress, 1981.

Bachelard, Gaston. *The Poetics of Reverie.* Boston: Beacon Press, 1960.

Barell, John. *Playgrounds of Our Minds.* New York: Teachers College Press, 1980.

Barrett, William. *A Time of Need: Forms of Imagination in the Twentieth Century.* New York: Harper and Row, 1972.

Barritt, Loren, Ton Beekman, Hans Bleeker, and Karel Mulderij. *Researching Educational Practice*. Grand Forks: University of North Dakota Press, 1983.

―――. "The World Through Children's Eyes: Hide and Seek and Peekaboo." *Phenomenology and Pedagogy* 1, no. 2 (1983): 140–61.

Barrow, Robin. "Skill Talk." *Journal of Philosophy of Education* 15, no. 1 (1981): 87–96.

―――. *Understanding Skills: Thinking, Feeling, and Caring*. London, Ontario: Althouse Press, 1990.

Beck, Ulrich. "From Industrial Society to Risk Society: Questions of Survival, Social Structure and Ecological Enlightenment." *Theory, Culture and Society* 9 (1992): 97–123.

Beckworth, Jay, and Jeremy J. Hewes. *Build Your Own Playground: A Sourcebook of Play Sculptures*. Boston: Houghton Mifflin, 1974.

Beekman, Ton. "Human Science as a Dialogue With Children." *Phenomenology and Pedagogy* 1, no. 1 (1983): 36–44.

―――. "Stepping Inside: On Participant Experience and Bodily Presence in the Field." *Journal of Education* 168, no. 3 (1986): 39–45.

Begley, Marita. Risky Business. *Backpacker* 14, no. 3 (1986): 34–39.

Bengtsson, Arvid. *Adventure Playgrounds*. New York: Praeger, 1972.

Benjamin, Joe. *Grounds for Play*. London: Bedford Square Press, 1974.

Benjamin, Jonathan, Lin Li, Chavis Patterson, Benjamin D. Greenberg, Dennis L. Murphy, and Dean H. Hamer. "Population and Familiar Associations between D4 dopamine Receptor Gene and Measures of Novelty-Seeking." *Nature Genetics* 12, no. 1 (1996): 81–84.

Berk, Laura E., and Adam Winsler. *Scaffolding Children's Learning: Vygotsky and Early Childhood Education*. Washington, D.C.: National Association for the Education of Young Children, 1995.

Bettelheim, Bruno. *Dialogues With Mothers*. New York: Avon Books, 1962.

―――. *The Uses of Enchantment: The Meaning and Importance of Fairy Tales*. New York: Vintage Books, 1975.

―――. *A Good Enough Parent: A Book on Child-Rearing*. New York: Vintage Books, 1987.

Beugelsdijk, Fons, and Siebren Miedema. "The Connection Between Geisteswissenschaftliche and Critical Pedagogy: Eric Weniger as an Example." Unpublished manuscript, 1984.

Bledsoe, Jim. "The World of the Cave Kid: The Rightful Recognition of Children's Knowledge." *Interchange* 8, nos. 1–2 (1977–78): 119–27.

Boas, George. *The Cult of Childhood*. London: Warburg Institute, 1980.

Bollnow, Otto F. "The Meaning of Hope." *Universitas* 4, no. 3 (1961): 263–73.

———. *Crisis and New Beginning: Contributions to a Pedagogical Anthropology.* Pittsburgh, Pa.: Duquesne University Press, 1966/1987.

———. "Risk and Failure in Education." *Modern Philosophies of Education.* New York: Random House, 1971, pp. 520–35.

———. "Existentialism's Basic Ethical Position." *Contemporary European Ethics,* edited by Joseph J. Kockelmans. New York: Doubleday, 1972.

———. "Encounter and Education." Translated by Donald Vandenberg and Christiana M. Smith. *The Educational Forum* 36, no. 3 (1972): 303–12, 465–72.

———. "The Objectivity of the Humanities and the Essence of Truth." *Philosophy Today* 18, nos. 1/4 (1974): 3–18.

———. "Practice as the Human Way." *Education* 10 (1974): 61–75.

———. "On the Virtues of the Educator." *Education* 20 (1979): 69–79.

———. "On Silence—Findings of Philosophico-Pedagogical Anthropology." *Universitas* 24, no. 1 (1982): 41–47.

———. "On the Right Way to Practice at School and in Life: A Study in Educational Anthropology." *Universitas* 29 (1987): 61–75.

———. *Die Pädagogische Atmosphäre.* Heidelberg: Quelle und Mayer, 1970. Translated by Max van Manen, in *Phenomenology and Pedagogy* 7 (1989): 5–63.

Boone, Tommy. "Safety, Spotting, and Gymnastics are Synonymous." *The Physical Educator* 42, no. 1 (1985): 18–23.

Boorman, Pauline. "The Contributions of Physical Activity to Development in the Early Years." In Blenkin, Geva M., and A. V. Kelly (eds.), *Early Childhood Education: A Developmental Curriculum.* London: Paul Chapman, pp. 231–50.

Bowlby, John. *Attachment and Loss.* Vol. 1, *Attachment.* New York: Basic Books, 1969.

———. *Attachment and Loss.* Vol. 2, *Separation: Anxiety and Anger.* New York: Basic Books, 1973.

———. *The Making and Breaking of Affectional Bonds.* London: Tavistock, 1979.

———. *Attachment and Loss.* Vol. 3, *Loss: Sadness and Depression.* New York: Basic Books, 1980.

Bradshaw, John. *Homecoming: Reclaiming and Championing Your Inner Child.* New York: Bantam Books, 1992.

Bredekamp, Sue. *Developmentally Appropriate Practice in Early Childhood Programs Serving Children from Birth Through Age 8.* Washington, D.C.: National Association for the Education of Young Children, 1987.

Brett, Arlene, Robin C. Moore, and Eugene F. Provenzo. *The Complete Playground Book.* Syracuse, N.Y.: Syracuse University Press, 1993.

Bromiley, Philip, and Shawn P. Curley. "Individual Differences in Risk Taking." *Risk Taking Behavior*, edited by J. Frank Yates. New York: John Wiley and Sons, 1992, pp. 87–132.

Bruya, Lawrence D., and Stephen J. Langerdorfer. *Where Our Children Play: Elementary School Playground Equipment*. Reston, Va.: American Alliance for Health, Physical Education, Recreation and Dance, 1988.

Buckley, Helen E. *Michael is Brave*. New York: Lothrop, Lee and Shepard, 1971.

Butcher, Janice. "Development of a Playground Skills Test: Relationship With Perceived Confidence." Paper presented at the CAHPER/HPEC '88 conference, Edmonton, University of Alberta, 1988.

Buytendijk, Frederick J. J. "Philosophic Basis of Human Relations." *Philosophy Today* 2 (1958): 108–12.

Canada Safety Council. *Policies, Guidelines and Checklists for a School Safety Program*. Ottawa: Canada Safety Council, 1984.

Carr, David. "On Mastering a Skill." *Journal of Philosophy of Education* 15, no. 1 (1981): 87–96.

Casey, Edward S. *Remembering: A Phenomenological Study*. Bloomington: Indiana University Press, 1987.

Cataldi, Sue L. *Emotion, Depth, and Flesh: A Study of Sensitive Space*. Albany: State University of New York Press, 1993.

Chlad, Dorothy. *Playing on the Playground*. Chicago: Children's Press, 1987.

Cobb, Edith. *The Ecology of Imagination in Childhood*. New York: Columbia University Press, 1977.

Conaway, Judith. *Sometimes It Scares Me*. Milwaukee, Wis.: Raintree, 1977.

Corsaro, William A. "Entering the Child's World: Research Strategies for Field-Entry and Data Collection in a Preschool Setting." In *Ethnographic Approaches to Face-To-Face Interactions*, edited by J. Green and C. Wallat. Norwood, N.J.: Ablex, 1981, pp. 117–46.

Crawford, Michael E., and Norma S. Griffin. "Testing the Validity of the Griffin/Keogh Model for Movement Confidence by Analyzing Self-Report Playground Involvement Decisions of Elementary School Children." *Research Quarterly for Exercise and Sport* 57, no. 1 (1986): 8–15.

Crowe, Brenda. *Play Is a Feeling*. London: Allen and Unwin, 1983.

Csikszentmihalyi, Mihaly. *Flow: The Psychology of Optimal Experience*. New York: Harper and Row, 1990.

Curtis, H. S. *The Play Movement and its Significance*. Washington, D.C.: McGrath and National Recreation and Park Association, 1917/1977.

Danner, Helmut. *Methoden Geisteswissenschaftlicher Padagogik*. Munchen, Basil: E. Reinhardt, 1979.

Dauenhauer, B. P. *Silence: The Phenomenon and Its Ontological Significance*. Bloomington: Indiana University Press, 1980.

Davidson, Keay, and Katherine Seligman. "Bullies: A Problem Dismissed Too Lightly." *San Francisco Examiner*, reprinted in *The Edmonton Journal*, D6, August 23, 1987.

De Mause, Lloyd. *The History of Childhood*. New York: Psychohistory Press, 1974.

Denske, Ien. "Narrative Knowledge and Science I: On the Nature and Value of Narrative Knowledge." *Journal of Learning About Learning* 1, no. 1 (1988): 19–27.

Dewey, John. *The Child and the Curriculum*. Chicago: University of Chicago Press, 1902/1956.

———. *Interest and Effort in Education*. Carbondale and Edwardsville: Southern Illinois University Press, 1913/1975.

———. *Experience and Education*. New York: Macmillan, 1938/1963.

Dietrich, Theo. "Peter Petersen's Educational Philosophy and Its Importance for the Present." *Education* 36 (1987): 109–22.

Dold, Catherine. "What Makes a Woman an Adrenaline Junkie?" *Cosmopolitan* (April 1996): 222–25.

Dostoevsky, Fydor. *The Brothers Karamazov*. Kingswood, Surrey: Windmill Press, 1912.

Douglas, Mary. "Risk as a Forensic Resource." *Daedalus: Journal of the American Academy of Arts and Sciences* 119, no. 4 (1990): 1–16.

Douglas, Mary, and Aaron Wildavsky. *Risk and Culture: An Essay on the Selection of Technological and Environmental Dangers*. Berkeley: University of California Press, 1983.

Dowley, Edith M. "Cues for Observing Children's Behavior." *Childhood Education* 45, no. 9 (1969): 517–21.

Downs, Robert B. *Heinrich Pestalozzi: Father of Modern Pedagogy*. Boston: Twayne, 1975.

Dreikurs, Rudolf. *The Challenge of Child Training: A Parent's Guide*. New York: Hawthorn Books, 1972.

Earle, Timothy C., and George Cvetkovich. "Risk Communication: The Social Construction of Meaning and Trust." In *Future Risks and Risk Management*, edited by Berndt Brehmer and Nils-Eric Sahlin. Dordrecht: Kluwer Academic, 1994, pp. 141–81.

Ebstein, Richard P., Olga Norvick, Roberto Umansky, Beatrice Priel, Yamina Osher, Darren Blaine, Estelle R. Bennett, Lubov Nemanov, Miri Katz, and Robert H. Belmaker. "Dopamine D4 Receptor (D4DR) Exon III Polymorphism Association with Human Personality Trait of Novelty Seeking." *Nature Genetics* 12, no. 1 (1996): 78–80.

Egan, Kieran. *Primary Understanding: Education in Early Childhood*. New York: Routledge, 1988.

Eifermann, Rivka. "Children's Games, Observed and Experienced." In *The Psychoanalytic Study of the Child*, vol. 42, edited by Peter B. Nevbauer and Albert J. Solnit. New Haven, Conn.: Yale University Press, 1987, pp. 127–44.

Ellis, Michael J. *Why People Play.* Englewood Cliffs, N.J.: Prentice-Hall, 1973.

Erikson, Erik H. *Identity: Youth and Crisis.* New York: Norton, 1968.

Evans, John. *Children At Play: Life in the School Playground.* Geelong: Deakin University Press, 1989.

Finnan, Christine R. "The Ethnography of Children's Spontaneous Play." In *Doing the Ethnography of Schooling*, edited by George Spindler. New York: Holt, Rinehart and Winston, 1982, pp. 355–81.

Fishoff, Baruch, Stephen R. Watson, and Chris Hope. "Defining Risk." *Policy Sciences* 17 (1984): 123–39.

Flitner, Andreas. "Educational Science and Educational Practice." *Education* 25 (1982): 64–75.

Flitner, Wilhelm. "The Abundance of Subject Matter: Exemplary Learning, Concentration and Selection." Translated by Helmut Danner. In *The Principle of the Exemplary*, edited by B. Gerner. Darmstadt: Wissenschaftliche Buchgemeinschaft, 1972.

Friedan, Betty. "Children's Crusade: A Gathering Heralds a Shift Toward a New Paradigm." *The New Yorker* (June 3, 1996), pp. 5, 6.

Frost, Joe L. "The American Playground Movement." In *When Children Play*, proceedings of the International Conference on Play and Play Environments, edited by Joe L. Frost and Sylvia Sunderlin. Wheaton, Md.: Association for Childhood Education International, 1985, pp. 165–70.

Frost, Joe L. and B. L. Klein. *Children's Play and Playgrounds.* Boston: Allyn and Bacon, 1979.

Gadamer, Hans-Georg. *Truth and Method.* New York: Seabury Press, 1975.

———. "Culture and Words—From the Point of View of Philosophy." *Universitas* 24, no. 3 (1982): 91–118.

Gallahue, David. L. *Developmental Physical Education for Today's Children.* Dubuque, Iowa: William C. Brown, 1993.

Gardner, Howard. *Frames of Mind: The Theory of Multiple Intelligences.* New York: Basic Books, 1983.

Geertz, Clifford. *The Interpretation of Cultures.* New York: Basic Books, 1973.

Glasser, William. *Positive Addiction.* New York: Harper and Row, 1976.

Goffin, Stacie G. *Curriculum Models and Early Childhood Education: Appraising the Relationship.* New York: Macmillan College, 1994.

Gordon, Edmund W. "Culture and the Sciences of Pedagogy." *Teachers College Record* 97, no. 1 (1995): 32–46.

Graeber, Laurel. "What Scares Kids: An Age-by-Age Guide to Helping Kids Overcome Their Fears." *Parents* 71, no. 10 (1996): 49–52.

Graham, George. *Teaching Children Physical Education: Becoming a Master Teacher.* Champaign, Ill.: Human Kinetics, 1992.

Greer, Germaine. *Sex and Destiny.* New York: Harper and Row, 1984.

Griffin, Norma S., and Jack F. Keogh. "A Model of Movement Confidence." In *The Development of Movement Control and Co-ordination,* edited by J. A. Scott Kelso and Jane E. Clark. New York: John Wiley, 1982, pp. 213–36.

Grubb, W. Norton, and Marvin Lazerson. *Broken Promises: How Americans Fail Their Children.* New York: Basic Books, 1982.

Grumet, Madeleine R. *Bitter Milk.* Amherst, Mass.: University of Massachusetts Press, 1988.

Haberman, Martin. "What Knowledge Is of Most Worth to Teachers of Young Children?" *Early Child Development and Care* 38 (1988): 33–41.

Hart, Craig H., and Robert Sheehan. "Pre-schooler's Play Behavior: Effects of Traditional and Contemporary Playgrounds." *American Educational Research Journal* 23, no. 4 (1986): 668–78.

Hart, Roger. *Children's Experience of Place.* New York: Irvington, 1979.

Hart, W. A. "Against Skills." *Oxford Review of Education* 4, no. 2 (1978): 205–16.

Haywood, D. Geoffrey, Marilyn Rothenberg, and Robert Beasley. "Children's Play and Urban Playground Environments: A Comparison of Traditional, Contemporary, and Adventure Playground Types." *Environment and Behavior* 6, no. 2 (1974): 131–68.

Heidegger, Martin. *An Introduction to Metaphysics.* New Haven, Conn.: Yale University Press, 1959.

———. *Being and Time.* Oxford: Basil Blackwell, 1962.

Hellison, Don. *Teaching Responsibility Through Physical Activity.* Champaign, Ill.: Human Kinetics, 1995.

Herbart, Johann F. *The Science of Education, its General Principles Deduced from its Aim and the Aesthetic Revelation of the World.* Boston: D. C. Heath, 1806/1896.

Hildebrandt, Reiner. The Changes of Consciousness in the Didactics of Physical Education. *International Journal of Physical Education* 24, no. 3 (1987): 13–17.

Hill, Polly. "Toward the Perfect Play Experience." In *Innovation in Play Environments,* edited by Paul F. Wilkinson. New York: St. Martin's Press, 1980, pp. 23–33.

Hoffman, Hubert, Jane Young, and Stephen Klesius. *Meaningful Movement for Children.* Boston: Allyn Bacon, 1981.

Huizinga, Johann. *Homo Ludens: A Story of the Play Element in Culture.* Boston: Beacon Press, 1950.

Husserl, Edmund. *The Crisis of European Sciences and Transcendental Phenomenology: An Introduction to Phenomenological Philosophy.*

Translated by David Carr. Evanston, Ill.: Northwestern University Press, 1970.

Hyland, Drew A. *The Question of Play.* New York: University Press of America, 1984.

Jago, Leo. "Learning Through Experience," 1970. In *Adventure Playground Information Kit No. 2.* Children's Environments Advisory Service, 1979.

Jensen, Mary A., and Stacie G. Goffin. *Visions of Entitlement: The Care and Education of America's Children.* Albany: State University of New York Press, 1993.

Keen, Sam. *Fire in the Belly: On Being a Man.* New York: Bantam Books, 1991.

Kelly-Byrne, Diana. *A Child's Play Life: An Ethnographic Study.* New York: Teachers College Press, 1989.

Kennedy, David. "The Hermeneutics of Childhood." *Philosophy Today* (1992, spring): 44–58.

Keyes, Ralph. *Chancing It: Why We Take Risks.* Boston: Little, Brown, 1985.

King, Keith V. "The Role of Adventure in the Experiential Learning Process." *Journal of Experiential Education* 11, no. 2 (1988): 4–8.

Kirby, Andrew (ed.). *Nothing to Fear: Risks and Hazards in American Society.* Tucson: University of Arizona Press, 1990.

Kirchner, Glenn. *Physical Education for Elementary School Children.* 7th edition. Dubuque, Iowa: William C. Brown, 1988.

Klein, Ernest. *A Comprehensive Etymological Dictionary of the English Language.* Amsterdam: Elsevier, 1971.

Kluger, Jeffrey. "Risky Business." *Discover* 17, no. 5 (1996): 44–47.

Kneller, George F. "Establishing Education as an Autonomous Discipline." *American Educational Studies, News and Comment* 14 (1984): 5–10.

Konner, Melvin. *Childhood.* Boston: Little, Brown, 1991.

Krell, David F. "Towards an Ontology of Play: Eugen Fink's Notion of Spiel." *Research in Phenomenology* 2 (1972): 63–93.

Lady Allen of Hurtwood, Marjory. *Planning for Play.* Cambridge, Mass.: MIT Press, 1968.

Langeveld, Martinus J. "Disintegration and Reintegration of Pedagogy." *International Review of Education* 4 (1958): 51–64.

———. "Some Recent Developments in Philosophy of Education in Europe." In *Philosophy and Education,* proceedings of the International Seminar, Ontario Institute for Studies in Education. Toronto: OISE Monograph No. 3 (1966): 81–114.

———. "Personal Help For Children Growing Up." W. B. Curry Lecture, University of Exeter, 1975.

———. "The Stillness of the Secret Place." *Phenomenology and Pedagogy* 1, no. 1 (1983): 11–17.

Laudan, Larry. *The Book of Risks: Fascinating Facts About the Chances We Take Every Day.* New York: John Wiley, 1994.

Lawrence, David H. *Sons and Lovers.* Middlesex: Penguin Books, 1913/1981.

Lee, John A. "Three Paradigms of Childhood." *Canadian Review of Sociology and Anthropology* 19, no. 4 (1982): 591–607.

Lever, Janet. "Sex Differences in the Games Children Play." *Social Problems* 23 (1976): 478–87.

Levinas, Emmanuel. *Totality and Infinity: An Essay on Exteriority.* Pittsburgh, Pa.: Duquesne University Press, 1969.

Lindsay, Peter L. "The Physical Characteristics of Playground Games in Public Schools in Edmonton." *CAHPER Journal* 51, no. 2 (1984): 8–11.

Linschoten, Hans. *On the Way Toward a Phenomenological Psychology: The Psychology of William James.* Pittsburgh, Pa.: Duquesne University Press, 1968.

Lippitz, Wilfred. "Understanding Children, Communicating With Children: Approaches to the Child Within Us, Before Us, and With Us." *Phenomenology and Pedagogy* 4, no. 3 (1986): 56–65.

Lowenfeld, Margaret. *Play in Childhood.* Portway, Bath: Cedric Chivers, 1969.

MacCrimmon, Kenneth R., and Donald Wehrung. *Taking Risks: The Management of Uncertainty.* New York: Free Press, 1985.

Mairs, Nancy. *Remembering the Bone House: An Erotics of Place and Space.* New York: Harper and Row, 1989.

Marcus, Clare C. "Remembrances of Landscapes Past." *Landscape* 22, no. 3 (1978): 35–43.

McMurray, Foster. "Preface to an Autonomous Discipline of Education." *Educational Theory* 5 (1955): 129–40.

McNeill, John. *Curriculum: The Teacher's Initiative.* Englewood Cliffs, N.J.: Prentice-Hall, 1995.

Merleau-Ponty, Maurice. *Phenomenology of Perception.* Translated by Colin Smith. London: Routledge and Kegan Paul, 1962.

———. "The Child's Relations with Others." In *The Primacy of Perception: And Other Essays on Phenomenological Psychology, the Philosophy of Art, History and Politics,* edited by James M. Edie. Evanston, Ill.: Northwestern University Press, 1964.

———. *The Visible and the Invisible.* Translated by Alphonso Lingis. Evanston, Ill.: Northwestern University Press, 1968.

Metsuru, Senda. *Design of Children's Play Environments.* New York: McGraw-Hill, 1992.

Meyer-Drawe, Kate. "Kaleidoscope of Experiences: The Capability to be Surprised by Children." *Phenomenology and Pedagogy* 4, no. 3 (1986): 48–55.

Miller, Alice. *For Your Own Good.* New York: Farrar, Straus, and Giroux, 1983.

Ministry of Education and the Central Office of Instruction. *Moving and Growing: Physical Education in the Primary School* Part 1. London: Her Majesty's Stationery Office, 1952.

Moore, Peter G. *The Business of Risk.* Cambridge: Cambridge University Press, 1983.

Moore, Robin C. "Generating Relevant Urban Childhood Places: Learning From the 'Yard.'" In *Innovation in Play Environments*, edited by Paul F. Wilkinson. New York: St. Martin's Press, 1980, pp. 45–75.

————. *Childhood's Domain: Play and Place in Child Development.* London: Croom Helm, 1986.

Morell, Virginia. "The Risk Seekers: Are Daredevils Born or Made?" *Equinox* 6, no. 30 (1986): 17.

Mosher, Ralph. "Educational and Psychological Applications of Theories of Human Development: A Brief Overview." *Journal of Education* 177, no. 1 (1995): 1–15.

Nabhan, Gary P., and Stephen Trimble. *The Geography of Childhood: Why Children Need Wild Places.* Boston: Beacon Press, 1994.

Nel, B. F. "The Phenomenological Approach to Pedagogy." *Journal of Phenomenological Psychology* 3, no. 2 (1973): 201–15.

Noddings, Nel. *Caring: A Feminine Approach to Ethics and Moral Education.* Berkeley: University of California Press, 1984.

————. *The Challenge to Care in Schools.* New York: Teachers College Press, 1992.

Onions, C. T. (ed.). *Oxford Dictionary of English Etymology.* Oxford: Clarendon Press.

Opie, Iona. *The People in the Playground.* Oxford: Oxford University Press, 1994.

Opie, Iona, and Peter Opie. *Children's Games in Street and Playground.* Oxford: Clarendon Press, 1969.

Orlick, Terry, and Cal Botterill. *Every Kid Can Win.* Chicago: Nelson-Hall, 1975.

Paley, Vivian Gussin. *Wally's Stories.* Cambridge, Mass.: Harvard University Press, 1981.

Pellegrini, Anthony D. "Children on Playgrounds: A Review of 'What's Out There.'" *Children's Environments Quarterly* 4, no. 4 (1987): 2–7.

Pellegrini, Anthony D. (ed.). *The Future of Play Theory: A Multidisciplinary Inquiry into the Contributions of Brian Sutton-Smith.* Albany: State University of New York Press, 1995.

Perez, Cecilia, and Roger A. Hart. "Beyond Playgrounds: Planning For Children's Access to the Environment." In *Innovation in Play Environments*, edited by Paul F. Wilkinson. New York: St. Martin's Press, 1980, pp. 252–71.

Peters, F. E. *Greek Philosophical Terms: A Historical Lexicon.* New York: New York University Press, 1967.

Pinar, William. "*Currere*: Toward a Reconceptualization." In *Curriculum Theorizing: The Reconceptualists*, edited by William Pinar. Berkeley: McCutchan, 1975, pp. 396–414.

Pinar, William, William M. Reynolds, Patrick Slattery, and Peter M. Taubman. *Understanding Curriculum: An Introduction to the Study of Historical and Contemporary Curriculum Discourses.* New York: Peter Lang, 1995.

Plant, Martin, and Moira Plant. *Risk-Takers: Alcohol, Drugs, Sex and Youth.* London: Routledge, 1992.

Polakow (Suransky), Valerie. *The Erosion of Childhood.* Chicago: University of Chicago Press, 1982.

Polakow, Valerie. "Deconstructing Development." *Journal of Education* 171, no. 2 (1989): 75–86.

———. "The Other Childhood; The Classroom Worlds of Poor Children." In *Visions of Entitlement: The Care and Education of America's Children*, edited by Mary A. Jensen and Stacie G. Goffin. Albany: State University of New York Press, 1993, pp. 157–74.

Polakow, Valerie, and Lobna Sherif. "Exploring the Meaning of Home, Neighborhood and Special Places With Children." Paper presented at the Sixth International Human Science Research Conference, University of Ottawa, May 26–30, 1987.

———. "An Ethnographic Portrait of Young Children's Culture of Place." *Elements* 19, no. 1 (1988): 4–8.

Polkinghorne, Donald. *Methodology for the Human Sciences: Systems of Inquiry.* Albany: State University of New York Press, 1983.

Postman, Neil. *The Disappearance of Childhood.* New York: Dell, 1982.

Rescher, Nicholas. *Risk: A Philosophical Introduction to the Theory of Risk Evaluation and Management.* Washington, D.C.: University Press of America, 1983.

Ricoeur, Paul. "The Model of the Text: Meaningful Action as Text." *Social Research* 38 (1971): 529–62.

———. *Hermeneutics and the Human Sciences: Essays on Language, Action and Interpretation.* Cambridge: Cambridge University Press, 1982.

Rilke, Rainer Maria. *The Notebooks of Malte Laurids Brigge.* New York: Random House, 1910/1982.

Roche, Maurice. "The Life of Sport: An Analysis." *Maieutics* 1, no. 1 (1980): 69–73.

Rogoff, Barbara. *Apprenticeship in Thinking: Cognitive Development in Social Context.* New York: Oxford University Press, 1990.

Ross, Bruce M. *Remembering the Personal Past: Descriptions of Autobiographical Memory.* New York: Oxford University Press, 1991.

Russell, Bertrand. *On Education: Especially in Early Childhood.* London: George Allen and Unwin, 1926.

Ryan, Jeannie, and Pamela Stock. "The Mademoiselle Smart Report: Risk and Reward." *Mademoiselle*, October 1996, pp. 154–61.

Scarbath, Horst. "What is Pedagogic Understanding? Understanding as an Element of Pedagogic Action." *Education* 31 (1985): 93–111.

Schmidt, Wilfred H. O. *Child Development: The Human, Cultural, and Educational Context*. New York: Harper and Row, 1973.

Schutz, Alfred, and Thomas Luckmann. *The Structures of the Life-World*. Translated by Richard M. Zaner and H. Tristram Engelhardt, Jr. Evanston, Ill.: Northwestern University Press, 1973.

Segell, Michael. "The Second Coming of the Alpha Male: A Prescription for Righteous Masculinity at the Millenium." *Esquire* 126, no. 4 (1996): 74–81.

Serafino, Edward P. *The Fears of Childhood: A Guide to Recognizing and Reducing Fearful States in Children*. New York: Human Sciences Press, 1986.

Sewell, John. "Negative Aspects of Safety Features." *Globe and Mail*, (November 12, 1986).

Shapiro, Joel B. "The Subject of Risk: On the Phenomenology of Skiing." *Philosophy Today* 36, no. 3 (1992): 228–39.

Shipley, J. T. *Dictionary of Word Origins*. Ames, Iowa: Littlefield Adams, 1959.

Siegelman, Ellen Y. *Personal Risk: Making Change in Love and Work*. New York: Harper and Row, 1983.

Silin, Jonathan G. "On Becoming Knowledgeable Professionals." *Professionalism and the Early Childhood Practitioner*, edited by Bernard Spodek, Olivia N. Saracho, and Donald L. Peters. New York: Teachers College Press, 1988, pp. 117–34.

Silverman, Hugh. "What is Textuality?" *Phenomenology and Pedagogy* 4, no. 2 (1986): 54–61.

Silvers, Ronald J. Discovering Children's Culture. *Interchange* 6, no. 4 (1975): 47–54.

———. "Appearances: A Videographic Study of Children's Culture." In *School Experience*, edited by Peter Woods and Martyn Hammersley. London: Croom Helm, 1977, pp. 129–61.

———. "On the Other Side of Silence." *Human Studies* 6 (1983): 91–108.

Simpson, D. P. *Cassell's Latin Dictionary*. London: Cassell, 1959.

Sinclaire, Carollyne. *Looking for Home: A Phenomenological Study of Home in the Classroom*. Albany: State University of New York Press, 1994.

Slukin, Andy. *Growing Up in the Playground: The Social Development of Children*. London: Routledge and Kegan Paul, 1981.

———. "The Culture of the Primary School Playground." In *Children and Their Primary Schools: A New Perspective*, edited by Andrew Pollard. London: Falmer Press, 1987.

Smith, Claire. "Letting Go." *Phenomenology and Pedagogy* 5, no. 2 (1987): 135–46.

Smith, David G. "Living With Children." In *Texts of Childhood.* Lifeworld Series Monograph, University of Alberta, 1986, pp. 1–4.

Smith, Robert P. *"'Where Did You Go?' 'Out' 'What Did You Do?' 'Nothing?'"* New York: W. W. Norton, 1957.

Smith, Stephen J. "The Phenomenology of Educating Physically." In *Phenomenology and Educational Discourse,* edited by Donald Vandenberg. Durban: Heinemann, 1997, pp. 119–43.

Snyder, Martha, Ross Snyder, and Ross Snyder, Jr. *The Young Child as Person: Toward the Development of Healthy Conscience.* New York: Human Sciences Press, 1980.

Soltis, Jonas F. "On the Nature of Educational Research." *Educational Researcher* 13, no. 10 (1984): 5–11.

Spiecker, Ben. "The Pedagogical Relationship." *Oxford Review of Education* 10, no. 2 (1984): 203–9.

Spodek, Bernard. "Implicit Theories of Early Childhood Teachers: Foundations for Professional Behavior." In *Professionalism and the Early Childhood Practitioner,* edited by Bernard Spodek, Olivia N. Saracho, and Donald L. Peters. New York: Teachers College Press, 1988, pp. 161–72.

Spranger, Eduard. "The Role of Love in Education." In *Modern Philosophies of Education,* edited by John P. Strain. New York: Random House, 1971, pp. 536–46.

Sutton-Smith, Brian. *"Our Street."* Wellington: A. H. and A. W. Reed, 1950.

———. "School Play: A Commentary." In *School Play: A Source Book,* edited by James H. Block and Nancy R. King. New York: Garland, 1987, pp. 277–90.

———. "Conclusion: The Persuasive Rhetorics of Play." In Pellegrini, Anthony D. (ed.), *The Future of Play Theory: A Multidisciplinary Inquiry into the Contributions of Brian Sutton-Smith.* Albany: State University of New York Press, 1995, pp. 275–95.

Sutton-Smith, Brian, and Diana Kelly-Bryne. *The Masks of Play.* Proceedings of the Association for the Anthropological Study of Play, London, Ontario, 1982. New York: Leisure Press, 1984a.

———. "The Idealization of Play." In *Play in Animals and Humans,* edited by Peter K. Smith. Oxford: Basil Blackwell, 1984b, pp. 305–21.

Takeshita, Fumiko. *Benchi ga Hitotsu.* Tokyo: Kodansha, 1985. Translated as *The Park Bench.* Brooklyn: Kane/Miller, 1988.

Taylor, Charles. "Interpretation and the Sciences of Man." In *Interpretive Social Science,* edited by Paul Rabinow and William M. Sullivan. Berkeley: University of California Press, 1979.

Thomas, Bob. *Walt Disney: An American Original.* New York: Simon and Schuster, 1976.

Thorne, Barrie. *Gender Play: Girls and Boys in School.* New Brunswick, N.J.: Rutgers University Press, 1993.

Trimpop, Rüdiger M. *The Psychology of Risk Taking Behavior.* Amsterdam: North-Holland, 1994.

Tuan, Yi-Tu. *Landscapes of Fear.* Minneapolis: University of Minnesota Press, 1979.

Vandenberg, Donald. *Being and Education: An Essay in Existential Phenomenology.* Englewood Cliffs, N.J.: Prentice-Hall, 1971.

———. "Phenomenology and Educational Research." In *Existentialism and Phenomenology in Education,* edited by David E. Denton. New York: Teachers College Press, 1974, pp. 183–220.

———. "Openness: The Pedagogic Atmosphere." In *The Philosophy of Open Education,* edited by David Nyberg. London: Routledge and Kegan Paul, 1975, pp. 35–57.

———. "Existential and Phenomenological Influences in Educational Philosophy." *Teachers College Record* 81, no. 2 (1979): 166–91.

———. "Education or Experience?" *Educational Theory* 30, no. 3 (1980): 235–51.

———. "Interpretive, Normative Theory of Education." *Educational Philosophy and Theory* 19, no. 1 (1987): 1–11.

———. "Knowledge in Schooling." *Phenomenology and Pedagogy* 6, no. 2 (1988): 63–78.

———. *Education as a Human Right: A Theory of Curriculum and Pedagogy.* New York: Teachers College Press, 1990.

Van den Berg, Jan H. "The Handshake." *Philosophy Today* 3 (1959): 28–34.

———. *The Changing Nature of Man.* New York: Dell, 1961/1975.

———. *A Different Existence.* Pittsburgh, Pa.: Duquesne University Press, 1974.

van Manen, Max. "Linking Ways of Knowing With Ways of Being Practical." *Curriculum Inquiry* 6, no. 3 (1977): 205–28.

———. "An Experiment in Educational Theorizing: The Utrecht School." *Interchange* 10, no. 1 (1978-79): 48–66.

———. "The Phenomenology of Pedagogic Observation." *Canadian Journal of Education* 4, no. 1 (1979): 5–16.

———. "Edifying Theory: Serving the Good." *Theory Into Practice* 21, no. 1 (1982a): 44–49.

———. "Phenomenological Pedagogy." *Curriculum Inquiry* 12, no. 3 (1982b): 283–99.

———. "Practicing Phenomenological Writing." *Phenomenology and Pedagogy* 2, no. 1 (1984): 36–69.

———. *The Tone of Teaching.* Richmond Hill, Ontario: Scholastic, 1986a.

———. "We Need to Show Our Human Science Practice is a Relation of Pedagogy." *Phenomenology and Pedagogy* 4, no. 3 (1986b): 78–93.

———. "Human Science and the Study of Pedagogy." Unpublished manuscript, University of Alberta, 1987.

———. *Researching Lived Experience: Human Science for an Action Sensitive Pedagogy.* Albany: State University of New York Press, 1990.

———. *The Tact of Teaching: The Meaning of Pedagogical Thoughtfulness.* Albany: State University of New York Press, 1991.

———. "The Vitality of the Pedagogical Relation." In *Reflections on Pedagogy and Method*, vol. 2, edited by Bas Levering, Siebren Miedema, Stephen Smith, and Max van Manen. Montfoort: Uriah Heep, 1992, pp. 173–92.

———. "On the Epistemology of Reflective Practice." *Teachers and Teaching: Theory and Practice* 1, no. 1 (1995): 33–50.

Viscott, David. *Risking*. New York: Pocket Books, 1977.

Weekley, E. *A Concise Dictionary of Modern English*. New York: Dutton, 1924.

Welch, Sharon D. *A Feminist Ethic of Risk*. Minneapolis, Minn.: Fortress Press, 1990.

Wildavsky, Aaron, and Karl Dake. "Theories of Risk Perception: Who Fears What and Why?" *Daedalus: Journal of the American Academy of Arts and Sciences* 119, no. 4 (1990): 41–60.

Wilkinson, Paul F., and Robert. S. Lockhart. "Safety in Children's Formal Play Environments." In *Innovation in Play Environments*, edited by Paul F. Wilkinson. New York: St. Martin's Press, 1980, pp. 85–96.

Wishon, Phillip M., and Marcia L. Oreskovich. "Bicycles, Roller Skates and Skateboards: Safety Promotion and Accident Prevention." *Children Today* 15, no. 3 (1986): 11–15.

Wood, Denis. "Free the Children! Down With Playgrounds!" *McGill Journal of Education* 12, no. 2 (1977): 227–42.

Woolf, Virginia. *Moments of Being: Unpublished Autobiographical Writings.* London: Hogarth Press, 1976.

Wordsworth, William. *The Prelude: Or Growth of a Poet's Mind.* Oxford: Clarendon Press, 1850/1959.

Yates, J. Frank, and Eric R. Stone. "The Risk Construct." In *Risk-Taking Behavior*, edited by J. Frank Yates. New York: John Wiley, 1992. pp. 1–25.

Yerkes, Rita. "What About the Young Child?" *The Journal of Experiential Education* 11, no. 2 (1988): 21–25.

Zelizer, Viviana A. *Pricing the Priceless Child*. New York: Basic Books, 1985.

Zerner, Charles J. "The Street Hearth of Play." *Landscape* 22, no. 1 (1977): 19–30.

Zuckerman, Marvin. *Sensation Seeking: Beyond the Optimum Level of Arousal.* Hillsdale, N.J.: Erlbaum, 1979.

# Index

215